Competition Policy and Merger Analysis in Deregulated and Newly Competitive Industries

Edited by

Peter C. Carstensen

University of Wisconsin Law School, USA

and

Susan Beth Farmer

Pennsylvania State University, USA

Edward Elgar

Cheltenham, UK • Northampton, MA, USA

Published by
Edward Elgar Publishing Limited
The Lypiatts
15 Lansdown Road
Cheltenham
Glos GL50 2JA
UK

Edward Elgar Publishing, Inc.
William Pratt House
9 Dewey Court
Northampton
Massachusetts 01060
USA

A catalogue record for this book
is available from the British Library

Library of Congress Control Number: 2008932900

ISBN 978 1 84542 313 1

Printed and bound in Great Britain by MPG Books Ltd, Bodmin, Cornwall

Contents

Figures

Tables

Contributors

Peter C. Carstensen is the George C. Young-Bascom Professor of Law at the University of Wisconsin Law School. Much of his scholarship has focused on the legal and economic issues at the intersection of regulation and competition. He co-chaired the drafting committee for the ABA Antitrust Section's monograph on statutory exemptions to antitrust law (*Federal Statutory Exemptions for Antitrust Law*, 2007).

Jim Chen is Dean and Professor of Law at the Louis D. Brandeis School of Law at Louisville University. Prior to his appointment as Dean he was the Associate Dean for Faculty and James L. Krusemark Professor of Law, at the University of Minnesota Law School. A wide-ranging scholar, he has worked extensively on issues involving various kinds of economic regulation and has published extensively on telecommunications regulation in particular.

Susan Beth Farmer is a professor of law at the Pennsylvania State University, Dickinson Law School, where she teaches in the fields of US and comparative antitrust, criminal law, white collar crime and gender & the law. She has also taught in the United Kingdom, and has lectured in Turkey, Italy, Belgium, Austria and France She is actively engaged in researching and writing about US and foreign antitrust and trade regulation law, including issues of federalism and comparative competition policy.

Thomas L. (Tim) Greaney is Chester A. Myers Professor of Law and Co-Director of the Center for Health Law Studies at Saint Louis University School of Law. He is co-author of the nation's leading health law casebook, *Health Law: Cases, Materials and Problems* (5th edition); and a treatise and hornbook on health law, all published by Thomson/West. Before joining the Saint Louis University faculty, he served as Assistant Chief of the Department of Justice, Antitrust Division, supervising health care antitrust litigation.

Curtis M. Grimm is the Dean's Professor of Supply Chain and Strategy at the Robert H. Smith School of Business of the University of Maryland. He has a Ph.D. in economics from the University of California-Berkeley and has published extensively on a variety of economic topics and has a long-standing specialization in railroad economics.

Diana L. Moss is an economist and the Vice President and a Senior Fellow of the American Antitrust Institute, a competition policy advocacy organization based in Washington, DC. She is also an adjunct professor of Economics at the University of Colorado at Boulder. Previously, she was senior staff economist coordinator for competition analysis at the Federal Energy Regulatory Commission. She has written extensively on energy related topics and is the editor of *Network Access, Regulation and Antitrust*, 2005.

Richard J. Pierce is Lyle T. Alverson Professor of Law at George Washington University. He has written a dozen books and over one hundred articles about government regulation and the effects of various forms of government intervention on the performance of markets, with particular emphasis on energy markets.

Bernard Shull is Emeritus Professor of Economics at Hunter College, CUNY, and a Special Consultant to National Economic Research Associates, Inc. He is the author of a number of books and articles on the structure and performance of the banking system including, *The Fourth Branch: The Federal Reserve's Unlikely Rise to Power and Influence*, 2005, *Bank Mergers in a Deregulated Environment* (with G. Hanweck) 2001, and 'The Separation of Banking and Commerce in the United States,' *Financial Markets, Institutions and Instruments*, 1999.

1.   Introduction and overview

Peter C. Carstensen
Susan Beth Farmer

Historically, the American economy operated in two spheres. One, the competitive sphere, gave enterprises substantial discretion to set their prices and other terms of trade as well as the products they would market. Antitrust law oversaw this sphere with a set of rules that prohibited some kinds of conduct and existing structures (e.g., price fixing among competitors and single firm monopoly) and intervened to block only those major mergers that might create an undue risk of anticompetitive conduct or create a monopoly. In the view of many antitrust scholars, courts and business people, merger law was a central force in retaining an open and competitive market structure that both enhanced the long-run dynamics of these industries and permitted a light-handed control over specific conduct.

The other sphere of the economy was the subject of direct economic regulation. This was most overt in the traditional fields of public utility service (gas, electricity and telecommunications) and transportation (rail, road and air). However, it also included health care and many elements of financial businesses (insurance, savings associations, banks and credit unions).

Within these spheres, regulation has varied with respect to the degree of direct control over the ultimate conduct of the businesses. Traditionally, in the areas of public utilities and transportation, all aspects of service and any combination among firms was subject to direct review and control by state and/or federal regulatory authorities. The same was true in financial sectors, with some greater discretion with respect to the pricing of many services, such as loans. While merger law has played a role in controlling the structure in some sectors for many decades (e.g, banking and natural gas), it has not been a pervasive influence and most often the regulatory agency has had the ultimate say on the validity of any combination.

Starting in the 1970s with airline and rail deregulation, and recently highlighted in the Telecommunications Act of 1996, economic policy in the United States has shifted strongly in favor of competitive markets as the means to encourage and discipline business enterprises in the formerly

regulated sectors. The basic vision of this policy was the belief that allowing firms to make their own price and output decisions would bring
about preferable results with respect to price, innovation and service to
the ultimate benefit of competition and consumers. Traditional regulation
was condemned as inefficient, ineffective and protective of established
interests.

The problematic character of this somewhat simplistic vision of economic organization became evident with the collapse of Enron (which
operated in gas and electricity markets), which contributed to the disrup-
tion of electric markets in the western United States, the bankruptcy of
WorldCom (telecommunications), which affected the organization of those
markets, and mergers between railroads, which generated a host of complaints about the quality and price of deregulated service on freight railroads, especially following the consolidation of the Union Pacific and
Southern Pacific. In addition, the unregulated market model has failed to
control the upward spiral of health care costs. In all of these fields, there
has been a great deal of continuing debate and discussion concerning the
appropriate policy. Indeed, after deregulation failed to being about the
promised benefits and, in some cases, caused serious and widespread economic harms, the public policy pendulum may be swinging back toward
more regulation. In the interim, however, massive merger movements have
taken place in formerly regulated industries.

The transformation of formerly regulated or noncompetitive industries
to competition is closely linked with merger movements. The historical
record demonstrates that once faced with competition, leading firms in
these industries began to merge. This has been the pattern in airlines, banks,
railroads, electric and gas utilities, health care and, with great prominence,
telecommunications. These merger waves seem, on their face, to conflict
with the model of a perfectly competitive market system with many participants. However, it must also be remembered that the prior patterns of ownership in all of these industries were determined through a regulatory
process and not a market one. Hence, substantial changes in the ownership
and organization of these markets are a predictable consequence of the
change in economic context in which the firms operated. Indeed, before
deregulation, industries from health care to railroads to electric power possessed excess (and probably inefficient) capacity only because of the lack of
competitive pressure. After 2000, with the collapse of the 'dot com' bubble
(excessive optimism about internet communications) and the exposure of
false income statements at WorldCom, there was pressure to merge economically strapped telecommunications firms. The airline industry, for
different economic reasons, is undergoing similar pressure to consolidate.
The same issues now face electricity and many banking services.

Along with these structural changes, some of these industries, e.g., telecommunications and health care, have experienced dramatic techno- logical innovation, often unleashed by deregulation. This has brought about substantial changes in the kinds of services and products provided to the market as well as in the structure of the enterprises themselves. Indeed, the potential for innovation in these industries can dramatically alter the implications of combinations among firms that in the past held dominant positions. For example, the development of wireless telecommu- nications increasingly provides a substitute for wire systems and so may greatly limit the market power of the dominant (previously regulated) local phone companies.

Against this backdrop, antitrust and regulatory authorities, who are now charged with facilitating competition, must evaluate mergers. What are the relevant markets? How should competitive impact be measured? How can and should decision makers incorporate expected future market contexts into their review? These questions are remarkably consistent over the entire range of previously regulated industries despite many industry-specific considerations.

This book includes a series of chapters that examine competition and merger policy experience in the key industries subject to the deregulatory process. In each chapter, a highly qualified expert in the field has reviewed the evolution of the industry, its transformation toward greater reliance on market institutions, and the resulting transformation of structure and conduct. These chapters reveal clear similarities in the economic, legal and public policy issues that have arisen following deregulation of these eco- nomic sectors. This set of industry studies provides a good basis to discern the consistency of the problems and the relative success of differing responses to these issues over a range of industries going through similar transformation. This book also provides guidance for decision makers to evaluate concerns for economic viability of individual firms in relation to the longer-term goal of enhancing the potential for workably competitive markets.

The American economy is not the only one undergoing a process of movement toward greater reliance on market mechanisms. Throughout the world, many formerly state-managed and state-owned economies are pri- vatizing enterprises and, at the same time, moving toward market competi- tion as the primary vehicle for allocating goods and services. The EU provides a particularly relevant point of comparison with the American effort. As a mature economy organized in a quasi-federal system, the EU has its own history and unique economic issues. It has a robust competition policy, perhaps even stronger today than the American model, and it faces the challenges of both integrating national economies into a regional economic unit (a challenge America overcame 200 years ago) and, at the same time, moving historically regulated industries toward a market model.

By developing a better understanding of the issues and analytical problems resulting from past large-scale deregulation in the United States, these case studies also provide important insights for future market deregulatory actions and contribute to better understanding of the merits of re-regulation in some contexts. Finally, these studies will offer a relevant counterpoint to efforts to understand the complex situation facing countries in Eastern Europe and Asia that are seeking, with mixed success, to move from state-managed to market-oriented economies. To assist in that comparison, this book also includes a chapter that contrasts the American experience with that of the EU with respect to some of the industries where the EU has also sought to move toward a more market-oriented regulatory scheme.

The next three chapters provide case studies on the traditional public utility industries of electricity (Chapter 2), natural gas (Chapter 3), and telecommunications (Chapter 4). Gas and electricity are subject to regulatory oversight by the same agency, the Federal Energy Regulatory Commission (FERC), yet the experience of merger review and subsequent market performance has been substantially different. The contrast rests on the inherent characteristics of the services involved in providing electricity and natural gas as well as the historical structure of the industries and the differences in the specifics of the overall legal regime governing the two types of energy providers. The experience with telecommunications provides a case study in regulatory lag in the face of a dramatic transformation of technology. The old telephone monopoly of AT&T held back the use of cost-saving, new technology such as microwave transmission, digital dialing and wireless communications. The creation of competition has gone hand in hand with both the commercialization of already existing technology and an increased pace of innovation. The consequence, as shown in Chapter 4, is that regulatory oversight was always behind and legislation often failed to address the most important aspects of the emerging technology at all. For example, the 1996 Telecommunications Act did not impose any regulation of the Internet, save for an attempted control over pornography.

The next two chapters examine key transportation industries, railroads (Chapter 5) and airlines (Chapter 6), that were freed from command and control regulation in the 1970s and 1980s. Both chapters conclude that deregulation has had positive effects. However, each chapter points to the failure on the part of those designing the new policies to foresee and appreciate the changed dynamics of the resulting markets. Consequently, the increased concentration in these markets resulting from mergers may have undermined the potential gains that deregulation might have made possible.

Chapter 7 turns to an examination of the transformation of health care with a focus on the merger of hospitals. While various new forms of organizations have come to be the primary method of providing health care services in the last 30 years, it is striking that there is no national agency charged with overseeing this transition in the health care field and formulating rules to facilitate market conduct. This chapter provides important lessons for public policy. The absence of any agency having overall responsibility for the development of market processes creates problems at least as bad as the problems of agency failure highlighted in the prior chapters. Despite some rhetorical commitment to the market, there was not the kind of legislative or regulatory action necessary to achieve viable market processes when interested parties, especially hospitals, made claims for special status.

Chapter 8 examines the banking industry. This industry was once subject to fairly detailed regulation of rates and other financial services. Different types of depository institutions such as commercial banks, savings banks, savings and loan associations, and credit unions, had distinct market niches. Regulators attempted to shield each type from undue competition from other types of depository institutions as well as to limit intra-industry competition. Starting in the 1960s, this model gradually disintegrated as banks and the other types of depository institutions expanded the range of their services resulting in more direct competition among the types of institutions. In addition, legislative and administrative actions expanded the permissible geographic scope of their activities thereby increasing the number of actual or potential competitors. This competition was an important factor in inducing much more innovation in financial services for both individuals and businesses. Nevertheless, banking remains a regulated industry because of the need to provide deposit insurance to protect consumers and to check the consequent risks of strategic conduct by banks. As the barriers to banking competition have come down and the ability of banks to expand (in both geographic area and product lines) has grown dramatically, a vast restructuring of the industry has taken place. The question, once again, is whether that restructuring is consistent with the public interest in obtaining the best advantages from the market process.

The final substantive chapter (Chapter 9) provides a comparison of the European Union's efforts to deregulate comparable industries with the American experience. The primary focus is on gas, electricity, banking and airlines. While the EU has also engaged in substantial supervision of telecommunications, the area was omitted from this survey because of the great complexity resulting from a simultaneous transformation in structure and in ownership (from public to corporate with respect to many of the systems). Europe generally uses public ownership for its railroads, with the exception of the United Kingdom, and therefore a comparison of the railroad industries is not possible. Similarly, European approaches to health care have largely precluded the use of market mechanisms to date. It is possible that in the future the EU may decide to move both railroads and health care toward more market-oriented ways of doing business, but that is not yet the case.

The EU legal system for dealing with competition policy, and mergers in particular, is different from the American system. The EU law provides much more exclusivity than does American law for specific decision makers dealing with specific types of transactions or conduct. Basically, the Commission itself has nearly exclusive jurisdiction over transactions or conduct that have substantial effect across the EU while national competition authorities have similarly exclusive authority with respect to more localized events. The EU has also been much more self-conscious about its overall decision to embrace competition as a fundamental policy to govern the various industry sectors. At the same time, the actual outcomes of the EU process of merger review and of industry deregulation have been similar overall to the American experience. For this reason, it is relevant to note that in one industry, airlines, it appears that the EU may have achieved better outcomes than the United States despite taking a somewhat more regulatory approach to the industry.

Chapter 10 concludes the book by identifying some of the common themes and implications of the specific case studies. This overview highlights the network nature of each industry and suggests that, overall, the case studies show a need for regulation that will both constitute and facilitate competitive markets. Too often, as the case studies show, the effort to move regulated industries toward a greater market orientation was frustrated because the regulators lacked the tools, the expertise or the commitment to govern the transition to competition. In addition, decision makers sometimes lacked an understanding of how unregulated markets would operate and failed to foresee problems. Their ignorance, however, is understandable given the often dramatic changes in the way these industries will operate once rigid and frequently inefficient regulatory commands were lifted. In an interesting and instructive contrast with the American model, the stated policy of the EU expressly recognizes the need for a comprehensive transition plan when industries are moved toward a market model. However, here too it is worth comparing the ambition of the EU policy with its actual accomplishment. Ultimately, the process of change is a continuing one. Success is highly dependent on thoughtful analysis and a responsible regulatory and legislative environment. Unfortunately, the political process, as the American experience demonstrates, has only rarely and never consistently provided this institutional framework.

Given the obstacles that effective reform and sound merger policy face, perhaps the most remarkable feature of the following case studies is that they all conclude that the economy is better off, or at least not worse off, as a result of the reforms.

2. Mergers in the US electric power industry

Richard J. Pierce

It is extraordinarily difficult to devise and implement a socially-beneficial merger policy in a network industry that is the subject of an ongoing restructuring process intended to increase reliance on market forces to obtain socially-desirable results. In order to decide which proposed mergers to approve or disapprove, antitrust agencies and regulatory agencies must know that which no one can know – how the restructuring process will evolve over the typical multi-decade period. This knowledge is required to complete a restructuring of a network industry. The agency responsible for announcing and applying a merger policy applicable to an industry that is in the process of restructuring must make a series of difficult, recurrent decisions. First, should the policy be designed to fit the present industry structure or should it instead be designed to fit some expected future structure? If the latter, which of the many potential future structures should the agency use as its baseline for evaluating the expected effects of a proposed merger? Finally, should the agency use its merger policy only as a means of reacting to changes in industry structure proposed by private market participants, or should the agency use its merger policy proactively as a means of encouraging the types of restructuring activities that it considers critical to the success of the agency's restructuring program? The US electric power industry illustrates well the daunting nature of the task. The following brief summary of the process of restructuring the US electricity market will help readers appreciate the difficulty that US antitrust and regulatory agencies have confronted, and continue to confront, in undertaking this task (for more detailed descriptions, *see* Pierce 2005; Joskow 2003).

AN OVERVIEW OF THE PROCESS OF RESTRUCTURING THE US ELECTRICITY MARKET

Until the 1980s, the US electricity industry consisted of approximately two hundred vertically integrated firms, each of which was a privately owned, state-franchised monopoly subject to pervasive cost-of-service regulation implemented by state regulators, plus a few government owned and operated entities like the Tennessee Valley Authority, the Bonneville Power Authority and rural electric cooperatives. Federal agencies had only minor regulatory roles and competition was nearly non-existent. In the 1980s, the federal agency with principal responsibility for regulating interstate electricity transactions, the Federal Energy Regulatory Commission (FERC), reached the well-supported conclusion that some forms of competition among suppliers could produce socially-beneficial results. FERC had little statutory power to introduce competition in the market at the time. However, it began to move in that direction through the use of the few sources of leverage it had – primarily through the pro-competitive conditions it imposed in its orders approving proposed mergers (Pierce 1996b, p. 31).

In 1992, Congress enacted the Energy Policy Act, a statute that increased FERC's power to introduce competition in the electricity market. The Act arguably gave FERC a mandate to create competitive wholesale electricity markets (*see generally* Watkiss and Smith 1993). In 1996, FERC issued a rule announcing the manner in which it would attempt to restructure the industry to create competitive wholesale markets (FERC 1996a). The restructuring plan FERC initially announced was largely ineffective, however. Therefore, it began to make changes in its restructuring program shortly after it announced its initial plan. The Commission's current restructuring plan is far more effective than the first plan. However, FERC has experienced significant resistance to its present restructuring plan from utilities and state regulators who oppose restructuring and who want to retain the traditional regulatory environment in which electricity is provided by vertically integrated, state-regulated monopolies. As of 2005, about half of the electricity in the US was provided by vertically integrated, state-regulated monopolies, and about half was provided in one of the four competitive wholesale markets that FERC has been able to create (*see generally* Pierce 2005; Joskow 2003). Throughout the lengthy and still incomplete restructuring process, FERC has been confronted with the need to announce and apply merger policies to an industry that was virtually certain to change in important, but unpredictable, ways in the near future.

THE NEED FOR MERGERS PRIOR TO RESTRUCTURING

In the 1970s, when almost all electricity was provided by vertically integrated, state-regulated monopolies, and there was no major change in the governance system on the horizon, it was relatively easy to identify a good merger policy. Stephen Breyer, then a young professor at Harvard Law School and now a Justice of the US Supreme Court, and Paul MacAvoy, then a young professor at Yale School of Management, wrote an excellent book in which they made the case for adoption of a policy that would encourage widespread mergers among utilities (Breyer and MacAvoy 1974, pp. 89–121). They argued persuasively that only a handful of the roughly two hundred electric utilities in the US were large enough to take advantage of the significant economies of scale and scope that are potentially available to perform the functions required to provide electricity service. They explained in a detailed and persuasive manner why a policy of widespread consolidation of electric utilities had the potential to save the US billions of dollars per year.

Breyer and MacAvoy recognized, however, that such a massive socially-beneficial consolidation of electric utilities was unlikely to take place unless the federal government mandated this change in structure or coerced market participants into implementing such a structure by making other fundamental changes in the policies applicable to the electricity industry. With each utility operating as a state-franchised monopolist, utilities had no incentive to attempt to implement mergers that would reduce their costs because they confronted no competition. Moreover, proposed electric utility mergers had to run a regulatory gauntlet that few could survive. They had to be approved by FERC, either the Department of Justice or the Federal Trade Commission, the Securities and Exchange Commission, and state regulators in each state in which the utility did business. State regulators were generally hostile to proposed utility mergers because many such mergers would create multi-state utilities that would be more difficult for state agencies to regulate. State agencies feared that they would eventually have to cede some of their regulatory powers over multi-state utilities to FERC. Thus, in most cases, state agencies either disapproved proposed mergers or imposed conditions that rendered them unprofitable to the parties, thereby discouraging utilities from proposing mergers. The only federal statutes applicable to electric utility mergers at the time were the Federal Power Act and the antitrust laws – statutes that clearly did not confer power on any federal agency to mandate or to encourage mergers – and the Public Utility Holding Company Act – a depression-era statute that made many potential socially-beneficial mergers unlawful (*see* Bilicic 2003) until it was repealed in the Energy Policy Act of 2005.

ELECTRIC UTILITIES BEGAN TO CONFRONT COMPETITION IN THE 1980s

In 1978, Congress enacted the Public Utilities Regulatory Policy Act (PURPA). The Act included provisions that instructed FERC to require utilities to purchase electricity from two statutorily prescribed types of qualifying facilities (QFs) owned by third parties (co-generators and small power producers) at state-determined estimates of the full cost the utility would avoid by making the mandatory purchase. PURPA was a failure as a means of improving the efficiency of the performance of electricity markets, primarily because some states made estimates of full avoided costs that required many utilities to pay supra-market prices for electricity generated by QFs. (Black and Pierce 1993, pp. 1347–1349). However, PURPA demonstrated the viability of an institutional regime in which utilities are required to transmit electricity generated by third parties – a critical prerequisite to creation of a competitive wholesale market.

In the 1980s, FERC recognized that changes in the basic technological and economic characteristics of generation and transmission of electricity had created a situation in which some functions that had been performed exclusively by vertically integrated, pervasively regulated monopolies were no longer natural monopoly functions (*see generally* Pierce 1986). FERC recognized that generation and wholesaling of electricity could be undertaken by unregulated firms operating in a competitive market. FERC also understood that substituting competitive market forces for regulation had the potential to allow the wholesale market to perform more efficiently. At the same time, industrial consumers in many states became angry with their local utilities for charging what the consumers perceived to be exorbitant prices attributable to the utilities' inefficiency. Industrial consumers in states with high electricity prices pressured both FERC and state officials to allow them to buy power from firms other than their local utility. Many industrial consumers also voted with their feet – they relocated to states with much lower electricity prices. FERC had little regulatory power to accede to the wishes of the industrial consumers. However, several major states enacted statutes that allowed industrial consumers in those states to buy electricity from non-utility providers or from utilities other than the utility that previously had the exclusive right to sell to the consumers (Black and Pierce 1993, pp. 1350–1354).

FERC ENCOURAGES COMPETITION BY CONDITIONING ITS APPROVAL OF MERGERS

As a result of the enactment of PURPA and of state statutes that allowed industrial consumers to buy from non-utility sources in some states, many electric utilities found themselves subject to competition for the first time. The resulting competitive pressures induced utilities to identify ways in which they could become more efficient and reduce costs. For the first time, large numbers of utilities looked favorably on the potential to participate in the mergers that Breyer and MacAvoy had previously identified as potential means of enhancing their efficiency. FERC was supportive of both the utility mergers that were proposed in the late 1980s and early 1990s and of the movement toward creation of the competitive wholesale markets that industrial consumers had persuaded many states to support. FERC would have liked to have been instrumental in implementing a broad transition to competitive wholesale markets in the 1980s by requiring all owners of transmission lines to provide third parties access to their lines (Pierce 1996b, p. 31). However, FERC believed that it lacked the statutory authority to issue such a broad mandate. It attempted to move the market in that direction, however, by conditioning its approval of the many mergers in the 1980s and early 1990s on the merged entity's willingness to agree to include in its tariff a provision that guaranteed equal access to its transmission lines (Pierce 1996b, p. 31). With guaranteed access to a utility's transmission lines, third-party generators could begin to compete with the utility to make sales to its customers.

   This merger policy – approve all proposed mergers subject to a condition that eliminates a major vertical restraint on trade – made a lot of sense at the time. It moved the industry gradually in the direction of greater reliance on market forces to govern the wholesale market. FERC's merger policy was inadequate alone, however, to induce most utilities to acquiesce in the actions required to further FERC's desired goal of creating competitive wholesale markets. Some utilities had no incentive to merge because they were already large enough to take advantage of available economies of scale and scope. Many other utilities would have enhanced their efficiency by merging, but they so feared the potential consequences of having to compete with third parties that FERC's policy of conditioning mergers on a guarantee that the utility would provide third parties access to their transmission lines deterred them from proposing many potential efficiency-enhancing mergers. Utilities that did not have tariff provisions that guaranteed third-party access to their transmission lines routinely denied third parties access, thereby insulating themselves from competition in the generation and wholesale markets.

FERC'S INITIAL RESTRUCTURING ORDER

In 1992, Congress enacted the Energy Policy Act, a statute that for the first time conferred on FERC the power to require a utility to provide third-party access to its transmission lines. FERC interpreted that statute as a mandate to create the conditions necessary to support competitive wholesale electricity markets (*see generally* Watkiss and Smith 1994). FERC conducted a rulemaking proceeding that culminated in the issuance of a 1996 rule requiring every investor-owned utility to provide third-party access to its transmission lines (FERC 1996a). In return for providing third-party access to its transmission lines, the FERC authorized each such utility to make wholesale sales at unregulated prices.

FERC's initial third-party access rule was ineffective in creating efficiently functioning competitive wholesale markets, however, for two reasons. First, it was somewhere between difficult and impossible to implement the rule in the context of the many utilities that had an incentive to resist competition and had an understanding of the capabilities of their transmission lines that was vastly superior to the knowledge any regulator or other third party could hope to obtain (this is an illustration of the familiar problem of information asymmetries). Many utilities simply claimed that they lacked the transmission capacity required to accommodate transactions proposed by third parties (*see generally* Pierce 1994).

Second, the 1996 rule was premised on a serious misunderstanding of the manner in which electricity flows on an integrated grid and of the competitive implications of alternative methods of pricing transmission (*see generally* Pierce 1997b). I will now embark on a lengthy digression about electricity transmission and transmission pricing policy. It is impossible to understand either the flaws in FERC's initial attempt to create competitive wholesale markets or the ways in which FERC's initial failed wholesale competition policy complicated the Commission's efforts to devise and implement a sound merger policy without first understanding the nature of transmission and the importance of a transmission pricing policy to the creation of competitive wholesale markets.

TRANSMISSION PRICING – THE FATAL FLAW IN FERC'S INITIAL RESTRUCTURING ORDER

Three integrated transmission grids support the provision of electricity service in the US – one east of the Rockies, one west of the Rockies, and a third grid that covers about two-thirds of Texas. Electricity flows on an integrated grid in inverse proportion to the impedance on each line that comprises the grid (*see generally* Hogan 1993; Joskow 2004). Electricity flows are unaffected by political boundaries, statutes, rules or contracts. Each of the two major grids in the US has thousands of nodes – points at which electricity either enters the grid from a generator or leaves the grid to serve a load center. The quantity of electricity that leaves the grid at each output node varies constantly, often by large amounts in short periods of time, as demand for electricity changes with weather conditions, the opening and closing of industrial and commercial facilities, etc. Similarly, the flow onto the grid from an input node can vary between zero and 2000 megawatts instantaneously as generators are turned on and off to meet constantly changing demand conditions. Unlike most markets, storage cannot temper the rapid, large changes in demand for electricity or assist in equating supply with the extraordinarily volatile demand for electricity. Electricity cannot be economically stored. As a result, the quantity of electricity generated and transmitted to a point must equal the quantity consumed at that point every second of the day, and the flows across an integrated grid are extraordinarily complicated and dynamic. A change in demand in Akron can have instantaneous large effects on capacity and flows into Des Moines, Boston or Atlanta.

It should be immediately apparent that an integrated grid should be owned and operated by a single entity – either a firm or a government agency – and that is the pattern of ownership and control of all integrated grids in the world except the US grid.[1] It is hard to imagine a worse mismatch between the characteristics of an integrated transmission grid and the pattern of ownership and control of the three integrated grids that support provision of electricity service to the continental US. Ownership and control of the three US grids is divided among 140 vertically integrated utilities (*see generally* Joskow 2004). This balkanized pattern of ownership and control yields massive inefficiencies, greatly increases the risks of cascading blackouts and greatly complicates the task of designing and implementing a plan for restructuring the industry in ways that produce efficiently functioning wholesale electricity markets.

To complicate the situation still further, FERC traditionally authorized utilities to charge for provision of transmission service on a utility-specific, average total cost basis. As a result, a generator that wanted to make a sale to a distribution company or an industrial consumer 100 miles away typically had to contract to pay high, average-cost-based transmission rates to the two, three or four utilities across whose lines the electricity was deemed to flow by the contracts between the generator and the utilities that comprised the fictional contract path between the generator and its customer (*see generally* Pierce 1997b). The resulting price of transmission service bore no relationship to the cost.

The per-unit price of transmission service should be based on marginal cost – a measure of cost that is usually a tiny fraction of average total cost in the context of electricity transmission and that does not depend on the pure happenstance of the number of utilities that lie between the buyer and the seller using some necessarily fictitious and arbitrary contract path (*see generally* Hogan 1997). The owner of the transmission assets can then supplement what otherwise would be its inadequate revenues attributable to unit prices based on marginal cost by charging all users of its assets postage stamp rates that reflect the embedded cost of its prior investments in transmission assets, and by requiring generators that propose to add generating capacity at a location that will require new investment in transmission assets to pay for that new transmission capacity (*see generally* Joskow 2003).

When FERC issued its initial rule to mandate third-party access to transmission lines in 1996, it made no change to its pre-existing method of pricing transmission service. As a result, the cost of transmission was so high that it was often uneconomic to transmit electricity over a fictitious contract path that included more than one utility. Thus, the wholesale markets created by the initial rule were small and highly concentrated.

FERC'S INITIAL MERGER POLICY

When FERC announced its first restructuring plan, it chose a merger policy that was designed to be compatible with its plan to create competitive wholesale electricity markets. FERC adopted the US Department of Justice/Federal Trade Commission (DOJ/FTC) horizontal merger guidelines as its own (*see generally* FERC 1996b). FERC's initial choice of merger policy has served it and the nation well. FERC continued to apply its 1996 policy as of 2005, recognizing that the DOJ/FTC Guidelines reflect a tremendous amount of accumulated experience and expertise. FERC also recognized that the Guidelines are sufficiently flexible to be applied to a market with any characteristics, including the idiosyncratic characteristics of electricity markets. By choosing to adopt the DOJ/FTC Guidelines as its own, FERC also minimized potential differences of opinion between itself and the antitrust agencies with which it shares jurisdiction over proposed electricity mergers. FERC and DOJ/FTC have had remarkably few differences of opinion about the appropriate response to a proposed merger in the electricity industry.

FERC has experienced major problems, however, in its attempts to apply its merger policies. The main source of the problem is the same in each case. The appropriate method of applying FERC's merger policy depends critically on the future environment in which the potentially merged firm is likely to operate. Yet FERC lacks both the regulatory power required to create those future conditions and the prescience required to predict how they will evolve over time. This problem has manifested itself primarily in two contexts. The first context is situations in which a proposed merger is likely to have adverse effects on the performance of a competitive retail electricity market that a state might, or might not, choose to create. The second context is situations in which a proposed merger is likely to have adverse effects on the performance of a wholesale market if, but only if, the wholesale market is designed in one of several potential ways.

HOW CAN YOU APPLY A MERGER POLICY WITHOUT KNOWING THE CHARACTERISTICS OF THE MARKETS POTENTIALLY AFFECTED BY PROPOSED MERGERS?

The proposed merger of Baltimore Gas & Electric with Potomac Electric Power Company was the first case in which FERC encountered the problem of applying its merger policy. In this case, the proposed merger would have adversely affected the performance of a retail electricity market if the state authorized the creation of such a market. However, the state had not yet decided whether to authorize creation of such a market. FERC's expert witness expressed the well-supported opinion that the proposed merger would create an unduly concentrated retail market. The expert witness for the merging companies agreed with that opinion. However, he expressed the view that, since FERC did not have the power to create a competitive retail market, FERC should not consider the potential effects of the proposed merger on the performance of such a market unless and until the state or states with the power to create retail markets decided to do so. FERC agreed as matter of policy. It approved the merger because only the State of Maryland had the power to create a competitive retail market in the area affected by the proposed merger and it had not done so (*see generally* Pierce 1997a). A few months later, to no one's surprise, Maryland announced the creation of a competitive retail electricity market. As a result, FERC had approved a merger that all of the expert witnesses before it agreed would have adverse effects on the performance of a newly created competitive retail market.

The second context in which FERC has encountered serious problems in its attempts to apply its merger policy is the ubiquitous situation in which a proposed merger is likely to have an adverse effect on the performance of a competitive wholesale market if, but only if, that market is structured in

one of several ways. When FERC announced its initial plan to create competitive wholesale markets, it made no changes to its pre-existing method
of pricing transmission. Since FERC's traditional method of pricing transmission produced artificially high transmission prices, it also produced
small, highly concentrated wholesale markets. When FERC applied its
merger policy to such a market, it determined the geographic scope of the
market based on the implicit assumption that FERC would retain its traditional method of pricing transmission. FERC instructed utilities to use a
hub-and-spoke method of defining the relevant geographic market to
include only those utilities whose operating areas were adjacent to the operating area of the merged utility or one utility removed from that operating
area.

A simple hypothetical will illustrate why this definition of the relevant
geographic market made sense if, but only if, FERC continued to use its
pre-existing method of pricing transmission service (*see generally* Pierce
1996a; Pierce 1997b; Pierce 1999). Imagine utilities Giant, Titan, Tiny,
Small One and Small Two. Giant is very large and is adjacent to Tiny, which
is very small. Titan is also very large, but it is separated from Giant by Small
One and Small Two. On those facts, FERC would approve a proposed
merger between Giant and Titan, even though the resulting firm would be
very large, because FERC would conclude that Giant and Titan are not
in the same geographic market. FERC would disapprove of a proposed
merger between Giant and Tiny, however, even though Tiny is much smaller
than Titan, because FERC would conclude that Giant and Tiny are in the
same small, highly concentrated market.

That combination of actions would make sense as long as FERC
retained its pre-existing transmission pricing policy. Due to application of
that policy, every market was small and highly concentrated. A merger
between Giant and Titan could not have adverse effects on the performance
of any market because Giant and Titan could not compete effectively
against each other, given the high cost of transmitting electricity across the
fictional contract path that includes Small 1 and Small 2. Conversely, a
merger between Giant and Tiny would increase significantly the degree of
concentration in the already highly concentrated, small market that
includes only Giant, Tiny and a few other utilities.

This hypothetical raises an obvious question: how long was FERC likely
to retain its pre-existing transmission pricing policy in the new environment
in which FERC was attempting to create efficiently functioning competitive
wholesale markets? FERC was highly unlikely to retain its pre-existing
transmission pricing policy for very long if it could implement a new policy.
Indeed, its pre-existing transmission pricing policy was inherently incompatible with creation of the large markets that are essential to support

effective competition in a wholesale electricity market (*see generally* Pierce 1997b). In fact, the FERC had repeatedly acknowledged the severe flaws in its transmission pricing policy for almost a decade before it announced its initial restructuring plan.

Any socially-beneficial change in transmission pricing policy that FERC might adopt in the future would increase the size of the wholesale markets in which sellers could compete with each other. With such a new transmission pricing policy in effect, the proposed mergers described in the hypothetical would have very different effects and might well elicit the opposite responses from FERC. FERC would conclude that Giant and Titan participate in the same geographic market, and FERC might well conclude that their proposed merger would create an undue increase in the concentration of that market. By contrast, FERC almost certainly would conclude that the proposed merger of Giant and Tiny would not create an intolerable increase in the degree of concentration of the then much larger and less concentrated market in which they compete with each other.

Of course, FERC could not make a well-informed decision with respect to the likely future effects of any proposed merger without knowing the transmission pricing regime that would exist in the future, since the size of the wholesale market relevant to any proposed merger of electric generating companies depends critically on the method that is used to price transmission. For reasons that will become apparent as I describe the status of FERC's ongoing attempts to restructure the market to support wholesale competition, FERC still does not know, and can not know, what transmission pricing policy will be in effect in the US in the near future.

FERC'S EFFORTS TO CHANGE TRANSMISSION PRICING

Shortly after FERC announced its initial restructuring plan and its hub-and-spoke method of defining geographic markets relevant to proposed mergers, it began an effort to change its transmission pricing policies. FERC sought pricing policies that would be much more conducive to creating efficiently performing competitive wholesale markets. These policies were inconsistent with the hub-and-spoke method of defining geographic markets relevant to proposed mergers. Once FERC achieved some success in implementing its new transmission pricing policy, the Commission adopted a new method of determining the geographic scope of a market relevant to a proposed merger that provides a better fit with its new transmission pricing policy. Unfortunately, by then FERC had applied its hub-and-spoke methodology as the basis for its actions in several merger cases.

Before I turn to a description of FERC's current method of determining the geographic scope of a wholesale market relevant to a proposed merger, however, I need to discuss two other structural impediments to FERC's efforts to create efficiently functioning competitive wholesale markets.

Shortly after it announced its initial restructuring plan, FERC recognized two major structural impediments to its attempt to create efficiently functioning competitive wholesale markets. First, vertical integration of the transmission and generating functions created an environment in which the many utilities that performed both functions had a powerful incentive to favor sales of their own generating capacity over sales of the generating capacity of their competitors (*see generally* Pierce 1994). It was extraordinarily difficult for FERC to enforce any duty to provide third parties with nondiscriminatory access to transmission lines (*see generally* Pierce 1994). The logical solution to that problem was to require all utilities to de-integrate their transmission and generating assets. However, FERC lacked statutory power to require utilities to take that action and only a minority of utilities responded favorably to FERC's gentle urgings by voluntarily spinning off their generating assets from their transmission assets. Second, the balkanized ownership and control of the three integrated transmission grids was a major obstacle to implementation of any new transmission pricing policy that would be compatible with FERC's attempt to create effectively competitive wholesale markets (*see generally* Joskow 2004; Pierce 1997b; Pierce 1999). The logical solution to that problem was to require consolidation of ownership of all the transmission assets that comprised each of the integrated grids into a single firm, but that action was also beyond FERC's statutory powers.

FERC'S EFFORTS TO OVERCOME STRUCTURAL BARRIERS TO RESTRUCTURING – ISOs AND RTOs

FERC attempted to overcome the two major structural obstacles to its creation of competitive wholesale markets by urging utilities to adopt a second-best solution – the creation of Independent System Operators (ISOs) (FERC 1999). An ISO controls all of the transmission lines owned by its members and operates a competitive wholesale market in the area covered by those lines. FERC believed that it lacked the power to require utilities to create ISOs, so it used a variety of carrots and sticks to encourage utilities to form ISOs voluntarily. By the end of 1999, FERC had succeeded in encouraging utilities to form five ISOs – one in California, one in Texas, one in New York, one in New England, and one in the Middle Atlantic States (referred to as PJM because it includes Pennsylvania,

New Jersey and Maryland). Each ISO was flawed in some respects, however, and each differed from the others in important ways. The deficiencies in the ISOs and the variations among the ISOs were attributable primarily to FERC's belief that it lacked the power to require a utility to create or to join an ISO. Since FERC could only encourage voluntary formation of ISOs, it had no practical choice but to acquiesce to the highly imperfect ISOs that utilities proposed to create (*see generally* Pierce 1999).

The PJM ISO came closest to furthering FERC's goals. It was by far the largest of the ISOs from its inception and has since been expanded significantly to include most of the Midwest, as well as the mid-Atlantic states. Moreover, PJM adopted a transmission pricing system based on locational marginal price (LMP). LMP is the pricing system that maximizes the size of a wholesale market. At the other end of the spectrum was the California ISO, which covered only a fraction of the integrated grid that supports the provision of electricity service to the western US. The California ISO also included two characteristics that made it unusually vulnerable to exercises of market power in the form of unilateral withholding of available capacity – a prohibition on long-term contracts and a below-market price cap on retail prices (*see generally* Joskow and Kahn 2001; Sweeney 2002; Pierce 2002; Wolak 2003; Pierce 2003; Rosenzweig, Fraser et al. 2003). In the absence of long-term contracts and any demand response to an increase in the wholesale price of electricity attributable to increased relative scarcity, even a firm that accounts for only a small share of a wholesale electricity market can engage in profitable unilateral withholding of capacity.

FERC RETURNS TO IMPOSITION OF PRO-COMPETITIVE CONDITIONS IN APPROVING MERGERS

In 2000, FERC returned to the tactic it had used with some success in the 1980s – use of its merger policy pro-actively to encourage creation of competitive wholesale markets (FERC 2000). American Electric Power Company (AEP), the largest utility in the Midwest, proposed to merge with Central and Southwest Corporation (CSW), a large utility in the southwest. FERC concluded that the proposed merger would create an unduly concentrated market if the two utilities continued to use the traditional method of pricing their transmission services. However, FERC also decided that the merger would not create an unduly concentrated market if the utilities took actions that had the effect of increasing significantly the size of the wholesale market relevant to the merger. Therefore, the

Commission conditioned its approval of the proposed merger between AEP and CSW on the merged firm's commitment to join an ISO. AEP eventually complied with that condition, over the objections of two of its state regulators, by joining the PJM ISO, thereby creating the world's largest competitive wholesale electricity market – a market that now covers the mid-Atlantic states and most of the Midwest (FERC 2004a).

FERC's new use of its conditioning power to further its pro-competitive goals suffers from the same serious limitation as its prior attempt to use its conditioning power for that purpose, however. A firm can avoid becoming subject to any pro-competitive condition FERC might impose in an order authorizing the firm to participate in a merger or acquisition simply by declining to propose any mergers or acquisitions. Utilities in the southeast and west would rather refrain from engaging in any mergers or acquisitions than subject themselves to a FERC order conditioning a merger or acquisition on the firm's agreement to expose itself to competition. As a result, the only entities that are engaged in acquisition of significant utility assets in the southeast and west are financial firms that had no pre-existing role in the industry (*see generally* Beck and Hart 2004; Burr 2004).

At the end of 1999, FERC issued a rule in which it announced another change in its approach to restructuring (FERC 1999). It renamed ISOs Regional Transmission Organizations (RTOs), defined RTOs to include most of the features of the PJM ISO and announced its intention to add more carrots and sticks to its efforts to encourage utilities to join RTOs. FERC then proposed to follow up on its 1999 rule with another rule that would mandate formation of RTOs using a standard market design (SMD) based primarily on the characteristics of the PJM RTO (FERC 2000).

THE CALIFORNIA DEBACLE AND THE ENRON SCANDAL DERAIL FERC'S RESTRUCTURING EFFORTS

By 2000, it appeared that FERC was well on its way to creating large, effectively competitive wholesale markets across the country. Then came the California electricity crisis and the Enron scandal (*see generally* Pierce 2003; Sweeney 2002). The price of electricity in California increased ten-fold for a period of several months due in large part to unilateral withholding of capacity by firms like Enron. The California price spike and the Enron scandal combined to provide the opponents of restructuring – primarily utilities and state regulators in the west and the southeast – the ammunition they needed to stall FERC's restructuring process. Since 2000, FERC has made little progress in its efforts to restructure the electricity market, and it seems to have abandoned efforts to mandate formation of RTOs based on an SMD, at least for the time being (*see generally* Pierce 2005). As a result, the wholesale electricity markets in the southeast and the west continue to be the small, highly concentrated markets that were created by FERC's initial ineffective restructuring rule in 1996.

FERC'S NEW WEAPON TO INDUCE RESTRUCTURING – THREATS TO WITHDRAW AUTHORITY TO MAKE UNREGULATED WHOLESALE SALES

FERC has not yet abandoned completely its efforts to create effectively competitive wholesale markets, however. In 2004, FERC added a new stick to its arsenal of weapons to encourage utilities to create the RTOs that are necessary to support effective competition. FERC announced a new test for determining whether a firm has market power for purposes of deciding whether the firm should be authorized to make unregulated wholesale sales (FERC 2004a). The new test is nearly identical to FERC's test for determining whether a proposed merger will create an undue concentration of power in the market. If the firm fails the new market power test, FERC says that it will withdraw the firm's authority to make wholesales at unregulated prices.

When FERC announced its initial restructuring plan, it included in the plan a market power test for determining whether a firm is authorized to make unregulated wholesale sales that was extremely easy to meet (FERC 1996a). The new test FERC announced in 2004 is based on FERC's experience with the performance of restructured markets of various types. Not surprisingly, FERC has discovered that small, highly concentrated markets perform poorly because one or more sellers have the ability to exercise market power unilaterally in such markets. By contrast, large markets perform well because even large firms lack the ability to exercise market power in such markets. Thus, FERC's new market power test yields results that are highly sensitive to the geographic scope of the market in which the firm sells.

Of course, the geographic scope of a market depends critically on the transmission pricing policy that applies to that market. Markets that lack RTOs are characterized by high transmission prices that have the effect of creating small, highly-concentrated markets. Markets with RTOs have low transmission prices that create large geographic markets (Pierce 1999). Thus, not surprisingly, the initial results of the application of FERC's new market power test form a clear pattern. Large firms that are not members of RTOs fail the test, while large firms that are members of RTOs pass the test (*see generally* Ecker 2004; Strangmeier 2004). FERC obviously hopes that this carrot-and-stick use of its power to authorize firms to make unregulated wholesales will induce resistant utilities to propose the creation of new RTOs or to join existing RTOs.

If FERC continues to adhere to its new policy with respect to a firm's eligibility to make unregulated wholesales, utilities in the southeast and west may finally choose to form the large RTOs required to support effective wholesale competition. If a utility 'voluntarily' agrees to join an RTO, state regulators who want to block the utility from doing so are unlikely to be successful. Section 205(a) of the Public Utilities Regulatory Policy Act of 1978 (PURPA) authorizes FERC to:

> 'exempt electric utilities . . . from any provision of State law, or from any state rule or regulation, which . . . prevents the voluntary coordination of electrical utilities . . . if the Commission determines that such voluntary coordination is designed to obtain economical utilization of facilities and resources in any area.'

FERC has already made a well-supported determination that any state law or rule that prohibits a utility from voluntarily joining an RTO precludes utilities from engaging in voluntary coordination that would increase the economical utilization of facilities and resources (FERC 2004b). That determination allows FERC to exempt any utility from any state law that restricts the utility's ability to join an RTO. Thus, the combination of FERC's new test for eligibility to make unregulated wholesales and its application of PURPA Section 205(a) has the potential to allow FERC finally to create the large, effectively-competitive wholesale markets it has been striving to create for over a decade. If FERC can accomplish that goal, it will finally know the scope of the geographic markets relevant to a proposed merger. Those markets will be large enough to support many more efficiency-enhancing mergers without increasing unduly the level of concentration of the markets.

WILL FERC COMPLETE THE RESTRUCTURING PROCESS?

Many contingencies could keep FERC from enjoying success in its efforts to complete the restructuring process, however. The Commission could lose its nerve and back down from imposition of either its new test for determining which utilities can make unregulated wholesales or its interpretation of PURPA Section 205(a) to authorize it to exempt utilities from state restrictions on their membership in RTOs. Even if FERC remains steadfast in the face of tremendous political pressure to change one or both of those policies, utilities in the southeast and west might choose to give up their authority to make unregulated wholesales rather than to subject themselves to real competition by joining an RTO. Finally, Congress could enact a statute that prohibits FERC from coercing utilities and states into acquiescing in FERC's restructuring plan. Since 2002, legislators from the southeast have repeatedly attempted to persuade Congress to enact such legislation (*see generally* Pierce 2005). Because of these multiple contingencies, FERC still cannot know the size of the geographic market in which a merged utility will participate in the near future.

HOW SHOULD AN AGENCY APPLY A MERGER POLICY WHEN IT CANNOT KNOW THE CHARACTERISTICS OF THE MARKETS THAT WILL BE AFFECTED BY PROPOSED MERGERS?

Looking back, I would give FERC an A minus for the merger policies it has adopted and applied. It was wise to adopt the DOJ/FTC merger guidelines and then to attempt to apply those flexible guidelines to the unique characteristics of the electricity market. FERC's inability to predict with confidence the size and nature of the markets relevant to the proposed mergers that it approved was regrettable, but beyond FERC's control. I think that FERC should have been more conservative in acting on the proposed mergers that came before it during the long period in which it could not (and still cannot) predict the nature and size of the markets that might be affected by those proposed mergers in the foreseeable future. Specifically, I would have preferred an approach in which FERC disapproved a proposed merger if it would create an undue concentration of power in any market that was likely to be created in the foreseeable future as a result of the ongoing process of restructuring the electricity market. FERC rejected that approach and adopted instead an approach in which it approved a proposed merger if it was not likely to create an undue concentration of power in any presently-existing market, even if the proposed merger would create an undue concentration of power in a market that was likely to be created in the foreseeable future (*see generally* Pierce 1996a; Pierce 1997a; Pierce 1999). FERC's approach created the obvious risk that it would allow a merger to proceed that would then have severe adverse effects on the performance of a market that was created by the restructuring process a year or two after FERC approved the merger.

I must admit, however, that I have not been able to identify a single case in which that risk actually manifested itself. I doubt that FERC's use of the hub-and-spoke method of geographic market definition in wholesale mergers has induced it to approve a merger that will create an undue concentration of power in the much larger wholesale markets that FERC has now created in some parts of the country and is attempting to create in the rest of the country.

Similarly, I doubt that FERC's failure to consider the potential effects of a proposed merger on a retail market that a state might create has done any harm. The proposed merger that most clearly raised this issue – the merger between Baltimore Gas & Electric and Potomac Electric Power Company – was never consummated for reasons independent of FERC's approval (The District of Columbia Public Service Commission disapproved the merger). More broadly, it has become clear that effectively competitive retail markets are extraordinarily difficult to create for reasons independent of the number of electric utilities that provide service in the area in which a state authorizes creation of such a market. Indeed, many proponents of FERC's restructuring plan, including many that once supported creation of retail markets, now believe that retail markets accessible to small customers are not viable today and are unlikely to become viable in the near future. There are many reasons for this growing belief that have been discussed in detail elsewhere (*see generally* Joskow 2000; Pierce 2005). For present purposes, it is enough to note that it is extraordinarily difficult, if not impossible, to design a retail market in which small consumers have a realistic prospect of attaining benefits that exceed the extremely high transactions costs they confront when attempting to participate in such a market. Of course, all consumers benefit substantially if indirectly from creation of effectively competitive wholesale markets even if some have no practical means of benefiting directly from participation in effectively competitive retail markets.

I would also give FERC high marks for using its power to condition approval of a proposed merger on the merged firm's willingness to engage in pro-competitive behavior. FERC's decision to condition approval of proposed mergers in the late 1980s and early 1990s on the merged firm's commitment to provide third-party access to its transmission lines opened some markets to competition for the first time. The Commission's decision to condition its approval of proposed mergers in the late 1990s on the merged firm's commitment to join an RTO allowed FERC to create the world's largest and most effective competitive wholesale electricity market – a market that now spans the mid-Atlantic states and most of the Midwest. FERC's power to attach conditions to its approval of proposed mergers can never be sufficient alone to empower FERC to create effectively competitive wholesale markets across the US, however. A firm can remain out of the reach of that conditioning power simply by declining to propose a merger – as the electric utilities in the southeast and west have shown.

The serious problems that have arisen in FERC's lengthy and still incomplete process of restructuring the electricity market are attributable to factors other than FERC's merger policy. Basically, Congress gave FERC a mandate to restructure the market but refused to give it the tools required to implement that mandate. To the extent that merger policy has played some role in rendering it difficult to implement a restructuring plan that will allow the country to rely primarily on competition to yield improved results in the electricity market, the problem is that we have had too few mergers, rather than too many. In that respect, the situation has not changed much since Breyer and MacAvoy completed their excellent study of the electricity market in 1974 (Breyer and MacAvoy 1974, 89–121).

THE NEED FOR MERGERS IN THE RESTRUCTURED MARKET

We still have too many firms that are too small to take advantage of the available economies of scale in generating and wholesaling power (*see generally* Bilicic 2003; Bilicic and Connor 2004; Marks 2004). That problem is likely to dissipate if, and to the extent that, FERC is successful in creating large wholesale markets by coercing utilities to join RTOs. The resulting competition will force participants in the generating and wholesale markets to consolidate to the extent required to become efficient participants in those markets. Of course, many of those socially-beneficial mergers could not take place until Congress took the long-overdue action of repealing the Public Utility Holding Company Act (*see generally* Bilicic 2003). It finally did so in the 2005 Energy Act. That would still leave us with a very poor industry structure in an even more important context, however. The balkanized pattern of ownership and control of the three integrated transmission grids that support provision of electricity service to the US is continuing to cause severe problems that eventually will doom any restructuring plan to failure unless they are addressed effectively (*see generally* Henney and Russell 2002; Joskow 2004; Pierce 2005).

FERC is attempting to address the problems caused by the balkanized structure of the transmission sector of the industry by inducing utilities to adopt the second-best solution of RTOs – entities that control but do not own large portions of an integrated grid. There is increasing evidence that this second-best solution addresses one set of problems reasonably well. However, RTOs create a new set of serious problems. Generally, any legal regime that separates ownership from control of major assets is certain to create problems. The problems that are emerging in the context of electricity transmission include inadequate incentives for any company to make the investments in new transmission capacity or the expenditures on maintenance of existing transmission assets that are essential both to maintain reliable service and to support newly created competitive wholesale markets (*see generally* Henney and Russell 2002; Joskow 2004; Hirst 2004; Pierce 2005). If we do not solve this problem quickly, we are certain to see a large increase in the incidence of cascading blackouts and the evolution of markets that are so geographically limited by transmission capacity constraints that they will perform poorly and will be extremely vulnerable to unilateral exercises of market power even by relatively small market participants.

In theory, it is easy to identify a solution to this problem. We need to induce the owners of the transmission assets that comprise each integrated grid to engage in the widespread consolidation of ownership required to create a single firm that owns and controls all of the assets that comprise each integrated grid. At the same time, of course, we need to induce each of those vertically integrated firms to split off into separate firms all of the generating plants and other assets that they use to participate in the newly competitive wholesale markets (*see generally* Pierce 1994). We then need to give FERC plenary and exclusive power to regulate transmission. Once we take those steps, FERC can adopt a performance-based method of regulating each of the new transmission-only firms that will encourage those firms to make all needed expansions of capacity and maintenance of existing capacity. I am afraid that the US has no chance of completing a beneficial restructuring of the US electricity industry unless Congress first enacts legislation to give FERC the necessary authority. Unfortunately, however, Congress is not likely to enact such legislation until the US experiences the large increase in the incidence of cascading blackouts that I see as inevitable without additional major changes in the structure of the market. Ironically, the changes the US desperately needs today are generally the same changes that Breyer and MacAvoy urged over 30 years ago (Breyer and MacAvoy 1974).

Finally, three recent developments have changed the regulatory environment in which mergers and acquisitions take place in the US electric power industry. First, FERC appears to have given up its efforts to restructure the industry in the southeast and west for now. It was not willing to continue to press its attempt to create effectively competitive wholesale markets in those regions over the opposition of utilities and politicians. As a result, providers that participate in effectively competitive wholesale electricity markets serve about half of the US population while vertically integrated, state-regulated franchised monopolies serve the other half. That dichotomous market structure will continue to complicate greatly FERC's efforts to devise and to implement sensible merger policies.

Second, Congress repealed the Public Utility Holding Company Act effective on 8 February 2006. That congressional action removes a major obstacle to socially-beneficial mergers. However, the third recent development illustrates the strength of the remaining obstacles to such mergers. On 14 September 2006, Exelon Corp. and Public Service Enterprise Group announced that they had abandoned the largest proposed merger in the history of the US electric power industry. Even though Pennsylvania, Illinois, the Department of Justice and FERC had approved the proposed merger, Exelon and Public Service concluded that the conditions imposed on the proposed merger by regulators in New Jersey would have rendered the proposed merger uneconomic.

NOTE

1. The European grid suffers from lesser versions of some of the same problems that plague the US grid, because the entity that owns and operates each part of the integrated European grid changes at each national border (Henney and Russell 2002).

REFERENCES

Beck, Mike and Hart, Craig (2004), After FERC's Market Power Ruling: Will Financiers Dominate the Market? Public Utilities Fortnightly 28–32, September.

Bilicic, George W. (2003), PUHCA Repeal: Whither Consolidation? Public Utilities Fortnightly 25–29, September 15.

Bilicic, George W. and Connor, Ian C. (2004), Electric Utility Reliability: The Merger Solution, Public Utilities Fortnightly 28–30, March.

Black, Bernard S. and Pierce, Richard J. (1993), The Choice Between Markets and Central Planning in Regulating the US Electricity Industry, Columbia Law Review 93(6): 1339–1441, October.

Breyer, Stephen and MacAvoy, Paul (1974), Energy Regulation by the Federal Power Commission, Brookings Institution, Washington DC.

Burr, Michael T. (2004), The Utility Sector: A Wall Street Takeover? Public Utilities Fortnightly 34–38, January.

Ecker, Jon (2004), Failing the Market Power Test: How FERC's Ruling Could Affect Wholesale Power Markets, Public Utilities Fortnightly 14–19, October.

Energy Policy Act of 1992, Pub. L. No. 102-486, 106 Stat. 2776 (1992).

Federal Power Act, 16 USC. §§824 et seq.

FERC Notice of Proposed Rulemaking, Remedying Undue Discrimination through Open Access Transmission Service and Standard Electricity Market Design, Docket No. RM01-12-000 (31 July 2002).

FERC Order No. 888, FERC Stats and Regs ¶31,036 (1996a), CCH.

FERC Order No. 592, FERC Stats and Regs ¶31,044 (1996b), CCH.

FERC Order No. 2000, FERC Stats and Regs ¶31,089 (1999), CCH.

FERC Opinion No. 442, American Electric Power Co., 90 FERC ¶61,129 (2000), CCH.

FERC Order, AEP Power Marketing, 107 FERC ¶61,018 (2004a), CCH.

FERC Opinion No. 472, New PJM Companies, 107 FERC ¶61,271 (2004b), CCH.

Henney, Alex and Russell, Tim (2002), Lesson from the Institutional Framework of Transmission System Operation, and Energy Markets in Most West European Countries and Some Other Countries the Case for Transcos, EEE Limited, London.

Hirst, Eric (2004), US Transmission Capacity: Present Status and Future Prospects, Edison Electric Institute, Washington DC.

Hogan, William W. (1993), Electric Transmission: A New Model for Old Principles, The Electricity Journal 5(2): 18–37, March.

Hogan, William W. (1997), Nodes and Zones in Electricity Markets: Seeking Simplified Congestion Pricing, Eighteenth Annual Conference of the US AEE/IAEE, San Francisco, September.

Joskow, Paul L. (2000), Why Do We Need Electricity Retailers? You Can Get It Cheaper Wholesale, Massachusetts Institute of Technology Faculty Website, Cambridge, February.

Joskow, Paul L. and Kahn, Edward (2001), A Quantitative Analysis of Pricing Behavior in California's Wholesale Electricity Market During Summer 2000, University of California Energy Institute, Berkeley, January.

Joskow, Paul L. (2003), The Difficult Transition to Competitive Electricity Markets in the US, AEI-Brookings Joint Center for Regulatory Studies Related Publication 03-13, Washington DC (July).

Joskow, Paul L. (2004), Transmission Policy in the United States, AEI-Brookings Joint Center for Regulatory Studies Related Publication 04-26, Washington DC, October.

Marks, Ken (2004), Dial M for Merger: When Will Utilities See the Next Round of Deals? Public Utilities Fortnightly 55–58, October.

Pierce, Richard J. (1986), A Proposal to Deregulate the Market for Bulk Power, Virginia Law Review 72(7): 1183–1235, October.

Pierce, Richard J. (1994), The Advantages of De-Integrating the Electricity Industry, The Electricity Journal 7(9): 16–21, November.

Pierce, Richard J. (1996a), Slow Down the Mega-Merger Feeding Frenzy, The Electricity Journal 9(1): 10–13, January/February.

Pierce, Richard J. (1996b), Antitrust Policy in the New Electricity Industry, Energy Law Journal 17(1): 29–58.

Pierce, Richard J. (1997a), Merger Policy and Federalism, The Electricity Journal 10(7): 49–55, August/September.

Pierce, Richard J. (1997b), FERC Must Adopt an Efficient Transmission Pricing Policy – Now, The Electricity Journal 10(8): 79–85, October.

Pierce, Richard J. (1999), Why FERC Must Mandate Efficiently-Structured Regional ISOs – Now, The Electricity Journal 12(1): 49–56, January/February.

Pierce, Richard J. (2002), How Will the California Debacle Affect Energy Deregulation? Administrative Law Review 54(1): 389–408.

Pierce, Richard J. (2003), Market Manipulation and Market Flaws, The Electricity Journal 15(1): 39–46, January/February.

Pierce, Richard J. (2005), Realizing the Promise of Electric Power Deregulation, Wake Forest Law Review 40(2): 451–496.

Public Utility Holding Company Act, 15 USC. §§79 et seq.

Public Utilities Regulatory Policies Act, 16 USC. §§ 824 et seq.

Rosenzweig, Michael B., Fraser, Hamish, Falk, Jonathon and Voll, Sarah (2003), Market Power and Demand Responsiveness: Letting Customers Protect Themselves, The Electricity Journal 16(4): 11–23, May.

Ruff, Larry (2002), Economic Principles of Demand Response in Electricity, Edison Electric Institute, Washington DC, October.

Strangmeier, Suzanna (2004), Seven Fail FERC Test of Market Power, Natural Gas Week 8, 20 December 2004.

Sweeney, James L. (2002), The California Electricity Crisis, Hoover Institution, Palo Alto.

Watkiss, Jeffrey and Smith, Douglas (1994), The Energy Policy Act of 1992: A Watershed for Competition in the Wholesale Power Market, Yale Journal on Regulation 10: 447–489.

Wolak, Frank A. (2003), Designing Market Rules for a Competitive Electricity Market, University of California Energy Institute, Berkeley.

3. Natural gas pipelines: can merger enforcement preserve the gains from restructuring?

Diana L. Moss[1]

INTRODUCTION

Of the sectors that have undergone major structural reform in the United States, the natural gas pipeline industry is unique in several ways. In comparison to electricity and local telecommunications, the two most transitionally challenged industries, the restructuring experience in natural gas may have more successfully proved the gains of reform in terms of less invasive regulation, workable competition and consumer choice.[2] For example, there is evidence of improved market performance resulting from access and a market-oriented regulatory approach; declines in natural gas transportation prices and development of spot markets as well as market hubs and hub services. There is also empirical evidence of market integration that signals more efficient market operation.

A number of reasons may account for this experience. First, pipeline markets are probably better characterized as network oligopolies (O'Neill 2005, 113) than monopoly essential facilities, reducing the need for more invasive regulation and improving prospects for competitive reforms. Second, restructuring has operated on an industry that was integrated largely through contract, instead of ownership. Policy makers were therefore not saddled with the troublesome job of vertical unbundling or, alternatively, imposing forced access on vertically integrated network owners.

Third, the economic distortions created by wellhead price regulation were arguably the primary impetus for regulatory reform. Pent-up forces perpetuated by years of intervention in the wellhead gas market may therefore have primed the industry for more rapid adjustment once the mechanisms for change were in place. Finally, entry into the critical pipeline network segment of the industry is controlled by federal, as opposed to state or regional entities (although there are always local environmental issues in the siting process). This avoids the jurisdictional friction and policy incongruities associated with the balkanized system found, for example, in electricity.

There are also similarities between the restructuring experience in natural gas and other industries. For example, reforms in natural gas have produced a mixed model of industry organization where parts of the industry remain more heavily regulated, while others are subject to lighter-handed regulation or left entirely to competition. Much like other formerly regulated or transitioning industries, restructuring in natural gas also triggered an intensive round of merger activity. This activity has fostered further changes in market participants, firm organization and industry structure.

In most restructuring industries, merger activity highlights the tension between the potential benefits of increased efficiency and innovation and possible trends toward market concentration. Quantitative assessments of changes in restructuring industries undergoing significant merger activity have yielded useful insights for reform policies (Peltzman and Winston 2000). However, qualitative assessments of the interplay between regulatory reform and merger activity are also enlightening. For example, evaluating the relationships between reforms and merger activity involving natural gas pipelines may answer several important questions. How has this pattern of restructuring affected the motivation for merger and types of mergers proposed? How has the expansion of products and services, development of market hubs and geographic market integration resulting from improved access affected the dimensions of relevant markets in merger review? What are the implications of merger activity for firm conduct, both at the horizontal pipeline level and in vertical relationships with upstream gas marketing and downstream electric generation or gas distribution?

This chapter attempts to address the foregoing questions. It proceeds as follows: the first section provides a brief regulatory history of the natural gas industry; the second section assesses the major changes in the commodity, technology, markets and institutions brought about by restructuring to date; third is an overview of pipeline mergers over the last 20 years; and the fourth section analyzes merger activity in the context of restructuring. The chapter concludes with major observations regarding the relationships between restructuring and merger activity and how they may inform the policy process.

REGULATORY HISTORY

Only a few industries have experienced complex and far-reaching packages of regulatory initiatives comparable to those that have characterized natural gas reform. In the 20-year period spanning 1984 to 2004, the Federal Energy Regulatory Commission (FERC) implemented more than 20 major orders designed to correct market malfunction, remove impediments to more efficient market operation and to create regulatory infrastructure more compatible with market-driven outcomes. Some argue that FERC's aggressive posture toward natural gas restructuring was unprecedented, as reflected in the magnitude and regularity of legal challenge. At the same time, however, the starting point for reforms was a highly fractured system, guaranteed to produce distorted and inefficient outcomes. Arguably, the only response under such circumstances was an aggressive program of restructuring.

The regulatory infrastructure for natural gas was created in the early 1900s in response to the anticompetitive abuses of large holding companies. Among other things, the Natural Gas Act (NGA) of 1938 granted the Federal Power Commission (FPC) two important types of authority. First was the authority to set 'just and reasonable' rates for the transmission or sale for resale of gas in interstate commerce. Second was the authority to grant certificates of public convenience and necessity. These certificates allowed for the construction and operation of pipeline facilities and provision of services, as well as the abandonment of those facilities and services (15 U.S.C. § 717).

The regulatory history of the natural gas industry after the passage of the NGA separates into three periods. The first spans the mid-1950s through the late 1970s, during which concerns over market power extended regulation from local distribution and interstate pipelines to the production segment of the industry. The second era covers the late 1970s through the mid-1980s and is marked by market distortions and inefficiency created by an intractable mix of wellhead price decontrol, declines in demand due to conservation and pipelines' contractual liabilities. The third and current era began in the late 1980s. It reflects the bulk of the transition from regulation to more competitive markets attributable to mandatory open access under FERC's Order 636 (FERC 1992). This era is marked by the development of spot markets, new market institutions, participants, products and services and, in limited instances, retail access.

The First Era: Regulation

The NGA did not initially apply to the production, gathering or local distribution of natural gas. It was not until 1954 that the Supreme Court interpreted the NGA in the far-reaching *Phillips Petroleum Co. v. Wisconsin* (1954) (*Phillips*) decision to mean that the FPC's authority extended to the regulation of rates of producer sales in interstate commerce for resale, certifications and abandonments. But the multitude of gas producers and contracts between producers and pipelines made cost-of-service regulation of wellhead price impractical. This forced a shift to a system of regional price regulation. While the first ceilings were not implemented until 1968, interim ceilings dampened incentives for producers to explore for and develop gas reserves.

Demand for gas grew significantly within this period. However, prices held below market clearing levels were unable to respond, creating short-ages. Producers thus shifted their sales to the unregulated intrastate markets, exacerbating shortages and forcing pipelines to curtail deliveries to their local delivery companies (LDCs) and industrial customers in the early 1970s.[3] FERC issued Orders 431 and 467 to address various aspects of these economically devastating curtailments (Breyer 1980, 253–254). However, in the end, Congress enacted the Natural Gas Policy Act (NGPA) in 1978, which attempted to correct the distortions in the intrastate and interstate markets by replacing producer price regulation with a variety of ceilings for wellhead prices (15 U.S.C. §§ 3301–3332).

The Second Era: Distortions

Despite increases in wellhead price ceilings over time, the NGPA controls proved as equally mismatched with market dynamics as price regulation under *Phillips*. In this era, pipelines signed long-term take-or-pay contracts at prices close to the maximum NGPA ceilings. But energy conservation put downward pressure on the demand for natural gas, converting the shortage of the 1970s to a surplus (the gas 'bubble') in the 1980s. Unable to pass on their high gas costs to fuel-switchable industrial customers, pipelines thus found themselves with significant take-or-pay liabilities. FERC implemented a number of adjustments to deal with the take-or-pay problem. Order 380 (1984) released LDCs from their obligations under long-term contracts to take-or-pay for a certain amount of gas (i.e., their minimum bills). A series of orders granted pipelines blanket certificates to transport gas for fuel-switchable (i.e., industrial) customers. Another (unsuccessful) policy initiative allowed producers to sell directly to such customers, for which the pipelines provided transportation-only service. This relieved the pipelines of their obligation to purchase gas from producers.[4]

FERC responded to legal challenges by the D.C. Circuit to its efforts to resolve the take-or-pay crisis with its first access initiative – Order 436 (1985). The order encouraged unbundling of pipelines' sales and trans-portation services. Customers with bundled service were allowed to convert to transportation-only service, initiating the dismantling of the pipeline's 'merchant' function. FERC also authorized blanket certificates under the condition that a pipeline offer open-access transportation on a first-come, first-served basis. The D.C. Circuit remanded Order 436 on the basis that it did not adequately address the take-or-pay issue. FERC responded with Order 500 (1987). The order attempted to allocate transition costs associated with renegotiating and terminating long-term contracts by shifting some of the liability to producers, LDC customers and even to other pipelines. Further legal reversals and remands ensued, bringing an end to a trying era (Kearney and Merrill 1998, 1379).

The Third Era: Transition

The third era of natural gas restructuring was ushered in by the Natural Gas Wellhead Decontrol Act (NGWDA) of 1989, which provided for the phase-out of wellhead price controls (15 U.S.C. § 3301). The NGWDA ratified and codified what the Commission had already done. The legislation removed all remaining ceilings on wellhead prices, eliminating disparities created by the NGPA and contributing to the expansion of the spot gas market. During this era, FERC persevered in its efforts to remove obstacles to competition. Order 490 (1988) allowed for the abandonment of contracts with pipelines when the contracts expired, furthering the ability of certain customers to bypass the pipeline. Despite a general lack of compliance with the voluntary provisions of Order 436, it was apparent that the pipeline's merchant function was disappearing. By 1991, for example, pipeline sales of gas fell to under 15 per cent of total volumes transported, while transportation volumes increased to over 85 per cent (Smith 1995, 80).

It was not until 1992 that FERC fully unbundled commodity sales and transmission sales with Order 636 (1992). Order 636 highlighted the limitations of voluntary access under Order 436 (Moss 2005, 267). Under its provisions, interstate pipelines were required to provide open-access transportation and storage. This was achieved through the principle of comparability, under which the pipeline was required to provide service under the same terms and conditions it provided to 'itself.' Unbundling of sales and transportation service allowed customers to choose among competing providers for elements of their service. The Straight-Fixed Variable rate (SFV) design allowed the pipeline to recover all its fixed transportation and storage costs through the demand (i.e., reservation) charge, reducing the risk of non-recovery.

The access initiative also established a framework by which firm transportation and storage customers could 'release' unwanted or excess capacity. To promote access to information on capacity, FERC implemented the seminal electronic bulletin board (EBB) system under which pipelines were required to disclose real-time information on capacity availability, improving transparency in market transactions.[5] Order 636, among other things, provided more flexibility by segmenting pipeline capacity. In sum, open access focused significantly on a greater reliance on contracts, information to promote transparency and market rules.

RESTRUCTURING CHANGES

The term 'restructuring' is used in a number of contexts, so it is helpful to clarify its meaning here. Natural gas, electricity, telecommunications and transportation are industries that have undergone fundamental transformations in the transition to market-oriented regulation. Federal regulation of natural gas no longer deals exclusively with permissions to enter along with allowable rates and profits for the purpose of protecting the consumer. It also addresses a broader set of regulatory objectives for promoting competition among rivals through a number of mechanisms. These include flexible rate designs such as incentive, negotiated and market-based rates, removal of entry barriers, streamlining processes to facilitate business decisions and realignment and developing infrastructure to support increased demand and reliability. This migration away from more invasive regulation is a central component of industry 'restructuring'.

Restructuring has important implications for merger activity and enforcement. However, as noted earlier, consolidation also produces a feedback effect, changing some of the industry characteristics upon which restructuring policies operate. Capturing this two-way effect is an important aspect of policy making, particularly under the 'mixed model' presented by natural gas pipelines. Before attempting that analysis, however, it is important to note the major areas in which the natural gas industry has been transformed by restructuring. These include: (1) relationships among market participants; (2) products and services; (3) capacity expansion and (4) patterns of prices and costs.

Relationships among Market Participants

Perhaps the most striking result of a changed regulatory regime in natural gas is the redefinition of buyer–seller relationships in a relatively undisturbed industry structure (Pierce 1994, 342). Numerous FERC initiatives have attempted to address the inability of contractual relationships to respond to distortions introduced by wellhead price regulation. For years, industrial consumers and LDCs purchased gas from the pipeline as a commodity bundled with transportation service. The elimination of minimum bills, abandonment of gas purchase contracts and bypass allowed buyers greater flexibility in managing their gas acquisition costs. Many of these former purchasers of bundled service thus became sophisticated buyers in a move from procurement under a standard tariff to a more flexible contract-base system of acquisition (Kearney and Merrill 1998, 1330–1331). Arguably, without drastic modification of historical buyer–seller relationships, competition would be slow to emerge. And it did emerge, but not without legal challenges to FERC's natural gas restructuring policies.

Together with increased competition for end users created by the loss of the pipeline's merchant function, many of the alterations in buyer–seller relationships ushered in shorter-term contracts and spurred the development of competing end-to-end networks. For example, the term of transportation contracts decreased from an average of 11 years in 1994 to about eight years in 1999 (Mariner-Volpe 2000, 14). The redefinition of relationships in the gas transportation segment of the industry was shepherded along by the emergence of the affiliated and unaffiliated gas marketer, that provided many of the customer management functions that the pipeline performed before access.[6]

Products and Services

A second result of changed regulation was the development of new products and services. Prior to access, sales of bundled gas constituted at least half of pipeline services. By the early 1990s, these sales had all but disappeared and were replaced with sales of released capacity on the secondary market created by Order 636, so-called no-notice service and a greater role of firm transportation relative to interruptible service (Mariner-Volpe 2000, 21). Access to information on pipeline capacity also improved through electronic postings, access and trading.

The development of regional market centers or 'hubs' was also a seminal development in providing interconnections among various regional pipelines. Hubs gave rise to a host of new products and services that allowed consumers additional flexibility and ability to manage gas acquisition costs. These services included wheeling, parking, loading, peaking, balancing and compression. The strategic importance of storage as an inventory and risk management tool also increased, as has the frequency of reporting on available storage capacity.

Capacity Expansion

A third result of regulatory changes has been expansion of pipeline and high-deliverability storage. Relieving capacity-constraints and access to new reserves in the Gulf of Mexico and in parts of Canada have been important drivers of expansion projects. Between 1990 and 1998, for example, 18 new pipeline systems were constructed in the US (Mariner-Volpe 2000, 7). Extensions from existing pipelines, looping and additional compression have all been used to increase capacity on existing pipelines.

Prices and Costs

Finally, regulatory changes have induced different patterns of prices and costs in the industry. With the removal of price ceilings by the mid-1980s, delivered gas prices fell steadily in real terms until the early 1990s. The development of spot markets for gas and increased price transparency brought not only gains in economic efficiency but also greater exposure to price volatility beginning in the early 1990s.[7] The emergence of the futures market signaled the importance of risk management, including the need for hedging and forward contracting. Since the early 1990s, wellhead prices have risen. However, transmission and distribution costs declined annually for commercial, industrial and electric utility customers from 1984 to 1995 (Mariner-Volpe 2000, 23). This was due largely to increased throughput from higher demand and better utilization of existing systems.

OVERVIEW OF PIPELINE MERGERS

Regulatory and Antitrust Review

The roles of regulation and antitrust in restructuring industries are in many cases most clearly defined by merger activity. Savings clauses contained in a number of regulatory statutes or seminal court decisions have preserved a role for antitrust in many regulated industries. For example, the Supreme Court's decision in *United States v. Otter Tail* (1973) mandating access to electricity transmission preserved a role for antitrust. In the *Verizon Communications Inc. v. Trinko* (2004) decision, the Supreme Court specifically acknowledged the savings clause in the 1996 Telecommunications Act even though it did not find antitrust liability. But in reality, antitrust has played a very limited role in non-merger enforcement. Successful anti-monopolization cases under Section 2 of the Sherman Act in regulated industries are relatively rare (e.g., *Trinko* 2004).

The foregoing means that regulation rather than antitrust is often the first line of defense against anticompetitive conduct (LaRue 1990, 40). This is not so in the case of merger enforcement, unless a regulatory agency is solely vested with review authority (e.g., railroad mergers and the Surface

Transportation Board). Merger enforcement is often carried out by both an antitrust and regulatory agency but under different standards. Regulatory agencies apply a 'public interest' standard which takes into consideration competitive effects and the effect of a merger on other factors such as rates and quality of service. Antitrust agencies, on the other hand, apply the 'no harm' standard which focuses only on the effect of a merger on competition.

Natural gas presents a different case. Merger review is carried out primarily by the antitrust agencies. This role was decided in 1962 by the Supreme Court in *California v. Federal Power Commission* (1962). In that case, the court decided that the federal courts retained antitrust jurisdiction over natural gas mergers, a finding reinforced two years later in *United States v. El Paso Natural Gas* (1964) (Balto and Mongoven 2001, 537). Since then, the Federal Trade Commission has assumed primary responsibility for evaluating natural gas pipeline mergers.

At the same time, however, Section 7 of the NGA confers on FERC the responsibility for finding that a certificate of public convenience and necessity for the acquisition or abandonment of pipeline facilities is in the public interest (15 U.S.C. §717). While FERC could arguably undertake a review of the competitive effect of pipeline mergers in discharging the public interest requirement of its certificate authority, the Commission has never done so.[8] On the other hand, FERC does review certain mergers involving pipelines through its authority under Section 203 of the Federal Power Act (FPA) (16 U.S.C. §824b(a)).

Under Section 203, the Commission is required to find transactions involving the disposition of jurisdictional electricity assets to be consistent with the public interest. This could include transactions involving electricity and other types of assets (e.g., natural gas, coal, etc.). The Commission's ability to reach natural gas under Section 203 is therefore effectively limited to vertical mergers that combine electricity generation with gas pipelines. FERC has exercised its authority in a number of high-profile cases such as *Pacific/Enova* (1997) and *Dominion/CNG* (1999). In those cases, FERC employed conduct-based remedies while the DOJ (*Pacific/Enova*) and the FTC (*Dominion/CNG*) required divestitures to remedy potential competitive harm.[9]

This sorting out of merger enforcement jurisdiction has had important implications for the consistency of review, treatment of policy issues and remedies imposed on natural gas pipeline mergers. That horizontal pipeline mergers are reviewed exclusively by the FTC could be considered beneficial for the consistency, transparency and predictability it creates for merger review. For example, dual review authority (e.g., of electric/gas mergers) could raise the potential for conflicts in the application of the 'public interest' and 'no harm' standards. Theories of competitive harm can also differ, as can the types of remedies employed.

Challenged Mergers

Table 3.1 lists the 16 horizontal and vertical natural gas mergers challenged by the antitrust agencies and/or the FERC from 1985 to 2003. Mergers involving pipeline gathering systems are excluded, in the interest of focusing attention on the parts of the industry most affected by reforms – interstate transportation and retail gas distribution. Column 4 notes whether the merger was horizontal, vertical or both, and Column 5 notes the major theory of competitive harm in each case.

About two-thirds of the challenged mergers in Table 3.1 were horizontal combinations that combined pipeline assets. Motivations for these types of mergers likely included market extension, i.e., expansion into new service territories or to develop a nationwide 'footprint'. Such mergers potentially enhance efficiency by decreasing costs through better utilization of pipeline capacity (e.g., increased throughput). However, in most cases, they increase market concentration in relevant markets, creating or enhancing the ability and/or incentive of the merged firm – unilaterally or in coordination with other firms – to adversely affect prices and output.

The remaining one-third of the transactions listed in Table 3.1 were vertical mergers. Most of these were the so-called 'convergence' mergers that combined gas transportation or distribution with electric generation. Motivations for these transactions likely included economies of coordination between fuel supply and generation, management of fuel price and supply risk and elimination of double margins. At the same time, however, such mergers create or enhance the ability and/or incentive to adversely affect upstream gas transportation prices *and* downstream electricity price and output through a variety of exclusionary strategies.

The numerous gas pipeline mergers and acquisitions that went unchallenged by the antitrust agencies or by FERC are not listed in Table 3.1. A number of these included diversification into complementary lines of business such as energy marketing, financial risk management and commodity trading. These transactions would bring under the firm's umbrella the tools for conducting business in a more market-driven environment. In the case of Enron, for example, successive mergers created a large, integrated business 'platform' ranging from fuel supply to delivered energy products.

Figure 3.1 shows a histogram of the mergers listed in Table 3.1. One series of horizontal mergers coincided closely with Order 436 in 1985. This was followed by a second series of mergers beginning around 1996 – after the issuance of Order 636. This series lagged behind Order 636 by a few years and was propelled in part by concurrent reforms in electricity and growing complementarities between natural gas and gas-fired electric generation. It is risky to draw too many conclusions about the significance of

Table 3.1   *Natural gas mergers challenged by the antitrust agencies and/or the Federal Energy Regulatory Commission*

	Year	Merging parties	Type of merger	Theory of competitive harm	Remedy
(1)	(2)	(3)	(4)	(5)	(6)
1	1985	InterNorth/ Houston Natural	Horizontal – pipeline/pipeline	Collusion	FTC – Pipeline divestiture
2	1986	Occidental/ MidCon	Vertical – gas producer/ pipeline	Regulatory evasion	FTC – Pipeline divestiture
3	1986	MidCon/ United Energy	Horizontal – pipeline/pipeline	Unilateral/ collusion	FTC – Pipeline divestiture
4	1989	Panhandle/ Texas Eastern	Horizontal – pipeline/pipeline	Unilateral	FTC – Pipeline divestiture
5	1989	Arkla/TransArk	Horizontal – pipeline/pipeline	Lessening of competition	FTC – Pipeline divestiture
6	1995	Questar/Kern River	Horizontal – pipeline/pipeline	Potential competition	FTC – Injunction
7	1998	Enova/Pacific	Vertical – pipeline/electric generation	Raising rivals' costs	DOJ – Electric generation divestiture FERC – Codes of conduct, electronic posting of capacity information
8	1999	Dominion/ CNG	Vertical – pipeline/electric generation	Raising rivals' costs	FTC – Gas distribution divestiture FERC – vacated and remanded
9	1999	El Paso/Sonat	Horizontal – pipeline/pipeline	Collusion/ potential competition	FTC – Pipeline divestiture
10	1999	CMS/Duke Energy	Vertical – (1) pipeline/gas distribution and (2) pipeline/electric generation	Raising rivals' costs	FTC – Designated capacity for interconnection, electronic posting of capacity information

Table 3.1   (continued)

	Year	Merging parties	Type of merger	Theory of competitive harm	Remedy
(1)	(2)	(3)	(4)	(5)	(6)
11	2001	El Paso/PG&E	Horizontal – pipeline/pipeline	Unilateral	FTC – Pipeline divestiture, operating agreement
12	2001	El Paso/Coastal	Horizontal – pipeline/pipeline	Lessening of competition/ potential competition	FTC – Pipeline divestiture, development fund to finance construction
13	2001	Entergy/Koch	Vertical – (1) pipeline/gas distribution and (2) pipeline/ electric generation	Regulatory evasion	FTC – Transparent gas purchasing, electronic posting of gas supply information FERC – No conditions
14	2001	Detroit Edison/ MichCon	Horizontal – electric distribution/gas distribution Vertical – gas distribution/ electric generation	Horizontal – lessening of competition Vertical – raising rivals' costs	FTC – Divestiture, easement agreement
15	2003	Southern Union/CMS	Horizontal – pipeline/pipeline	Unilateral/ Coordinated interaction	FTC – Termination of management agreement
16	2004	Enterprise/ GulfTerra	Horizontal – pipeline/pipeline	Lessening of competition	FTC – Divestiture

Source: see Notes for case citations.

periods of merger activity or lags between major restructuring initiatives and the onset of merger activity. However, lags likely reveal market participants' perceptions of the risks and incentives that restructuring creates. Larger lags, for example, could indicate more uncertainty about the

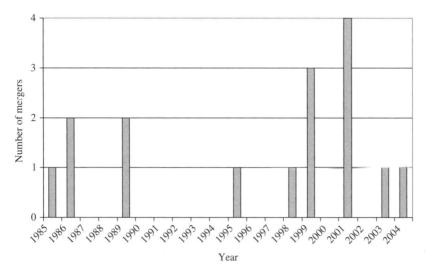

Figure 3.1   Mergers in the US involving gas pipelines (interstate transportation and local distribution) (1985–2004)

pattern, magnitude of transition costs and likelihood of legal challenges to regulatory initiatives. Smaller lags could indicate that pent-up forces associated with years of distortionary regulation were dissipated through a more reactive merger response.

KEY MERGER AND RESTRUCTURING ISSUES

An analysis of natural gas merger cases reveals a number of interesting observations. First, the record sketches out a picture in which relevant markets are consistently highly concentrated with prohibitively large entry barriers. Challenged natural gas mergers were problematic because they eliminated significant and direct competitors, raising industry concentration well beyond the DOJ/FTC 1992 *Horizontal Merger Guidelines* (*Guidelines*) thresholds. For example, In *El Paso/Sonat* (2000), the merger-induced increase in concentration in the Gulf coast of Louisiana was 1000 HHI, yielding post-merger concentration of 4400 HHI. In most horizontal pipeline cases, the FTC relied heavily on structural market analysis as the basis for its findings – leading in most problematic cases to divestiture requirements. Only in vertical cases did the FTC impose conduct-based remedies, probably to preserve merger-related efficiencies.

THEORIES OF COMPETITIVE HARM

Theories of competitive harm in challenged natural gas mergers from 1985 to 2004 range from eliminating potential competition, to the increased likelihood of unilateral exercise of market power (e.g., withholding capacity or raising rivals' costs) or anticompetitive coordination. For example, the FTC argued in *InterNorth/Houston Natural Gas* (1985) (later renamed Enron), *MidCon/United Energy* (1986), *El Paso/Sonat* (1999) and *Southern Union/CMS* (2003) that combining pipelines would increase the likelihood of collusion. The FTC also successfully challenged the *MidCon/United Energy* (1986), *Southern Union/CMS* (2003) and *El Paso/PG&E* (2001) mergers on the basis that the combined companies would likely exercise unilateral market power. It is also notable that the FTC applied the potential competition doctrine in *Questar/Kern River* (1995), *El Paso/Sonat* (1999) and *El Paso/Coastal* (2001). In *Questar/Kern River* (1995), the FTC obtained an injunction to stop the merger.[10]

The ability to support a variety of theories of competitive harm in pipeline mergers suggests a number of things. One is that anticompetitive effects may be easier to defend in well-established infrastructure industries – particularly in physical network-based sectors – where entry and innovation play limited roles in disciplining market outcomes.[11] This applies to horizontal unilateral theories which have been difficult to support in recent years and to the vertical foreclosure/raising rivals' costs theory put forward in *Enova/Pacific* (1998), *Dominion/CNG* (1999), *CMS/Duke Energy* (1999) and *DTE/MichCon* (2001) and the regulatory evasion theory articulated in *Occidental/MidCon* (1986) and *Entergy/Koch* (1999).[12]

It is, also, likely that merger-induced concentration and post-merger concentration is sufficiently high in challenged natural gas mergers to support a number of theories of competitive harm. Take, for example, *MidCon/United Energy* (1986) and *Southern Union/CMS* (2003), in which the FTC reasoned that the merger would increase the likelihood of *both* the unilateral and coordinated exercise of market power. Moreover, the FTC in a number of cases limited its allegations to a lessening of competition (e.g., *Arkla/TransArk* (1989), *El Paso/Coastal* (2001) and *Enterprise/GulfTerra* (2004)) without proposing a specific theory of harm. This may imply that concentration was high enough for the combination to be *presumptively* anticompetitive.

Relevant Markets

Product market definition in pipeline mergers has changed with the effects of regulatory reform over the last two decades. For example, in the 1962

United States v. El Paso case, the relevant product was defined as natural gas. By the early 1980s merger cases, this definition had expanded to include gas transportation *and* the sale of natural gas. In the late 1980s *Arkla/ TransArk* (1989) case, the FTC included firm capacity in the secondary release market in the product market (Balto and Mongoven 2001, 69). In *El Paso/Coastal* (2001), the FTC defined long-term firm transportation and 'tailored services' such as peaking storage as separate relevant product markets.

Approaches to relevant geographic markets definition have remained relatively unchanged over time. For example, one market is typically defined around the ability of gas producers to obtain transportation service *out* of producing regions. In *El Paso/PG&E* (2001), for example, this market was defined as production out of the Permian basin. A second geographic market is defined around the ability of end-use customers (e.g., LDCs, electric utilities, industrial customers) located along pipeline corridors to obtain delivered gas. These markets are defined in horizontal pipeline mergers and as downstream input markets in gas/electric mergers.[13] In *Southern Union/CMS* (2003), for example, the consumption market included counties in the vicinity of Kansas City.

Based on the foregoing, it appears that new products and substitution possibilities brought about by the emergence of capacity release markets and hub market services is reflected in product market definitions over time. However, these cases are few relative to the majority of challenged pipeline mergers, in which product markets remain focused on transportation service. While geographic production area markets will reflect the expansion of capacity in existing and new areas, they are likely to remain highly concentrated. This is because only a few firms in such markets will continue to control the bulk of pipeline capacity (e.g., through total and partial controlling interests).[14] For the same reasons, concentration in most consumption markets will probably remain high, despite bypass opportunities for larger customers brought about by access and other FERC initiatives.

Entry Barriers

High entry barriers support the notion that concentration is a pervasive problem in pipeline markets – despite concerted efforts to streamline the certification process. The FTC recognized these barriers in most merger cases. Merger complaints cite numerous contributors to the difficulty of entry into pipeline markets, including: (1) significant sunk costs; (2) high fixed costs; (3) long lead-times necessary to construct new pipelines or extensions to existing pipelines over long, narrow rights-of-way; (4) the necessity of obtaining long-term contracts to obtain construction financing; (5) the need for certificates and various other regulatory approvals and (6) environmental concerns associated with siting and construction. Difficult entry conditions exist in many wholesale markets that are capital intensive and subject to regulatory restrictions and constraints, including chemicals, refineries and electric generation. These pervasive conditions highlight the challenge of easing entry into natural gas markets that have otherwise responded positively to many restructuring initiatives.

IMPLICATIONS AND POLICY RECOMMENDATIONS

What does the foregoing imply for the future of the gas pipeline industry? And what can we expect with regard to the terms of competition and firm conduct after two significant phases of merger activity? A number of implications come to mind. First, based on the historical pattern of merger enforcement, further consolidation in the pipeline industry will continue to raise competitive problems similar to those witnessed over the last 20 years. This means that restructuring has not demonstrably altered the long-recognized and natural tendency toward concentration in the pipeline industry. And as long as incumbent firms account for the bulk of capacity expansions, this balance is unlikely to be disturbed.

Second, the rapid pace of merger activity during restructuring in the 1990s may well have increased concentration in regional pipeline markets. While regional market concentration analysis is data intensive, aggregate changes in the industry may be a second-best estimate. For example, market shares and concentration based on annual deliveries for pipelines owned by 14 parent firms in 1992, 1997 and 2001 are shown in Table 3.2. These firms account for over 80 per cent of interstate gas pipeline activity. Entries at the bottom of the table show concentration based on HHI and the 8-firm and 4-firm concentration ratios.

It is clear from Table 3.2 that merger activity during the period 1992–2001 has produced significant consolidation. The HHI statistics on line 16 indicate that the industry was only moderately concentrated in the 1990s, with little change in structure from 1992 to 1997. Concentration increased significantly with the second period of merger activity from 1997 to 2001 – primarily through a series of acquisitions by El Paso, now the largest pipeline owner in the US. This increase occurred despite significant divestitures negotiated in various consent decrees. Regional markets are likely to parallel this broader trend, particularly since the major pipelines have pursued national expansion strategies. Thus, despite a consistent and fairly aggressive approach by the FTC toward pipeline mergers over the last 20 years, merger activity may simply have moved ahead of the slower pace of merger

Table 3.2   Changes in concentration in US gas pipelines (1992–2001)

No.	Firm	Market share (per cent)		
		1992	1997	2001
1	Coastal (becomes El Paso)	23	18	0
2	Columbia Energy Group	15	20	20
3	Consolidated Natural Gas (becomes Dominion Resources)	4	3	3
4	Duke Energy	4	10	8
5	El Paso	8	11	32
6	Enron	11	8	8
7	KN Energy	1	1	4
8	MDU Resources	1	0	0
9	Northern States Power (becomes Xcel)	1	0	0
10	PG&E (becomes El Paso)	3	3	3
11	Reliant	5	3	0
12	Questar	3	1	12
13	Sonat (becomes El Paso)	8	3	0
14	Williams	14	20	12
15	Total market share	100	100	100
16	HHI	1266	1398	1858
17	8-firm ratio	88	92	99
18	4-firm ratio	63	68	75

Source: EIA (October 1999), p. ix and FERC (2001).

enforcement. If so, it could suggest the need for a higher level of vigilance in merger enforcement to preserve the gains from restructuring thus far.

Third, there has been a significant increase in pipeline integration into downstream electricity generation, gas distribution and expansion into gas marketing. However, integration against a backdrop of incrementally higher market concentration potentially creates or enhances the incentive for the merged firm to adversely affect gas transportation and electricity prices by excluding rivals or by evading rate regulation in order to pass on artificially inflated input costs. Federal and state regulation has not been recognized by the antitrust agencies as able to constrain such conduct.

For example, FERC addressed anticompetitive information sharing between pipelines and their marketing affiliates numerous times. Order 2004 (2003) solidified the agency's policies by establishing standards of conduct governing information exchange between transmission (i.e., gas and electricity) companies and their affiliates. Given strong incentives to share information, coupled with limitations of FERC's conduct-based approach, anticompetitive information sharing between the pipeline and its gas marketing (or electric generation) affiliates will continue to be problematic.[15] While the FTC experimented with more innovative conduct-based remedies in vertical merger cases, a trend toward pipeline concentration may require the use of divestiture instead.

In light of the foregoing observations, the gas pipeline industry presents something of a paradox. On one hand, reforms have been relatively successful and there is evidence of improved market performance resulting from access and market-oriented reforms. Demonstrated declines in transportation prices for industrial, commercial and electricity utility pipeline customers and decreases in residential gas bills (O'Neill 2005, 111) all point to the benefits of access and other reforms. Development of spot markets, market hubs and various hub services, expansion of customer choice and the advent of risk management tools all imply that restructuring has improved efficiency. Transition costs that were significant when incurred, but in retrospect appear to be outweighed by the benefits of restructuring, indicate a fundamentally sound set of policy objectives. Finally, empirical evidence of market integration demonstrates that nondiscriminatory access removed, in part, many of the impediments to more efficient market operation (De Vany and Walls 1993). On the other hand, the pipeline industry continues to possess structural features that limit the probability of competitive outcomes. If merger activity proceeds without close scrutiny, it could erode the gains from restructuring.

Restructuring thus presents a high-stakes game for policy makers and merger enforcement as the industry moves forward. Without ongoing scrutiny and vigilance, further efforts to pursue the benefits of restructuring may be in jeopardy. Competition and consumers would be the direct victims of this failure. Such scrutiny includes vigorous merger enforcement, market-based and negotiated rate decisions based on diligent market analysis, support for customer bypass, infrastructure development that improves information flow and transparency and a certification process that reflects ongoing changes in market conditions.

NOTES

1. Thanks to Richard O'Neill, Jim Chen, Richard Pierce and Peter Carstensen for helpful comments.
2. See, e.g., Kwoka's 2006 review of the studies on the costs and benefits of electricity market restructuring.
3. Until the 1970s natural gas was considered a low valued by-product of oil production and a large amount was flared due to market economics. Intrastate markets had no explicit commodity regulation, but many state conservation commissions limited production under conservation laws.

4. Other orders capped recovery of take-or-pay costs and attempted to streamline the construction approval process. The FERC order allowing sales directly from producers to consumers was remanded and vacated by the Court of Appeals for the District of Colombia (D.C. Circuit) because its application to fuel-switchable customers was deemed discriminatory.

5. Order 563 (1994) standardized EBB requirements and Order 587 (1998) required EBB systems to be replaced with internet web sites. Released capacity competed in some instances with interruptible transportation service offered by the pipeline.

6. Marketers increased their share of the transportation market in the two-year period between 1997 and 1999 from 22 per cent to 27 per cent – reflecting reallocation mostly away from LDCs (Mariner-Volpe 2000, 16).

7. Weather, economic conditions, capacity, storage levels, operational problems and information availability all contribute to price volatility.

8. In non-merger contexts, FERC has examined competitive conditions in markets in certification proceedings. See, for example, Hughes and Hall 1990, 262.

9. FERC's decision in *Dominion/CNG* was eventually vacated and remanded by the D.C. Circuit. In *Pacific/Enova,* divestitures in the DOJ consent decree obviated the need for FERC's conduct remedies (*U.S. v. Enova* [1998]).

10. Potential competition was also at issue in *U.S. v. El Paso* (1964).

11. See, e.g., the Antitrust Modernization Commission's 2007 final report, which focuses intensively on the role of innovation in merger review.

12. These cases demonstrate the inapplicability of the single monopoly rent theory in a regulated industry context (Riordan and Salop 1994–95, 517).

13. The downstream output market in a vertical pipeline/electric generation market is electricity or electricity during certain times (e.g., high-demand periods).

14. Balto and Mongoven argue that minority interests in pipelines can raise concerns if that interest confers veto power regarding contracts and pipeline expansions (Balto and Mongoven 2001, 554).

15. For example, El Paso has been embroiled in litigation concerning allegations that the pipeline preferentially favored its marketing affiliate (*CPUC v. El Paso* [2004]).

REFERENCES

Balto, D. and J. Mongoven (2001), 'Deregulation and Merger Enforcement in the Natural Gas Industry,' Antitrust Law Journal 69, 527–568.

Breyer, Stephen (1982), Regulation and Its Reform, Cambridge, MA: Harvard University Press.

Burrit McArthur, J. (1997), 'Antitrust in the New [De]regulated Natural Gas Industry,' Energy Law Journal 18, 1–112.

De Vany, A. and W.D. Walls (1993), 'Pipeline Access and Market Integration in the Natural Gas Industry: Evidence from Cointegration Tests,' Energy Journal 14, 1–19.

Federal Energy Regulatory Commission (2001), 'Form 2 – Major Natural Gas Pipeline Annual Report, Historical Data,' Washington, D.C. Online. Available http://www.ferc.gov/docs-filing/eforms/form-2/data/historical.asp#skipnavsub. Accessed May 23, 2005.

Hughes, W.R. and G.R. Hall (1990), 'Substituting Competition for Regulation,' Energy Law Journal 11, 243–267.

Jess, M. (March 1997), 'Restructuring Energy Industries: Lessons from Natural Gas,' Natural Gas Monthly, Washington, D.C.: Energy Information Administration.

Johnson, S., J. Rasmussen, and J. Tobin (October 1999), 'Corporate Realignments and Investments in the Interstate Natural Gas Transmission System,' Natural Gas Monthly, Washington, D.C.: Energy Information Administration.

Kearney, J.D. and T.W. Merrill (1998), 'The Great Transformation of Regulated Industries Law,' Columbia Law Review 98, 1323–1409.

LaRue, P.H. (1990), 'Antitrust and the Natural Gas Industry,' Energy Law Journal 11, 37–51.

Mariner-Volpe, B. (May 2000), 'The Evolution of Gas Markets in the United States,' Washington, D.C.: Energy Information Administration, Online. Available http://www.eia.doe.gov/pub/oil_gas/natural_gas/presentations/2000/evolution_gas/index.htm. Accessed May 23, 2005.

Morrison, S.A. and C. Winston (2000), 'The Remaining Role for Government Policy in the Deregulated Airline Industry,' in Sam Peltzman and Clifford Winston (eds), Washington, D.C.: AEI-Brookings Joint Center for Regulatory Studies.

Moss, D. (2005), 'Part III: Policy Recommendations and Analysis,' in Diana L. Moss (ed), Network Access, Regulation and Antitrust, London: Routledge, 255–272.

O'Neill, R. (2005), 'Natural Gas Pipelines,' in Diana L. Moss (ed.), Network Access, Regulation and Antitrust, London: Routledge, 107–120.

Peltzman, Sam and C. Winston (eds) (2000), Deregulation of Network Industries: What Next?, Washington DC: AEI-Brookings Joint Center for Regulatory Studies.

Pierce, R.J. (1994), 'The State of the Transition to Competitive Markets in Natural Gas and Electricity,' Energy Jaw Journal 15, 323–350.

Riordan, M.H. and S.C. Salop (1994–1995), 'Evaluating Vertical Mergers: A Post-Chicago Approach,' Antitrust Law Journal 63, 513–568.

Smith, Jr., S.K. (1995), 'Future Structures for the Regulated Energy Industries in the United States,' Journal of Energy and Natural Resources Law 13, 75–95.

US Department of Justice and the Federal Trade Commission Horizontal Merger Guidelines, Trade Reg. Rpts. § 13,104.

Cases

Arkla, Inc., Complaint and Analysis and Draft Complaint to Aid Public Comment, FTC Docket No. C-3265 (June 8, 1989).

California v. Federal Power Commission, 369 U.S. 482 (1962).

CMS Energy Corp., Complaint and Analysis and Draft Complaint to Aid Public Comment, FTC Docket No. C-3877 (June 2, 1999).

DTE Energy Co., Complaint and Analysis and Draft Complaint to Aid Public Comment, FTC File No. 001–0067 (March 22, 2001).

Dominion Resources, Inc. and Consolidated Natural Gas Co., 89 FERC ¶61,162 (November 10, 1999).

Dominion Resources, Inc. and Consolidated Natural Gas Co., Complaint and Analysis and Draft Complaint to Aid Public Comment, FTC Docket No. C-3901 (December 9, 1999).

El Paso Energy Corporation and The Coastal Corporation, Complaint and Analysis and Draft Complaint to Aid Public Comment, FTC Docket No. C-3996 (January 29, 2001).

El Paso Energy Corporation and PG&E Corporation, Complaint and Analysis and Draft Complaint to Aid Public Comment, FTC Docket No. C-3997 (January 30, 2001).

El Paso Energy Corporation, Complaint and Analysis and Draft Complaint to Aid Public Comment, FTC Docket No. C-3915 (January 6, 2000).
Entergy Corp. and Entergy-Koch LP, Complaint and Analysis and Draft Complaint to Aid Public Comment, FTC File NO. 001–0172 (January 31, 2001).
Enterprise Products Partner, L.P. and Dan L. Duncan, Complaint and Analysis and Draft Complaint to Aid Public Comment, FTC Docket No. C-4123 (November 23, 2004).
Federal Trade Commission v. Questar Corp., No. 2:95CV 1137S (D. Utah 1995).
InterNorth, Inc., Consent Order, FTC Docket No. C-3168 (October 29, 1985).
MidCon Corp., Consent Order, FTC Docket No. 9198 (March 12, 1986).
Occidental Petroleum Corp., Consent Order, 109 F.T.C. 167, FTC Docket No. C-3191 (June 25, 1986).
Phillips Petroleum Co. v. Wisconsin, 347 U.S. 672 (1954).
Public Utilities Commission of the State of California v. El Paso Natural Gas, 106 FERC ¶61,315 (March 30, 2004).
San Diego Gas & Electric and Enova Energy, Inc., 79 FERC ¶61,372 (June 25, 1997); Enova Corp. and Pacific Enterprises, 79 FECR ¶61,107 (April 30, 1997).
Southern Union Company and CMS Energy, Complaint and Analysis and Draft Complaint to Aid Public Comment, FTC File No. 031-0068 (May 29, 2003).
United States v. El Paso Natural Gas, 376 U.S. 651 (1964).
United States v. Enova Corp., No. 98-CV-583 (D.D.C.) (March 9, 1998).
United States v. Otter Tail Power Co., 410 U.S. 366 (1973).
Verizon Communications, Inc. v. Trinko, 540 U.S. 398 (2004).

Statutes and Regulations

Federal Power Act of 1935, 16 U.S.C. § 824b(a).
Natural Gas Act of 1938, 15 U.S.C. §§ 717(a)–717(w) (1982).
Natural Gas Policy Act of 1978, 15 U.S.C. §§ 3301–3432 (1982).
Natural Gas Wellhead Decontrol Act of 1989, 15 U.S.C. § 3301.
Federal Energy Regulatory Commission, Order 380, 49 Fed. Reg. 22,778 (1984).
Federal Energy Regulatory Commission, Order 436, 50 Fed. Reg. 42,408 (1985).
Federal Energy Regulatory Commission, Order 500, 52 Fed. Reg. 30,334 (1987).
Federal Energy Regulatory Commission, Order 636, 57 Fed. Reg. 15,267 (1992).
Federal Energy Regulatory Commission, Order 497, 59 Fed. Reg. 32,884 (1994).
Federal Energy Regulatory Commission, Order 2004, Final Rule, 105 FERC ¶61,248 (November 25, 2003).

4. Telecommunications mergers

Jim Chen[1]

MERGER MANIA AND THE TELECOMMUNICATIONS ACT OF 1996

The Telecommunications Act of 1996 promised to 'promote competition and reduce regulation', 'secure lower prices and higher quality services . . . and encourage the rapid deployment of new telecommunications technologies' (Telecommunications Act 1996, 110 Stat. 56 (1996)). Detractors argue that the Act in practice has disappointed the expectation that legislative reform would 'open all telecommunications markets to competition' (1996 S. Conf. Rep.,1). Among the gauges by which critics have assailed the Telecommunications Act, the record of mergers among telecommunications firms since 1996 figures prominently.

A dozen years after comprehensive legislative reform, all significant segments of the telecommunications industry are highly concentrated. Three firms dominate local exchange and wireless sectors alike. Miniature versions of the old Bell system have emerged. Verizon and AT&T have reinvented and revived the end-to-end telephone company combined with a geographic division of the United States. The cable industry is only slightly less concentrated, and nothing stands between further consolidation and integration in that industry except laws predating the 1996 Act that had been designed to protect competition within media markets rather than telecommunications markets. If, as appears increasingly likely, Voice over Internet Protocol (VOIP) eventually overcomes every other form of terrestrial telecommunications technology, control of telecommunications will be divided between providers of broadband Internet access and wireless network operators. Firms that are the most facile in integrating wireless and wireline services, for residential and business customers alike, will dominate the industry.

In the quarter century since the conclusion of the dismantling of AT&T, no significant telecommunications merger has failed to receive the ultimate approval of the Federal Communications Commission (FCC) and the Department of Justice. In implementing the 1996 Act, federal authorities have extracted significant concessions in exchange for their approval of major telecommunications mergers. The prospect that the Commission or the Justice Department would actually bar a merger, however, has diminished to a historic nadir.

This chapter reviews the mergers and related competition policies that have reshaped telecommunications since the passage of the 1996 Act. Much of the FCC's merger policy has grown out of its response to mergers involving incumbent telecommunications carriers. The Telecommunications Act's cable provisions and certain legal tools independent of the 1996 legislative reform have facilitated an alternative approach to merger policy. That alternative path has assumed ever greater importance as broadband Internet access has achieved greater prominence within the market for telecommunications services.

The Telecommunications Act has accelerated rather than retarded the trend toward consolidation and concentration in telecommunications. Because the Act focused on legal issues whose technological and economic roots lay deep in the Bell breakup decree, it failed altogether to deal with the Internet. This oversight was one of several mistaken technological assumptions underlying the Act.

FCC MERGER POLICY SINCE 1996

The Statutory Framework

Section 7 of the Clayton Act bans mergers that 'may tend substantially to lessen competition' or 'tend to create a monopoly'. The Clayton Act also authorizes the FCC to review and to reject mergers involving at least one 'common carrier engaged in wire or radio communication or radio transmission of energy' (15 U.S.C. § 21(a)). In addition, the FCC under the Communications Act of 1934 (48 Stat. 1064 (1934)) must approve any merger involving a regulated enterprise. The Act originally authorized the FCC to immunize certain telecommunications mergers from antitrust scrutiny (47 U.S.C. § 221(a) (1994)), but the 1996 Act repealed the Commission's authority in this regard. Indeed, while other comparably 'detailed regulatory scheme[s]' 'ordinarily' shield the entities subject to them 'from antitrust scrutiny altogether' (*Verizon Commc'n, Inc., v. Law Offices of Curtis V. Trinko, LLP (Trinko)* 540 U.S. 398, 406 (2004)), § 601(b)(1) of the 1996 Act provides that 'nothing in this Act or the amendments made by this Act shall be construed to modify, impair, or supersede the applicability of any of the antitrust laws' (47 U.S.C. § 601 (2000)). The Supreme Court has held that section 601 'bars a finding of implied immunity' from 'claims that satisfy established antitrust standards' (*Trinko*, 540

U.S. at 406–7). Thus, FCC approval is a necessary but never sufficient condition for the completion of a merger among telecommunications firms.

Although the FCC does invoke its Clayton Act jurisdiction (WorldCom, 13 FCC Rcd 18 025, 18 030–18 031 (1998); NYNEX, 12 FCC Rcd 19 985, 20 001 (1997); Pacific Telesis, 12 FCC Rcd 2624, 2631 (1997)), it never squarely rests on that authority (Weiss and Stern 1998, 198). Instead, the FCC usually reviews telecommunications mergers under the 'public interest, convenience, and necessity' standard that pervades the Communications Act of 1934 (48 Stat. 1064 (1934)), 'so construed as to secure for the public the broad aims of' the statute (*W.U. Div., Commercial Telegraphers' Union v. United States*, 87 F. Supp. 324, 335 (1949)). The Commission usually 'find[s] [its] jurisdiction under the Communications Act to be sufficient to address all competitive effects' of a proposed merger, 'including the [Clayton Act] issue of whether [a] proposed transfer [of licenses] may substantially lessen competition or tend to create a monopoly' (Pacific Telesis, 12 FCC Rcd at 2631; McCaw & Am. Tel. & Tel. Co., 9 FCC Rcd 5836, 5843–44 (1994)). The FCC normally reviews telecommunications mergers under the Communications Act's public interest standard instead of invoking its Clayton Act jurisdiction. The FCC is 'entrusted with the responsibility to determine when and to what extent the public interest would be served by competition' (*United States v. FCC*, 652 F.2d 72, 88 (1980)) because the 'public interest' standard 'necessarily subsumes and extends beyond the traditional parameters [of] . . . the antitrust laws' (NYNEX, 12 FCC Rcd at 19 987; Teleport Communications Group, 13 FCC Rcd 15 236, 15 242-15 243 (1998); *Schurz Commc'n, Inc. v. FCC*, 982 F.2d. 1043, 1049 (1992)).

The 'public interest', as defined in the Communications Act, undoubtedly treats 'competition [as] a relevant factor' (*FCC v. RCA*, 346 U.S. 86, 94 (1953)), and the Commission may quite properly consider a licensee's anticompetitive conduct or other issues sounding of antitrust in the course of discharging its fundamental statutory mandate (*FCC v. Nat'l Citizens Comm. for Broad.*, 436 U.S. 775, 795–96 (1978); *Nat'l Broad. Co. v. United States*, 319 U.S. 190, 222–23 (1943)). The FCC's antitrust-related obligations are effectively discharged once the Commission 'seriously considers the antitrust consequences of a propos[ed] [merger] and weighs those consequences with other public interest factors' (*United States v. FCC*, 652 F.2d 72, 88 (1980); NYNEX, 12 FCC Rcd at 20 003–4; OTI, 6 FCC Rcd 1611, 1612 (1991)).

Conventional antitrust law examines mergers according to the relationship of the merging parties. The most common area of concern arises when a merger eliminates actual competition between the parties and results in a substantial increase in concentration within a relevant product and geographic market. Such mergers are 'horizontal' from the perspective of antitrust law. Where the firms are customers and suppliers of each other, the merger is treated as a vertical merger. Contemporary policy holds that vertical mergers create few risks to competition unless they result in a significant foreclosure of the potential for entry into or access to a concentrated market. Finally, the parties may neither compete with each other nor have a customer-supplier relationship. Such conglomerate mergers may still cause anticompetitive effects if there is a significant loss of potential competition. This concept in turn has two elements. The first, the so-called 'wings' effect, involves the immediate loss of pressure on a concentrated market presented by a potential entrant. The second competitive concern arises from the loss of future actual competition in the market resulting from the combination of a potential entrant and a dominant firm in that market.

The 'actual potential competition doctrine' addresses mergers that will leave concentration in the market exactly as it was, neither hurt nor helped, and that are challengeable under Section 7 only on grounds that the company could, but did not, enter de novo or through 'toe-hold' acquisition (*United States v. Falstaff Brewing Corporation*, 410 U.S. 526, 537 (1973)). Such a merger eliminating a potential competitor may be declared anticompetitive upon a demonstration of three factors. First, the market must be concentrated. Second, the acquiring firm must have been among those firms that were likely and uniquely well situated to enter. Finally, but for the acquisition, such entry would have deconcentrated the market or resulted in other procompetitive effects (*United States v. Marine Bancorp., Inc.*, 418 U.S. 603, 633 (1974); *Tenneco, Inc. v. FTC*, 689 F.2d 346, 352 (1982); *Yamaha Motor Co., Ltd. v. FTC*, 657 F.2d 971, 977 (1981); *Mercantile Texas Corp. v. Bd. of Governors of the Fed. Reserve Sys.*, 638 F.2d 1255, 1264 (1981)). The Supreme Court has declined, however, to decide whether this doctrine operates 'solely on the ground that such a [market-extension] merger eliminates the prospect for long-term deconcentration of an oligopolistic market that in theory might result if the acquiring firm were forbidden to enter except through a de novo undertaking or through the acquisition of a small existing entrant' (*United States v. Marine Bancorp., Inc.*, 418 U.S. at 625). There has been little judicial development of this theory in the past 30 years (*see generally* Bush and Massa 2004).

The FCC's approach to telecommunications mergers has transcended antitrust law's merger doctrines. Nothing in the Communications Act's ubiquitous 'public interest' standard binds the FCC 'to analyze proposed mergers under the same standards that the Department of Justice . . . must apply' under Section 7 of the Clayton Act (*Ne. Util. Serv. Co. v. FERC*, 993 F.2d 937, 947–48 (1993)). Especially in its review of mergers among the former Bell operating companies, the 'wide discretion afforded to the Commission has inspired "imaginative interpretation" of the public interest' (*FCC v. RCA*, 346 U.S. (1953) at 90). Although the public interest standard is as 'supple' and 'as concrete as the complicated factors for judgment in such a field of delegated authority permit' (*FCC v. Pottsville Broad. Co.*, 309 U.S. 134, 138 (1940); *FCC v. WNCN Listeners Guild*, 450 U.S. 582, 593 (1981)), this statutory 'criterion is not to be interpreted as setting up a standard so indefinite as to confer an unlimited power' (*Fed. Radio Comm'n v. Nelson Bros. Bond & Mortg. Co.*, 289 U.S. 266, 285 (1933)).

The public interest standard is presumably broader than the antitrust standard underlying Section 7 of the Clayton Act. If the FCC were to confine its analysis to matters addressable under the antitrust laws, such an approach might fail to discharge the Commission's statutory obligation to uphold the public interest (*United States v. Radio Corp. of Am. & Nat'l Broad. Co., Inc.*, 358 U.S. 334, 351–52 (1959)). Indeed, the public interest standard arguably obliges the FCC to police or even to bar mergers that might be permitted under a strict view of economic efficiency under the antitrust laws. Nevertheless, the FCC has not invalidated a single major telecommunications merger since 1996. In weighing successive petitions proposing telecommunications mergers, however, the Commission has continually tightened the terms and conditions under which it will approve a merger (WorldCom, 13 FCC Rcd at 18 031–18 032; NYNEX, 12 FCC Rcd at 20 012; 47 C.F.R. § 1.110 (2005)). This practice of extracting concessions represents the FCC's primary tool for shaping telecommunications mergers.

BOC MERGERS

The FCC's approval of three BOC mergers involving former Bell operating companies (BOCs), SBC's 1997 acquisition of Pacific Telesis (Pacific Telesis, 12 FCC Rcd at 2624), Bell Atlantic's 1999 acquisition of NYNEX (NYNEX, 12 FCC Rcd at 19 985) and SBC's 1999 acquisition of Ameritech (Ameritech, 14 FCC Rcd at 14 716 (1999)), effectively established the Commission's approach to telecommunications mergers. More than any other legal development since 1996, horizontal BOC merger reviews have stretched the Communications Act's public interest standard well beyond core antitrust principles. These mergers all involved combinations of firms engaged in similar activities but serving different geographic markets. As such, the only antitrust standard implicated was that of potential competition which was and is a very much under-developed concept in both economic and legal terms.

SBC's bid for Pacific Telesis gave the FCC its first opportunity under the Act to review a merger of major local exchange carriers (LECs). Finding an absence of actual potential competition, the Commission approved the merger (Pacific Telesis, 12 FCC Rcd at 2624). First, the FCC reasoned that there were 'more than a few other potential entrants into [PacTel's] markets' (ibid. at 2637). At that time, SBC looked no more likely than any other major local exchange or interexchange carrier to encroach on PacTel's turf. Second, the FCC found no evidence 'that SBC would enter or would have entered' those markets 'but for the proposed merger' (ibid. at 2637). Thereupon the Commission concluded its analysis under the actual potential competition doctrine without discussing the merger's purported benefits (ibid. at 2638).

The FCC's review of the SBC/PacTel merger effectively equated the Communications Act's traditional public interest test with Clayton Act standards. The Commission abruptly changed course in its 1997 approval of Bell Atlantic's acquisition of NYNEX (NYNEX, 12 FCC Rcd at 19 985). The FCC found that each of these companies was a potential entrant in the other's service territories. The Commission found that Bell Atlantic had formulated concrete plans to enter NYNEX markets (ibid. at 19 990–19 991, 20 025–20 028) and that NYNEX was at least 'a possible entrant into Bell Atlantic territories' (ibid. at 19 991). By contrast, SBC and PacTel, which lacked geographically contiguous territories and did not enjoy significant goodwill or name recognition in each other's markets, could not be distinguished from 'a large number of . . . [other] significant market participants' (ibid. at 20 024).

The Bell Atlantic/NYNEX merger also raised a regulatory concern over benchmarking. Benchmarking matured as a centerpiece of regulatory policy shortly before the Bell breakup. Regulators, competitors and even incumbent carriers themselves set baselines according to the performance of existing regulated monopolists (*People of the State of California v. FCC*, 39 F.3d 919, 927 (1994); *Ne. Util. Serv. Co. v. FERC*, 993 F.2d at 1580; *United States v. W. Elec. Co.*, 900 F.2d 283, 299 (1990)). A 'reduction in the number of separately owned firms engaged in similar businesses' would compromise the 'Commission's ability to identify, and therefore to contain, market power' (NYNEX, 12 FCC Rcd at 20 058). In particular, the FCC feared that it might lose the ability to treat the uncoordinated activities of a sufficiently large number of unrelated LECs as 'regulatory "benchmarks" for evaluating the conduct of other carriers or the industry as a whole' (ibid. at 19 994). 'As diversity among carriers declines, both this Commission and state commissions may lose the ability to compare performance between similar carriers that have made different management or strategic choices' (ibid. at 20 058). In the immediate wake of the Bell Atlantic/

NYNEX merger, the FCC made heavy use of benchmarking. Periodically revised local telephone rates set by states established critical baselines against which the Commission assessed its own ratemaking proceedings (*WorldCom, Inc., v. FCC*, 308 F.3d 1 (2002); *Sprint Commc'n Co., L.P. v. FCC*, 274 F.3d 549 (2001)).

The identification of benchmarking as a component of the public interest represented the most innovative aspect of the FCC's Bell Atlantic/ NYNEX order. Benchmarking is a peculiarly bureaucratic concern. It focuses on the government's ability to measure (and ultimately to discipline) a regulated firm's performance, as distinct from the classic economic concern that dominant firms can influence prices by controlling input instead of having to take such prices as prevail in a competitive market (*Eastman Kodak Co. v. Image Technical Serv., Inc.*, 504 U.S. 451, 469–70, fn.15–16 (1992); *Jefferson Parish Hosp. Dist. No. 2 v. Edwin G. Hyde*, 466 U.S. 2, 36–37 (1984); Pitofsky 1990, 1806–13). This is one of the strongest ways in which the Bell Atlantic/NYNEX order purportedly took the FCC's merger policy beyond 'the realm of general competition law' (Shelanski 2002, 340–41).

The FCC nevertheless approved the Bell Atlantic/NYNEX merger. The decisive factor was a set of commitments that these firms accepted as a condition of approval. The merging companies agreed to cooperate in the monitoring of their operating support systems, especially 'with respect to resold services, unbundled network elements and combinations of unbundled network elements' (NYNEX, 12 FCC Rcd at 19 992). 'Bell Atlantic and NYNEX also agree[d] to offer, in interconnection negotiations and arbitrations, payment mechanisms . . . consistent with the Commission's decision in its Second Physical Collocation Order' (ibid. at 19 993). Most of all, the firms 'commit[ted] to offer interconnection, unbundled network elements and transport and termination at rates based on forward looking economic cost' (ibid. at 19 992).

This final set of commitments represented a very significant concession. As the effective price for FCC approval, Bell Atlantic conceded significant ground in two of its most fiercely contested battles against the Commission's program for introducing competition into local telephone service: physical collocation of competitive local exchange carriers' equipment within incumbents' central offices and the total element long-run incremental cost (TELRIC) methodology used to price unbundled network elements to competitors seeking interconnection with incumbent local carriers (*Ashcroft v. ACLU*, 535 U.S. 564, 567 (2002); *AT&T Corp. v. Iowa Util. Bd.*, 525 U.S. 366 (1999)).

Physical collocation and TELRIC lay at the heart of constitutional attacks on the Telecommunications Act (Sidak and Spulber 1997,

232–40; Spulber and Yoo 2003, 947–59; Worstell 1998, 441). The Telecommunications Act's requirement that an incumbent carrier permit physical or virtual collocation of facilities if necessary for interconnection or unbundled access (47 U.S.C. § 251(c)(6) (2000)) arguably compels a physical invasion of incumbent local exchange carrier (ILEC) property subject to the 'physical takings' doctrine (e.g., *Loretto v. Teleprompter Manhattan CATV Corp.*, 458 U.S. 419, 426 (1982)). Courts struck down the FCC's pre-1996 collocation rules because the Commission lacked the power to take LEC property and reassign it to a competitor (*Bell Atl. Telephone Cos. v. FCC*, 24 F.3d 1441, 1446–7 (1994); *GTE Nw., Inc. v. Pub. Util. Comm'n of Oregon*, 321 Orc. 458, 474 (1995)). The FCC's post-1996 collocation rules have also encountered judicial resistance based on disagreements over the definition of the statutory term 'necessary' (*US West Commc'n, Inc. v. Jennings*, 46 F. Supp. 2d 1004, 1026 (1999); *MCI v. Bell Atl.*, 36 F. Supp. 2d 419, 428, fn.10 (1999); *US West Commc'n, Inc. v. AT&T Commc'n of Pac. Nw., Inc.*, 31 F. Supp. 2d 839, 854, fn. 9 (1998)). However, takings doctrine has not felled those rules. *Quest Corp. v. United States*, 48 Fed. Cl. 672 (2001); *GTE S., Inc. v. Morrison*, 6 F. Supp. 2d 517 (1998)).

TELRIC represented the FCC's effort to enforce the Telecommunications Act's requirement that incumbent local exchange carriers permit competitors to interconnect (47 U.S.C. § 251(c)(2) (2000)) and to offer unbundled network elements for sale (ibid. § 251(c)(3)). Rates for unbundled elements must be 'just, reasonable, and nondiscriminatory' (ibid.). Those rates 'may include a reasonable profit' and 'shall be based on the cost . . . of providing the interconnection or network element' (ibid. § 252(d)). However, 'cost' must be 'determined without reference to a rate-of-return proceeding' (ibid.). The FCC has elected to price unbundled network elements according to a definition of 'forward-looking economic cost' comprising 'the sum of (1) the total element long-run incremental cost of the element' and '(2) a reasonable allocation of forward-looking common costs' (47 C.F.R. § 51.505(a) (2005)). TELRIC excludes all 'opportunity costs' such as 'the revenues that the incumbent LEC would have received for the sale of telecommunications services, in the absence of competition' (ibid. § 51.505(d)(3)).

Nearly a decade of litigation has not enabled the Commission to implement TELRIC industry-wide. In 1999, the Supreme Court upheld the FCC's authority to 'design a pricing methodology' that could bind state public utility commissions (*AT&T Corp. v. Iowa*, 525 U.S. at 385), but remanded the case to the FCC for failing to take proper account of the statutory term 'impair' (ibid. at 387). In 2002, the Supreme Court upheld TELRIC against a battery of challenges based on the 'confiscatory ratemaking' doctrine in takings law (*Verizon Commc'n Inc. v. FCC*, 535 U.S. 467, 483–44, 524–55 (2002)). TELRIC remains the subject of fierce litigation, most of it addressed to the Commission's interpretation of the terms 'necessary' and 'impair' (*US Telecom Ass'n v. FCC*, 290 F.3d 415, 415 (2002)) and its abortive attempt to delegate determinations of impairment to state public utility commissions (*US Telecom Ass'n v. FCC*, 359 F.3d. 554 (2004)). The conditions on the approval of the Bell Atlantic/NYNEX merger permitted the FCC to proceed with TELRIC-based pricing of unbundled network elements offered for sale to the combined firms' competitors.

The last of this initial trio of BOC mergers, SBC/Ameritech, barely passed regulatory muster. The FCC identified three threats to the public interest. First, the merger would 'significantly decrease the potential for competition in local telecommunications markets by large incumbent LECs' by eliminating SBC and Ameritech as potential competitors in each other's local exchange (LX) markets. The FCC also expressed concern for competition 'in out-of-region markets', where the BOCs could 'offer wireline local exchange services, potentially bundled with cellular and other offerings', to customers of their wireless affiliates (Pleading Cycle Est. for Comments on Conditions Proposed by SBC & Ameritech, 14 FCC Rcd 14 592, 14 741 (1999)).

Second, by further diluting the effectiveness of 'comparative practice analyses (or "benchmarking")', a merger of 'two of the six remaining major incumbent LECs' would presumably 'frustrate the ability of the Commission (and state regulators) to implement the local market-opening provisions' of the 1996 Act (Pleading Cycle Est. for Comments on Conditions Proposed by SBC & Ameritech, at 14 741). This merger added nuance to the Commission's deepening concern over benchmarking. The FCC said, the 'elimination of Ameritech as an independently-owned regulated Bell operating company (RBOC) is likely to reduce significantly the amount of innovation that regulators and competitors could observe and analyse' (ibid.). Just as the Bell divestiture sparked 'an unprecedented flowering of innovation' (*United States v. W. Elec. Co.*, 890 F. Supp. 1, 1 (1995)), the FCC feared that the effective restoration of the Bell system through horizontal BOC mergers could smother telecommunications' inventive spirit.

Third, the SBC/Ameritech merger allegedly 'would increase the incentives and ability' of the combined firm 'to discriminate against rivals in retail markets where the new SBC will be the dominant incumbent LEC' (Pleading Cycle Est. for Comments on Conditions Proposed by SBC & Ameritech, at 14 742). The sheer size of SBC's enlarged empire would expand the number of geographic markets where raised costs could cripple a rival (ibid. at 14 742–43). The FCC expressed 'particular concern' over this effect 'in the retail market for advanced services' (ibid. at 14 743).

Despite concluding that the SBC/Ameritech merger offered few competitive benefits, the FCC approved the merger (ibid. at 14 712). SBC and Ameritech, the Commission wrote, had overstated the impact of their merger on the combined firm's incentive to enter out-of-region markets (ibid. at 14 840). Indeed, the firms' activities before the announcement of their merger – especially SBC's 1998 purchase of Southern New England Telephone (Southern New England Tel., 13 FCC Rcd 21 292 (1998)) – showed that the unmerged carriers already had ample incentive and opportunity to expand their geographic reach (Pleading Cycle Est. for Comments on Conditions Proposed by SBC & Ameritech, at 14 841).

The merging firms' voluntary commitment to grant favorable interconnection terms to competitive local exchange carriers (CLECs) and to enter 30 out-of-region local markets (ibid. at 14 595–97) enabled the Commission to recalibrate 'the public interest balance in their favor' (ibid. at 14 854–55). The public interest balance marginally favored permitting the merger. The FCC cautioned, however, that its acceptance of these conditions had no bearing on the merged company's compliance with other provisions of the Communications Act, especially Section 271 of the 1996 Act (ibid. at 14 857).

In none of these mergers did the Department of Justice seek further review in court under the Clayton Act. This inaction suggests that the Antitrust Division's lawyers and economists did not regard the loss of potential competition as sufficient to justify a conventional antitrust case.

THE BOC MERGER APPROVALS AS A REGULATORY PROGRESSION

The FCC's approvals of the BOC mergers progressively toughened what once had been a modest regulatory barrier. The SBC/PacTel order explicitly warned that the Commission's approval of that merger 'should not be taken as an indication that [it would] approve all subsequent proposed combinations of major carriers' (Pacific Telesis, 12 FCC Rcd at 2640). In the Bell Atlantic/NYNEX proceeding, the FCC warned that applicants might not always be able to deflect regulatory attention merely by 'propos[ing] pro-competitive public interest commitments' (NYNEX, 12 FCC Rcd at 19 993). The SBC/Ameritech merger rested squarely on such conditions. The Commission had concluded that the merger's 'significant harms' outweighed the merger's otherwise 'speculative and small' benefits (Ameritech, 14 FCC Rcd at 14 717–18).

The mere existence of earlier telecommunications mergers, especially unions involving incumbent carriers, counsels ever closer scrutiny of future mergers. After almost summarily approving the SBC/PacTel merger, the FCC became progressively more reluctant to approve mergers between carriers. The Commission's successive approvals of the PacTel, NYNEX, Ameritech and GTE acquisitions made it difficult for the FCC to approve further consolidation. Reducing the number of BOCs from seven to four and eliminating the two largest independent local exchange carriers in the United States increased the likelihood of collusion, eroded regulatory benchmarks and aggravated the loss of actual potential competitors who might challenge these carriers and other established telecommunications companies.

The SBC/Ameritech order enabled the FCC to rationalize its approach to reviewing telecommunications mergers under the Communications Act's public interest standard (ibid. at 14 737–38). This approach consists of four distinct inquiries:

First, will the transaction result in a violation of the Communications Act or other applicable statute? (Tele-Communications, Inc., 14 FCC Rcd 3160, 3221–24 (1999); Southern New England Tel., 13 FCC Rcd at 21 309–10). For instance, a BOC's authorizations to provide long-distance telephone service may overlap with its post-merger local service area, in violation of the presumptive bar to BOC provision of interexchange service to local exchange customers under 47 U.S.C. § 271.

Second, will the transaction result in a violation of applicable FCC rules? (Tele-Communications, Inc., 14 FCC Rcd at 3207–08, n. 287). For instance, FCC rules implementing Sections 11 and 13 of the Cable Act of 1992 bar any entity from owning cable facilities reaching more than 30 per cent of the nationwide audience (47 C.F.R. § 76.505 (2005)). Unless the Commission waives those rules, its rules would bar the consummation of a merger that would enable a single firm to consolidate so large a share of the nation's cable infrastructure.

Third, will the merger 'substantially frustrate or impair the Commission's implementation or enforcement of the Communications Act'? (Tele-Communications, Inc., 14 FCC Rcd at 3224–26; Southern New England Tel., 13 FCC Rcd at 21 309–10). This open-ended factor provides the most flexible channel by which the FCC may apply traditional doctrines of public utility law asserting that competition alone 'is not enough' to protect the public interest in 'industr[ies] so regulated and so largely closed' as telecommunications (*FCC v. RCA*, 346 U.S. at 97; *Hawiian Tel. Co. v. FCC*, 498 F.2d 771, 776 (1974)).

Fourth, does the merger confer affirmative 'public interest' benefits (Tele-Communications, Inc., 14 FCC Rcd at 3229–39; Puerto Rico Tel. Auth., 14 FCC Rcd 3122, 3149 (1999)), including the potential to 'enhance competition?' (WorldCom, 13 FCC Rcd at 18 032–33; NYNEX, 12 FCC Rcd at 19 987). This final factor distinguishes the FCC's inquiry into 'whether a merger produces affirmative benefits' from the conventional antitrust inquiry into 'whether a merger will produce harms' (Shelanski 2002, 341).

More than any other combination of telecommunications companies, mergers between incumbent carriers have required the FCC to balance three related regulatory concerns against three goals at the heart of the Commission's local competition initiatives. Actual potential competition, natural safeguards against collusion, and benchmarking all become increasingly tenuous with each merger that is approved. In allowing every BOC merger that has come before it, the FCC has conceded substantial amounts of ground on these matters. By the same token, however, the Commission persuaded Bell Atlantic to withhold its attacks on two of the most contentious policies underlying the FCC's post-1996 plan to induce competition in local telephone service: physical collocation and the use of TELRIC in pricing unbundled network elements sold to competitors requesting interconnection. It also secured competitive entry commitments from the combined SBC/Ameritech.

As demonstrated in the Bell Atlantic/NYNEX and SBC/Ameritech orders, the FCC's interpretation of the Communications Act's public interest standard includes the signature tactic of extracting concessions from and imposing conditions on merging parties. The Commission approaches every proposed merger with bluff and bluster regarding the potential threat to competition. However, it eventually secures voluntary commitments as the price for its eventual approval of the merger. This technique arose out of the FCC's adaptation to incumbent carriers' litigation tactics. The FCC's earliest merger approvals assumed the full and proper implementation of the local competition provisions of the 1996 Act (NYNEX, 12 FCC Rcd at 20 126). For years after the Act's passage, incumbent carriers waged all-out war on TELRIC, the collocation requirement and other aspects of the FCC's program for introducing local competition into the telecommunications industry. The earliest lawsuits against the FCC's original local competition rules represented, in retrospect, 'just the first salvo in what promises to be a prolonged battle . . . over the terms and pace of new competition' (Robinson 1996, 308, n. 54). Once incumbent carriers succeeded in delaying implementation of the Act's local competition provisions through seemingly ceaseless litigation, the FCC responded by tightening its merger policy and extracting concessions from parties seeking regulatory approval of their proposed mergers (NYNEX, 12 FCC Rcd at 20 126).

One branch of the BOCs' litigation strategy illustrates how incumbent resistance to competitive restructuring has affected the FCC's merger policy. The 1996 Act finally gave the BOCs potential access to the in-region markets for long-distance carriage. Section 271 gave the BOCs conditional access to this lucrative market. A BOC must show that some competitor

stands ready to provide local carriage 'either exclusively over [its] own telephone exchange service facilities or predominantly over [its] own . . . facilities in combination with the resale of the telecommunications services of
another carrier' (47 U.S.C. § 271(c)(1)(A) (2000); 1996 H.R. Conf. Rep.,
147–48). Such a 'competing provider' must offer an actual commercial
alternative to the BOC's local services (*SBC Commc'n, Inc. v. FCC*, 138
F.3d 410, 416 (1998)). Alternatively, if 'no [competing] provider' in any
given state 'has requested . . . access [to] and interconnection' with a BOC
within '10 months after February 9, 1996', the BOC may provide
interLATA service in that state by filing 'a statement of the terms and conditions' by which it 'generally offers to provide . . . access and interconnection' to local competitors (47 U.S.C. § 271(c)(1)(B) (2000)). On either of
these tracks, Section 271 also requires a petitioning BOC to bear the burden
of proof (47 U.S.C. § 271(d)(3) (2000); Proceedings for Bell Operating Co.
Applications, 11 FCC Rcd 19 708 (1996)) and to satisfy a 14-step 'competitive checklist' (47 U.S.C. § 271(c)(2)(B) (2000)).

For three years after the passage of the 1996 Act, Section 271 imposed
an impenetrable firewall against BOC entry into interLATA carriage. From
1997 through 1998, the Commission denied every Section 271 petition that
came before it. In 1999, however, the FCC approved Bell Atlantic's petition
for New York (Bell Atl. New York, 15 FCC Rcd 3953 (1999)); the following year, the FCC allowed SBC to provide interLATA service in Texas (SBC
Communications, 15 FCC Rcd 18 354 (2000)). These approvals roughly
coincided with the approval of the SBC/Ameritech merger, which in retrospect marked the practical end of the Section 271 firewall. Section 271
approvals began to issue routinely (Verizon Pennsylvania Inc., 16 FCC Rcd
17 419 (2001); SBC Communications, 16 FCC Rcd 20 719 (2001)).

CABLE MERGERS

The 1996 Act did add a specific merger-related tool to the FCC's legal
arsenal. Section 652 of the Act, codified at 47 U.S.C. § 572 (2000), presumptively bans the cross-ownership of cable and telephone companies.
This prohibition arose from Congress's apparent hope that the separation
of LECs and cable operators would keep each group as a potential competitive check on the other. The Telecommunications Act effectively directs
federal antitrust enforcement to presume that geographically overlapping
combinations of cable and telephone companies are anticompetitive until
proven otherwise (Botein 1996, 570).

Under Section 652, a telephone company may not acquire 'more than a
10 percent financial interest, or any management interest, in any cable

operator providing cable service' in the same service area (47 U.S.C. § 572(a) (2000)). The reverse is also true; no cable operator may acquire a comparable stake in a telephone company within its franchise area (ibid. § 572(b)). Moreover, the Act bans joint ventures between cable and telephone companies (ibid. § 572(c)). Cable-telco mergers and joint ventures are legal when they involve small cable systems in non-urban areas, in rural areas generally, in putatively 'competitive' markets, and whenever the FCC waives Section 652's presumptive prohibition (ibid. § 572(d)(6)). In addition, Section 652 does not 'apply to any situation where an existing cable company initiates telephone service within the cable company's franchise area' (Southcast Tel. Ltd., 12 FCC Rcd 2561 (1996)). To provide otherwise would undermine Congress's hope of fostering 'a technological convergence that would permit the use of the same facilities for the provision of telephone and cable service' (Annual Assessment of the Status of Competition in Markets, 13 FCC Rcd 13 044, 13 050 (1998)).

The cable-telephone provisions imposed one of the strongest forms of structural separation in the entire 1996 Act. The House–Senate conference committee on the Telecommunications Act accepted 'the most restrictive provisions of both the Senate bill and the House amendment in order to maximize competition between local exchange carriers and cable operators within local markets' (1996 H.R. Conf. Rep. No. 104–458, 389). Congress did not presumptively ban any other type of telecommunications merger.

The FCC's 1999 approval of AT&T's $31.6 billion merger with Tele-Communications, Inc (TCI), marked a significant turning point in telecommunications merger policy (Tele-Communications, Inc., 14 FCC Rcd at 3160). The most serious objection to the AT&T/TCI merger was the prospect that an enlarged AT&T 'could bundle its bottleneck broadband transmission service with any or all of the numerous residential services under its wide corporate umbrella – cable television, long distance voice, local voice, and wireless, as well as Internet services' (ibid. at 3218). Though acknowledging that AT&T might enjoy monopoly or market power over cable in certain locations, the Commission declined 'to impose a blanket rule prohibiting the bundling of cable services with other services in which a cable operator might have a financial interest' (ibid. at 3219).

Section 652 of the 1996 Act did not impede AT&T's acquisition of TCI. In 1998, AT&T acquired Teleport, then the largest independent competitive local exchange company in the United States (Teleport Communications Group, 13 FCC Rcd 15 236, 15 239 (1997). Thus arose the possibility that Section 652 would 'prohibit AT&T from acquiring any TCI systems in areas served by Teleport' (Tele-Communications, Inc., 14 FCC Rcd at 3221). The timing of Teleport's entry into local exchange markets proved decisive: because Teleport had not begun providing 'telephone exchange service' as of January 1, 1993 (47 U.S.C. § 572(e) (2000)), Section 652 did not require AT&T to divest any cable systems it acquired from TCI or to seek a waiver from the FCC (ibid. at 3223–24).

AT&T's acquisition of MediaOne faced few initial obstacles. The FCC found an affirmative consumer benefit in 'the merged entity's ability' to deliver 'facilities-based local telephone service and other new services to residential customers' (MediaOne Group, Inc., 15 FCC Rcd 9820 (2000)). The combination of a major multiple-system cable operator with what was then the country's largest long-distance carrier promised to transform cable carriage into a formidable telecommunications medium. Cognizant of the merger's impact on the cable broadband market, the FCC conditioned the merger on the completion of open-access agreements with unaffiliated Internet service providers (ISPs) (ibid. at 9866–67).

The AT&T/MediaOne merger did trigger anti-concentration measures that predated the 1996 Act. Section 11(c) of the 1992 Cable Act ([1992] 106 Stat. p. 1486) directed the FCC to 'establish reasonable limits on the number of cable subscribers a person is authorized to reach through cable systems owned by such person' (47 U.S.C. 4 § 533(f)(1)(A) (2000)). Acquiring MediaOne would have enabled AT&T to reach 51.3 per cent of cable subscribers in the United States (MediaOne Group, Inc., 15 FCC Rcd 9816, 9819 (2000)), well beyond the FCC's horizontal cable ownership rules. In 1994, the FCC promulgated rules prohibiting any entity from owning an attributable interest in cable systems 'reach[ing] more than 30 per cent of all homes . . . nationwide', plus an additional margin of 5 per cent 'provided [that] the additional cable systems . . . are minority-controlled' (Implementation of Sec. 11 and 13, 8 FCC Rcd 8565, 8567 (1993)). While the AT&T/MediaOne petition lay before it, the FCC revised those horizontal cable ownership rules. The Commission's 1999 rules based the 30 per cent ceiling on 'cable subscribers served rather than on cable homes passed' and eliminated the additional 15 per cent allowance for minority-controlled systems. The FCC also changed the denominator used in computing the ownership limit. Instead of basing the limit on cable subscribers alone, the new rules capped ownership at 30 per cent of the market consisting of all multichannel video programming distributors. Critically, this market included direct broadcast satellite (DBS) services (Implementation of Sec. 11(c), 14 FCC Rcd 19098, 19101 (1999)). Practically speaking, the rule change eased the barrier to any major merger among cable companies.

The cable ownership rules, long a subject of bitter litigation, remain in limbo (*Time Warner Entm't Co. v. FCC*, 240 F.3d 1126 (2001)). In striking down the 30 per cent limit on the number of cable subscribers that any set of commonly owned and operated cable systems may reach nationwide, the D.C. Circuit complained that 'the Commission has pointed to nothing in the record supporting a non-conjectural risk of anticompetitive behavior' among either affiliated cable systems, 'by collusion or other means' (ibid. at 1136). The appeals court likewise struck down vertical limits on the number of channels that any cable operator may assign to programmers in which the operator holds an attributable interest (ibid. at 1139).

In the wake of this decision, the FCC suspended its divestiture conditions on the AT&T/MediaOne merger (MediaOne Group, Inc., 16 FCC Rcd 5835 (2001); MediaOne Group, Inc., 16 FCC Rcd 20 587 (2001)). This action had the practical effect of approving the AT&T/MediaOne merger outright. The horizontal cable ownership rules themselves are still pending (Implementation of Sec. 11(c), 16 FCC Rcd 17 312 (2001)). With those rules in suspended animation, AT&T consummated an even bigger acquisition in 2002. It purchased Comcast for $72 billion. At a projected 28.9 percent of the market for multichannel video programming distribution, the combined AT&T Comcast fell just under the 30 per cent threshold imposed by the cable ownership rules (Comcast Corp., 17 FCC Rcd 23 246, 23 248 (2002)). The FCC approved the merger as one 'likely to result in some public interest benefits associated with accelerated deployment of broadband services' (ibid. at 23 249).

The AT&T/TCI merger sparked a dispute over open access to cable-based platforms providing Internet access. As a condition of approving the transfer of TCI's franchise agreements to AT&T, local officials in Portland, Oregon, required AT&T to permit unaffiliated ISPs to interconnect with AT&T's cable modem platform. The Ninth Circuit concluded, in effect, that broadband Internet access over cable should be regarded as an amalgam of 'telecommunications service' and 'information service' within the meaning of the Telecommunications Act (*AT&T v. City of Portland*, 216 F.3d 871, 876 (2000)). To the extent that a cable-based ISP 'controls all of the transmission facilities between its subscribers and the Internet', the court concluded, 'Internet transmission over [that] cable broadband facility' constitutes 'a telecommunications service' (ibid. at 878). That classification promised to unite regulatory treatment of cable broadband with equivalent services offered by local telephone companies. Cable broadband services remained subject to the common carrier provisions of title II of the Communications Act of 1934 and to the incumbent carrier provisions of the Telecommunications Act of 1996 (Chen 2001, 688–92). The FCC, however, has never imposed open access on cable broadband platforms, either industry-wide or in response to a specific merger.

Instead, the Federal Trade Commission (FTC), in approving America Online's (AOL) purchase of Time Warner, sought to implement an open access policy (*see generally* Federal Trade Commission (2000) 'In re

America Online Inc. and Time Warner Inc.'). This merger combining Time Warner's media and cable empire with AOL's domination of the market for online services appeared likely to blunt AOL's preexisting incentives to promote digital subscriber line (DSL) services and other high-speed alternatives to cable broadband (Cooper 2000, 1041). The FTC responded by fashioning an open access rule. From 2001 through 2006, AOL/Time Warner agreed to allow its subscribers a choice of at least three non-affiliated ISPs offering Internet access over a cable broadband platform. The order's five-year term, described by FTC chairman Robert Pitofsky as 'the shortest duration of [any] competition order,' reflects 'the uncertainty of developments in' broadband markets and 'the dynamic quality of innovation' (Pitofsky 2001, 555). The combined firm also committed to continue offering DSL as an alternative mode of broadband access, and it promised not to interfere in the delivery of Internet content or interactive television by independent suppliers.

One year after the FTC extracted a commitment to open access as a condition of approving the AOL/Time Warner merger, the FCC reaffirmed its policy of insulating cable broadband from open access obligations. In 2002, the FCC ruled that cable companies offering broadband Internet access do not offer telecommunications services. This conclusion effectively excluded cable broadband from regulation under the common carrier provisions in title II of the Communications Act (although it did leave room for the FCC to impose open access requirements on cable broadband operators as providers of 'information service' within the meaning of the Telecommunications Act of 1996). The Telecommunications Act defines:

> '(t)he term "information service" [as] the offering of a capability for generating, acquiring, storing, transforming, processing, retrieving, or making available information via telecommunications, . . . but does not include any use of any capability for the management, control, or operation of a telecommunications system or the management of a telecommunications service' (47 U.S.C. § 153(20) (2000)).

The Ninth Circuit, however, invalidated the FCC's order to the extent that the Commission failed to treat the provision of Internet access over cable as a 'telecommunications service' (*Brand X Internet Serv. v. FCC*, 345 F.3d 1120, 1120, 1132 (2003)). The Supreme Court then vacated the Ninth Circuit's decision and reinstated the FCC's interpretation of 'telecommunications service' as excluding broadband Internet access over cable (*Nat'l Cable & Telecomm. Ass'n v. Brand X Internet Serv.*, 545 U.S. 967 (2005)). The Supreme Court's resolution effectively restored the FCC's previous treatment of cable broadband.

Before *Brand X*, the FCC had ruled that DSL services offered over the wireline telephone network are subject to common carrier regulation, including open access obligations (47 U.S.C. § 251(c)(3) (2000); Implementation of the Local Competition Provisions, 11 FCC Rcd 15 499, 15 689 (1996); Deployment of Wireline Service Offering Advanced Telecommunications Capability & Implementation of the Local Competition Provisions in the Telecommunications Act of 1996, 14 FCC Rcd 20 912, 20 916 (1999); Speta 2000, 67–69). As a result, the two leading technologies for high-speed Internet access were subject to very different access rules. The D.C. Circuit, however, blocked aspects of the FCC's open access regime for DSL on multiple occasions (*US Telecomm. v. FCC*, 290 F.3d at 415; *WorldCom, Inc., v. FCC*, 246 F.3d 690 (2001); *Bell Atl. Telephone Cos. v. FCC*, 206 F.3d 1 (2000); Speta 2003, 15). The Commission nevertheless declared its comfort with an asymmetrical regime under which cable broadband operators remained free of open access obligations (Oxman 1999, 6; Inquiry Concerning the Deployment of Wireline Services, 14 FCC Rcd 2398, 2423–24 (1999)) while their telephone company counterparts were at least nominally obliged to offer DSL-enabling elements of their networks at cost to their competitors (Inquiry Concerning High-Speed Access, 17 FCC Rcd 4798, 4825 (2002); *Nat'l Cable & Telecomm. Ass'n v. Brand X Internet Serv.*, 545 U.S. 967 (2005); Deployment of Wireline Services Offering Advanced Telecommunications Capability, 13 FCC Rcd 24 011, 24 031 (1998)).

In its restoration of the FCC's cable broadband policy, the Supreme Court took pains not to disturb the FCC's unbalanced treatment of DSL (*Nat'l Cable & Telecomm. Ass'n v. Brand X Internet Serv.*, 545 U.S. at 1001–2). The Commission, however, responded by reversing its prior policy (Appropriate Framework for Broadband Access to the Internet over Wireline Facilities, 20 FCC Rcd 14853 (2005)). The FCC determined that wireline broadband Internet access constitutes an 'information service' functionally integrated with a telecommunications component. This decision eliminated wireline broadband carriers' obligation to offer this service's transmissions component on a stand-alone, common-carrier basis.

Among the types of telecommunications mergers that Congress could have predicted and regulated in 1996, the only type of merger that the Telecommunications Act specifically banned was the cable-telephone company combination targeted by Section 652. Among the different branches of the FCC's merger policy that have emerged since 1996, the Commission's approach to mergers involving cable companies have deviated the most from the statutory template laid down in 1996. Section 652 of the Telecommunications Act failed to add a significant weapon to the FCC's merger arsenal. By contrast, the two collateral issues that arose in connection with AT&T's acquisition of cable operators do provide significant checks against concentration and other anticompetitive consequences of cable mergers.

One of the tools at issue, Section 11(c) of the 1992 Cable Act and the horizontal cable ownership rules promulgated under its authority, arose before 1996. Like Section 652 of the 1996 Act, the horizontal ownership rules were designed to target concentration among firms offering multichannel video programming delivery, a regulatory concern distinct from Internet access. The FCC has attempted to adapt both Section 652 and the horizontal ownership rules as tools for responding to the emerging problem of concentration in the market for broadband Internet access, especially over the technologically superior cable platform. The fact remains, however, that these provisions arose in response to a distantly related or even irrelevant regulatory concern. Once the horizontal cable ownership rules failed to survive judicial review in the 2001 *Time Warner* decision (*Time Warner Entertainment v. FCC*, 240 F.3d 1126 (2001)), the FCC lost much of the leverage it had evidently expected to exploit in reviewing significant mergers among cable operators. As a result, AT&T was able to absorb MediaOne and Comcast in rapid succession, with minimal regulatory resistance.

The second legal tool – namely, open access obligations on cable broadband operators – retains an uncertain status. The Commission has refrained from imposing any sort of open access requirement on cable broadband operators. The courts have endorsed the FCC's decision to tackle what is the industry-wide problem of equal access to cable platforms through rulemaking rather than ad hoc conditions imposed in connection with merger approvals (*Consumer Federation of Am. v. FCC*, 348 F.3d 1009, 1013 (2003); *SBC Commc'n v. FCC*, 56 F.3d 1485, 1491 (1995)). In all likelihood, the sharp contrast with the FCC's exuberant use of conditions in horizontal mergers between local exchange carriers arises from a basic statutory difference. Whereas open access to DSL is a natural outgrowth of the common carrier regime that the Communications Act historically imposed on companies providing wireline telecommunications services (47 U.S.C. § 251(c)(3) (2000); Implementation of the Local Competition Provisions, 11 FCC Rcd at 15 689); Deployment of Wireline Services Offering Advanced Telecommunications Capability & Implementation of the Local Competition Provisions in the Telecommunications Act of 1996, 14 FCC Rcd at 20 916; Speta 2000, 67–69), that statute and its subsequent amendments painstakingly insulate 'cable system[s]' from 'regulation as a common carrier or utility by reason of providing any cable service' (47 U.S.C. § 541(c) (2000)).

Growing concentration in the cable sector – the very phenomenon that neither Section 652 of the 1996 Act nor the ill-starred horizontal cable ownership rules have been able to obstruct – heightens the prospect that the FCC may exercise its authority to require open access to cable-based Internet access as an 'information service'. Then again, intermodal competition between cable broadband, DSL and its nascent wireless alternatives tempers the urge to subject all of these modes of transmission to open access requirements. The continuing growth of 'robust competition' (*US Telecomm. v. FCC*, 290 F.3d 415, 428 (2002); *Nat'l Cable & Telecomm. Ass'n v. Brand X Internet Serv.*, 545 U.S. at 1001–02) in the race to provide 'residential high-speed access to the Internet', especially as that contest 'evolv[es] over multiple electronic platforms' (Inquiry Concerning High-Speed Access, 17 FCC Rcd at 4820), suggests that all of these platforms will be freed from regulatory open access obligations. Once facilities-based competition emerges, especially for a market as technologically volatile as that for broadband Internet access, it makes no sense to shackle any of those modes of carriage on behalf of well-positioned competitors.

TECHNOLOGICAL MYOPIA AND REGULATORY MISMATCHES

FCC merger policy bears little resemblance to 'legal landscape' contemplated by the Telecommunications Act of 1996 (*AT&T Corp. v. City of Portland*, 216 F.3d at 876). Indeed, the leading tools for shaping merger policy within contemporary telecommunications law are at best tenuously connected to the 1996 Act. The FCC's authority to grant conditional approval of mergers stems from the public interest standard of the Communications Act of 1934. The horizontal cable ownership rules originate in 1992 legislation aimed at curbing concentration in mass media, not in telecommunications. A potentially vital tool for checking concentration in the industry that holds a commanding lead in the market for broadband Internet access owes its legal impetus to a statute designed to ensure diversity in news and entertainment. The success FCC has enjoyed in supervising telecommunications mergers has come not because of the 1996 Act, but in spite of it.

Legislative shortsightedness bears much of the blame. The 1996 Act conspicuously ignored the Internet except as a transmission vector for pornography (*Reno v. ACLU*, 521 U.S. 844, 857 (1997); Esbin 1999, 55; Podesta 1996, 1093). The Act's decency provisions and the litigation those provisions provoked have had no bearing on the market structure and industrial organization of telecommunications (Communications Decency Act of 1996, 110 Stat. 133 (1996); Internet Tax Freedom Act of 1998, 112 Stat. 2681–719 (1998); *Reno v. ACLU*, 521 U.S. 844 (1997); *Ashcroft v. ACLU*, 535 U.S. 564 (2002); *Ashcroft v. ACLU*, 542 U.S. 656 (2004)). Having failed to anticipate 'the fastest growing new medium of all time' and 'the information medium of first resort for its users' (*see generally* Lyman and Varian

2003), the Telecommunications Act gave the FCC no tools for responding more cogently to voice over Internet protocol or any other emerging technology. Even after the 1996 Act's technological shortcomings became undeniably clear, Congress continued to regulate the Internet primarily as a conduit for sexually explicit speech, secondarily as a duty-free shopping zone (Internet Tax Freedom Act of 1998, 112 Stat. 2681–719 (1998)) and barely as a dominant communications medium. The drafters of the 1996 Act systematically underestimated the rate of technological evolution in the industry (Epstein 2005, 320).

Those portions of the Telecommunications Act that did address competition policy focused on '[t]he two most noteworthy and most controversial changes in the status quo, authorizing competition in local telephone markets and, reciprocally, authorizing Bell operating company . . . entry into long distance' (Robinson 1996, 289). Much of the energy devoted to the first decade of implementing the Telecommunications Act was spent on bruising and ultimately inconsequential battles over incumbent carriers' pricing of unbundled network elements and BOC petitions under Section 271 to offer interexchange services to local exchange customers. As early as 1998, facilities-based competition began to take root. By 2000, facilities-based entry eclipsed entry based on unbundled network elements and resale of ILEC service – the categories of competitive entry dependent on Section 251 and the other local competition provisions of the 1996 Act (Shelanski 2002, 353). The enormous legal effort poured into Sections 251 and 271 has coincided with those provisions' slide into technological irrelevance.

The deregulatory model contemplated by the Telecommunications Act of 1996 was not inherently defective. Its roots can be traced to Harold Demsetz's work on imperfect competition (Demsetz 1968, 55). 'The Act sought to unleash three of the most deeply entrenched monopolists in the American economy – local exchange carriers, interexchange carriers and cable system operators – on each other's markets in the hope that competition among the large would dissolve these industrial giants.' Even if each combatant achieved only modest 'inroads', the mere presence of 'new entrant[s]' in each of these 'tight oligopoly industr[ies]' promised to 'shake things up a great deal' (Turner 1965, 1383; *BOC International LTD. v. FTC*, 557 F.2d 24, 27 (1977)). The Act anticipated the prospect that local carriage, the last of the great natural monopolies, would succumb to a technologically sophisticated intermodal assault. The Act contemplated a battle royal in which interexchange carriers and cable companies would attack the local exchange, while BOCs would breach the firewalls, traceable to the Bell breakup decree, that had kept them out of long-distance carriage (*United States v. Am. Tel. & Tel. Co.*, 552 F. Supp. 131, 188–91 (1982)) and video programming (Cable Communications Policy Act of 1984, 98 Stat. 2779 (1984)).

These head-to-head battles over the leading telecommunications markets of the 1980s never materialized. Incumbent local exchange carriers never successfully invaded the cable operators' core business of multichannel video programming and delivery. Erstwhile buzzwords such as 'video dialtone' and 'open video systems' now bear mute legal testimony to the failed aspirations of policy makers who had envisioned telephone companies as the video programming providers of choice. Nothing ever came of the 'hybrid fiber coax' technology once thought to be the conduit by which cable operators would carry switched voice messages (Minoli 1995, 129). In truth, video dialtone and hybrid fiber coax were the same technology (Botein 1996, 581 82) and it failed.

For all the hope that the 1996 Act lodged in facilities-based competition, the 104th Congress grossly underestimated the competitive potential of wireless telephone service (Price and Duffy 1997, 982). The legislative history of the Telecommunications Act explicitly rejected the possibility that wireless service could satisfy the statute's definition of 'facilities-based competition' (1996 H.R. Conf. Rep., 147). Ironically, under the state of communications technology that prevailed in 1996, wireless telephone service promised the most economically robust, facilities-based platform by which competitive carriers could undermine incumbent carriers' wireline legacy networks (Warner 1996, 52; Thoreson 1998, 336). Especially in rural areas, where wireless telephone service could most effectively address the problems that dispersed populations, forbidding climates and 'unaccommodating' terrain pose to the operator of a wireline network (*Alenco Commc'n, Inc. v. FCC*, 201 F.3d 608, 617 (2000); Grimes and Lyons 1994, 219), telecommunications law's bias against wireless telephone service has been perverse and unremitting (Chen 2003, 307). There is no historical basis for this bias. In the first decades of telephone service, AT&T and independent carriers so fiercely contested local markets that more than half of the American population had a choice of carriers (Lavey 1987, 178; Shelanski 2002, 343–44) and rural markets were the markets where most of this competition took place (Mueller 1993, 359–60).

In retrospect, the FCC's 1999 approval of the SBC/Ameritech merger marked a legal and technological turning point in American telecommunications policy. That proceeding marked the last of the significant horizontal BOC mergers. Bell Atlantic's acquisition of GTE, approved eight months later, seemed legally anticlimactic despite its $52.8 billion price tag. The merged firms' commitment to divest GTE's Internet backbone holdings (GTE Corp., 15 FCC Rcd 14 032, 14 036–14 037 (2000)) and overlapping wireless properties in 96 overlapping markets (ibid. at 14 039) effectively cleared all regulatory hurdles to the absorption of the country's largest independent local exchange carrier by the mightiest of the BOCs (ibid. at 14 036). In a long but legally inconsequential order, the FCC blessed the creation of Verizon.

The divestiture of Internet backbone associated with the birth of Verizon would eventually affect the telecommunications industry in unanticipated ways. One seemingly insignificant divestiture associated with the SBC/Ameritech proceeding, for its own part, had the effect of giving the future Verizon the breakthrough in wireless markets that Bell Atlantic had long coveted. In anticipation of its merger with SBC, Ameritech agreed to sell 20 of its wireless properties, including the Chicago and St. Louis markets, for $3.27 billion to a partnership led by GTE (Ameritech Corp., 15 FCC Rcd 6667 (2000)). The licenses acquired by GTE came to rest in Verizon's hands upon Bell Atlantic's absorption of America's last significant independent local exchange carrier. Meanwhile, Bell Atlantic eventually reached a compromise with Vodafone, which agreed to sell AirTouch's former properties in North America – precisely what the BOC had coveted in its failed 1999 bid for AirTouch (Holson 1999 (Sept 13), C1). By unifying the geographically comprehensive wireless assets that once belonged to Bell Atlantic, AirTouch, Ameritech and GTE, Verizon forged a wireless empire worth an estimated $70 billion at the time of the Bell Atlantic/GTE merger (Holson 1999 (Sept 22), C1). As of its creation in 2000, Verizon commanded a dominant position in wireless telephone service across the entire United States. Wireline dominance in telephone service had begun its inexorable decline.

Federal communications policy has long favored wireline over wireless infrastructure. On an annual basis, historic delays in the rollout of wireless capacity inflict roughly $33 billion in lost productivity across the American economy (Hausman 1997, 1). The FCC initially assigned two 25 megahertz (MHz) cellular licenses in the 800 MHz band in each local market, reserving one for the incumbent wireline carrier (Implementation of Sec. 6002(b), 19 FCC Rcd 20 597, 20 632 (2004)). In 1995, the FCC opened 120 MHz of spectrum in the 1900 MHz band for broadband personal communications services (PCS) (ibid. at 20 632–33; Omnibus Budget Reconciliation Act of 1993, 107 Stat. 312 (1993)). This action, which predated comprehensive statutory reform of the Communications Act by a single year, may have had a greater competitive impact than the Telecommunications Act of 1996. The first broadband PCS auction triggered an epochal change in American wireless telephone service. The old cellular duopoly gave way to a thoroughly competitive national marketplace. Between 2000 and 2004, the percentage of the United States population having access to three or more different choices in mobile telephone service increased from 88 to 97 per cent (AT&T Wireless Servs., 19 FCC Rcd 21 522, 21 553 (2004)). By 2004, six mobile operators operated nationwide networks: AT&T Wireless,

Cingular Wireless, Nextel, T-Mobile, Sprint and Verizon Wireless (At&T Wireless Services, 19 FCC Rcd 21 522, 21 553 (2004)). Further consolidation has whittled this number to three: AT&T, Verizon and T-Mobile. Along with market structure, the technological basis for wireless telephone service changed dramatically. From the end of 1998 (roughly contemporaneous with the horizontal BOC mergers) to 2004, the portion of mobile telephone subscribers using digital rather than analog cellular technology rose from 30 per cent to more than 90 per cent (Implementation of Sec. 6002(b), 19 FCC Rcd at 20 669).

Indeed, the wireless industry's pronounced absence from the most important FCC merger proceedings of the past decade teaches a deeper lesson about the impact of telecommunications law on this facet of the industry. In retrospect, neither comprehensive legislative reform in 1996 nor the first decade of regulatory experience under the Act has significantly changed the impact of mergers in this industry. Even though the 1996 Act terminated the consent decree governing AT&T's 1993 acquisition of McCaw Cellular Communications (Communications Decency Act of 1996, 110 Stat. 133, 143–44 (1996)), the AT&T/McCaw merger arguably still sets the baseline by which the law's impact on telecommunications mergers can be measured. Touted as one of the most significant developments in telecommunications before 1996 (Baumol and Sidak 1994, 16; Kellogg *et al.* 1993, 1224), AT&T's acquisition of McCaw's wireless network terrorized the BOCs by threatening to recreate 'the only facilities based national and local end-to-end service in the country since divestiture' (*SBC Commc'n Inc. v. FCC*, 56 F.3d 1484, 1490 (1995)). At the time, the union of AT&T and McCaw tantalizingly promised full-service telecommunications based on wireless local exchanges and fiber optic transmission – the technological mirror image of the copper-and-microwave combination that precipitated the Bell breakup decree (*United States v. W. Elec. Co.*, 46 F.3d 1198, 2101–02 (1995)).

No one today regards the AT&T/McCaw merger as more than a minor footnote in the rapidly evolving history of telecommunications. Though that merger signaled the rise of wireless telephone service as a significant competitive force in telecommunications, the designers of the 1996 Act took pains to minimize the role that wireless technologies would play in disputes over local competition. The once fearful combination of AT&T's interexchange kingdom with McCaw's wireless network played virtually no role in SBC's acquisition of AT&T. Rather than responding to these developments, the path of legal reform in telecommunications since 1996 has focused on other issues, such as unbundled access to the local exchange and Section 271 petitions permitting the provision of interexchange carriage to BOC customers.

The AT&T/McCaw merger did reverse the baseline by which the law approaches telecommunications mergers. Line-of-business firewalls separating local wireline carriage, interexchange carriage, wireless carriage and equipment manufacturing once characterized the Bell breakup decree (Kearney 1999, 1395). That legal regime scrutinized any proposed merger that would blur these operational boundaries. Yet the AT&T/McCaw merger proceeded almost without regard to the Bell breakup decree, notwithstanding the FCC's acknowledgement of Bell divestiture as a 'special circumstance' affecting the AT&T/McCaw merger's legality (*SBC v. FCC*, 56 F.3d at 1489–90). Ever since, both the FCC and the Department of Justice have been content to extract regulatory concessions from the parties in proposed telecommunications mergers. However, neither the FCC nor Justice has barred a major telecommunications merger outright in the tradition of the Bell breakup. In a legal realm whose 'regulatory measures' emphatically 'are temporary expedients, not eternal verities' (*Fed. Power Comm'n v. East Ohio Gas Co.*, 338 U.S. 464, 489 (1950)), meaningful barriers to telecommunications mergers have yielded in favor of presumptive regulatory comfort with convergence, consolidation, and concentration.

Concededly, '[e]conomic analysis and market predictions' are nowhere 'an exact science' (*United States v. W. Elec. Co.*, 900 F.2d 283, 297 (1990)), least of all in an industry whose 'unusually dynamic character' has confounded legal efforts to keep pace with technological change (*MCI Telecomm. Corp. v. Am. Tel. & Tel. Co.*, 512 U.S. (1994) at 235). The FCC has cobbled a merger policy from almost no legislative raw material and under conditions of rapid technological change and predictive uncertainty. The Commission's experience since 1996 finds an instructive parallel from the agency's earliest days. In response to the Congress's first request for an investigation of the telephone industry (Public Resolution, 49 Stat. 43 (1935)), the FCC concluded that the 'fundamental problem' of regulating interstate telephone service 'consist[ed] largely of developing ways and means . . . for continuous acquisition of basic factual data' on the industry (Federal Communications Commission 1939, 596). The Commission thus developed and pursued a policy of 'constant or continuing surveillance' of long-distance rates through 'informal negotiation' (Federal Communications Commission 1938, 68). Constant surveillance allowed the FCC to patrol long-distance rates without interminable hearings or the antagonistic atmosphere of command-and-control regulation, all the while gathering more knowledge of telephone service's underlying market structure (Welch 1963, p. 340). The Commission thus stumbled onto the aptly named regulatory strategy of 'muddling through' (Lindblom 1959, 86; Davis 1969, 733).

Merger policy, at most an afterthought in the 1996 Act, has become a major part of telecommunications reform. Ad hoc responses to numerous unanticipated legal and economic twists since 1996 have made merger policy an important component of the FCC's implementation of the Telecommunications Act. Although that policy has never stopped a proposed merger falling within the Act's comprehensive scope, the FCC's record of adaptation and response since 1996 suggests that there may be some virtue in allowing merger policy in any technologically volatile industry to unfold over a period of years, without conscious forethought, and in response to rather than in anticipation of market events. The FCC's record, however, is only as valuable as its most recent manifestation. VOIP, once fully deployed and embraced 'by a substantial majority of residential customers' (47 U.S.C. § 254(c)(1)(B) (2000)), will test the ability of the existing legal framework to respond to unanticipated anticompetitive threats. How telecommunications law affects this market depends on the ability of regulators to manage what may be the most significant innovation in communications since the invention of the telephone.

Chen (2007) provides a more extensive review of these issues.

NOTE

1. Andrew Davis, Jennifer L. Hanson, Matthew Krueger and Erica Tunick supplied very capable research assistance. Daniel A. Farber, Daniel J. Gifford, Gil Grantmore and Bernard Shull provided helpful comments.

REFERENCES

Baldwin, Thomas F., D. Stevens McVoy and Charles Steinfeld (1996), *Convergence: Integrating Media, Information, and Communications*, Thousand Oaks, CA: Sage Publications.

Baumol, William J. and J. Gregory Sidak (1994), *Toward Competition in Local Telephony*, Cambridge, MA: MIT Press.

Belson, Ken (Jan. 28, 2005), 'Dial M for Merger,' *N.Y. Times*, p. C1.

Belson, Ken (Jan. 31, 2005), 'SBC Near Deal to Acquire AT&T for $16 Billion,' *N.Y. Times*, p. A18.

Botein, Michael (1996), 'Cable/Telco Mergers and Acquisitions: An Antitrust Analysis,' *Sw. U. L. Rev.* 25, 569–604.

Bush, Darren and Salvatore Massa (2004), 'Rethinking the Potential Competition Doctrine,' *Wis. L. Rev.*, 2004, 1036–1160.

Chen, Jim (1997), 'The Legal Process and Political Economy of Telecommunications Reform,' *Colum. L. Rev.*, 97, 835–73.

Chen, Jim (2001), 'The Authority to Regulate Broadband Internet Access over Cable,' *Berkeley Tech. L.J.*, 16, 677–727.

Chen, Jim (2003), 'Subsidized Rural Telephony and the Public Interest: A Case Study in Cooperative Federalism and Its Pitfalls,' *Telecomms. and High Tech. L.J.*, 2, 307–73.

Chen, Jim (2007), 'The Echoes of Forgotten Footfalls: Telecommunications Mergers at the Dawn of the Digital Millennium,' *Hous. L. Rev.*, 43, 1312–71.

Committee Reports, 104th Congress; 2nd Session (1996), S. Rep. No. 104-230 [104 S. Rpt. 230] Telecommunications Act of 1996: conference report (to accompany S. 652).

Committee Reports, 104th Congress; 2nd Session (1996) H.R. Rep. No. 104–458 [104 H. Rpt. 230] Telecommunications Act of 1996: conference report (to accompany S. 652).

Cooper, Mark (2000), 'Open Access to the Broadband Internet: Technical and Economic Discrimination in Closed Proprietary Networks,' *U. Colo. L. Rev.*, 71, 1011–69.

Davis, Kenneth Culp (1969), 'A New Approach to Delegation,' *U. Chi. L. Rev.*, 36, 716–33.

Demsetz, Harold (1968), 'Why Regulate Utilities,' *J. Law & Econ.*, 11, 55–65.

Epstein, Richard A. (2005), 'Taking Commons and Associations: Why the Telecommunications Act of 1996 Misfired,' *Yale J. on Reg.*, 22, 315–48.

Esbin, Barbara (1999), 'Internet over Cable: Defining the Future in Terms of the Past,' *CommLaw Conspectus*, 7, 37–118.

Federal Communications Commission (1938), *Final Report of the Telephone Rate and Research Department*, Washington D.C.: United States Government Printing Office.

Federal Communications Commission (1939), *Investigation of the Telephone Industry in the United States*, Washington D.C.: United States Government Printing Office.

Federal Communications Commission (2006), 'Voice Over Internet Protocol,' http://www.fcc.gov/voip.

Federal Trade Commission (2000), 'In re America Online Inc. and Time Warner Inc.' *WL*, 2000, 1843019.

Grimes, Seamus and Gerald Lyons (1994), 'Information Technology and Rural Development: Unique Opportunity or Potential Threat?,' *Entrepreneurship and Regional Dev't*, 6, 219–38.

Hausman, Jerry A. (1997), 'Valuing the Effect of Regulation on New Services in Telecommunications,' *Brookings Papers on Economic Activity: Microeconomics*, Washington D.C.: Brookings Institution, 1–54.

Holson, Laura (Sept. 13, 1999), 'Bell Atlantic and Vodaphone, Once Enemies, Are Now Allies,' *N.Y. Times*, p. C1.

Holson, Laura (Sept. 22, 1999), 'Deal to Create Biggest U.S. Wireless Network,' *N.Y. Times*, p. C1.

Kearney, Joseph D. (1999), 'From the Fall of the Bell System to the Telecommunications Act: Regulation of Telecommunications Under Judge Greene,' *Hastings L.J.*, 50, 1395–1472.

Kellogg, Michael, K., John Thorne, and Peter W. Huber (1993), 'Telecommunications in Jericho,' *Cal. L. Rev.*, 81, 1209–39.

Kimelman, Gene (1998), 'Consolidation in the Telecommunications Industry,' Testimony Before Sen. Judiciary Comm., *WL*, 1998, 767370.

Lander, Mark (June 19, 1997), 'In Unusual Move, FCC Chief Criticizes a Possible Deal,' *N.Y. Times*, p. D1.

Lavey, Warren G. (1987), 'The Public Policies That Changed the Telephone Industry into Regulated Monopolies: Lessons from 1915,' *Fed. Comm, L.J.*, 39, 171–94.

Legg, Michael J. (2004), 'Verizon Communications, Inc. v. FCC – Telecommunications Access Pricing and Regulatory Accountability through Administrative Law and Takings Jurisprudence,' *Fed. Comm. L.J.*, 56, 563–85.

Lindblom, Charles (1959), 'The Science of Muddling Through,' *Pub. Admin. Rev.*, 19, 79–88.

Lyman, Peter and Hal R. Varian (2003), 'How Much Information,' http://www.sims.berkeley.edu/research/projects/how-much-info-2003/printable_report.pdf.

McFadden, Douglas B. (1997), 'Antitrust and Communications: Changes After the Telecommunications Act of 1996,' *Fed. Comm. L.J.* 49, 457–72.

Minoli, Daniel (1995), *Video Dialtone Technology*, New York: McGraw-Hill.

Mueller, Milton (1993), 'Universal Service in Telephone History,' *Telecom. Pol'y*, 17, 352–69.

Mueller, Milton (1997), *Universal Service: Competition Interconnection and Monopoly in the Making of the American Telephone System*, Cambridge, MA: MIT Press.

New York Times (June 13, 1997), 'FCC Sees Obstacles to an AT&T Merger,' *N.Y. Times*, p. D2.

Oxman, Jason (1999), *The FCC and the Unregulation of the Internet*, Washington DC: Office of Plans and Policy, Federal Communications Commission.

Pitofsky, Robert (1990), 'New definitions of Relevant Market and the Assault on Antitrust,' *Colum. L. Rev.*, 90, 1805–64.

Pitofsky, Robert (2001), 'Antitrust and Intellectual Property: Unresolved Issues at the Heart of the New Economy,' *Berkeley Tech. L.J.*, 16, 535–59.

Podesta, John D. (1996), 'Unplanned Obsolescence: The Telecommunications Act of 1996 Meets the Internet,' *DePaul L. Rev.* 45, 1093–1115.

Price, Monroe E. and John F. Duffy (1997), 'Technological Change and Doctrinal Persistence: Telecommunications Reform in Congress and the Court,' *Colum. L. Rev.*, 97, 976–1015.

Robinson, Glen O. (1996), 'The "New" Telecommunications Act: A Second Opinion,' *Conn. L. Rev.*, 29, 289–329.

Shelanski, Howard A. (2002), 'From Sector-Specific Regulation to Antitrust Law for US Telecommunications: The Prospects for Transition,' *Telecom. Pol'y*, 26, 335–55.

Sidak, Gregory and Daniel F. Spulber (1997), *Deregulatory Takings and the Regulatory Contract: The Competitive Transformation of Network Industries in the United States*, New York: Cambridge University Press.

Speta, James B. (2000), 'A Critique of Open Access Rules for Broadband Platforms,' *Yale J. on Reg.*, 17, 39–91.

Speta, James B. (2003), 'FCC Authority to Regulate the Internet: Creating It and Limiting It,' *Loy U. Chi. L.J.*, 35, 15–39.

Spulber, Daniel F. and Christopher S. Yoo (2003), 'Access to Networks: Economic and Constitutional Connections,' *Cornell L. Rev.*, 88, 885–1024.

Swedenburg, Eric M. (1999), 'Promoting Competition in the Telecommunications Markets: Why the FCC Should Adopt a Less Stringent Approach to Its Review of Section 271 Applications,' *Cornell L. Rev.*, 84, 1418–75.

Thoreson, Eric (1998), 'Comment: Fairwell to the Bell Monopoly? The Wireless Alternative to Local Competition,' *Or. L. Rev.*, 77, 309–36.

Turner, Donald, F. (1965), 'Conglomerate Mergers and Section 7 of the Clayton Act,' *Harv. L. Rev.*, 78, 1313–95.

Warner, Lisa M. (1996), 'Wireless Technologies Creating Competition in the Local Exchange Market: How Will Local Exchange Carriers Compete?,' *CommLaw Conspectus*, 4, 51–78.

Weiss, James R. and Martin L. Stern (1998), 'Serving Two Masters: The Dual Jurisdiction of the FCC and the Justice Department over Telecommunications Transactions,' *CommLaw Conspectus*, 6, 195–212.

Welch, Francis X. (1963), 'Constant Surveillance: A Modern Regulatory Tool,' *Villanova L. Rev.*, 8, 340–59.

Worstell, Jennifer L. (1998), 'Note, Section 253 of the Telecommunications Act of 1996: A Permanent Physical Appropriation of Private Property That Must Be Justly Compensated,' *Fed. Comm. L.J.*, 50, 441–81.

Cases

Alenco Commc'n, Inc. v. FCC, 201 F.3d 608 (2000).
Ashcroft v. ACLU, 535 U.S. 564 (2002).
Ashcroft v. ACLU, 542 U.S. 656 (2004).
AT&T Corp. v. Iowa Util. Bd., 525 U.S. 366 (1999).
AT&T Corp. v. City of Portland, 216 F.3d 871 (2000).
AT&T Corp. v. FCC, 220 F.3d 607 (2000).
Bell Atl. Tel. Cos. v. FCC, 206 F.3d 1 (2000).
Bell Atl. Tel. Cos. v. FCC, 24 F.3d 1441 (1994).
BellSouth Corp. v. FCC, 162 F.3d 678 (1998).
BOC Int'l, Ltd. v. FTC, 557 F.2d 24 (1977).
Brand X Internet Serv. v. FCC, 345 F.3d 1120 (2003).
Consumer Fed. of Am. v. FCC, 348 F.3d 1009 (2003).
Daniels Cablevision, Inc. v. United States, 835 F. Supp. 1 (1993).
Denver Area Educ. Telecomm. Consortium, Inc. v. FCC, 518 U.S. 727 (1996).
Eastman Kodak Co. v. Image Technical Serv., Inc., 504 U.S. 451 (1992).
FCC v. Nat'l Citizens Comm. for Broad., 436 U.S. 775 (1978).
FCC v. Pottsville Broad. Co., 309 U.S. 134 (1940).
FCC v. RCA Commc'n, Inc., 346 U.S. 86 (1953).
FCC v WNCN Listeners Guild, 450 U.S. 582 (1981).
Fed. Power Comm'n v. East Ohio Gas. Co., 338 U.S. 464 (1950).
Fed. Radio Comm'n v. Nelson Bros. Bond & Mortgage Co., 289 U.S. 266 (1933).
Fortner Enter., Inc. v. US Steel Corp., 394 U.S. 495 (1969).
FTC v. Proctor & Gamble Co., 386 U.S. 568 (1967).
Gordon v. New York Stock Exch., Inc., 422 U.S. 659 (1975).
GTE Nw., Inc. v. Pub. Util. Commn, 321 Ore. 458 (1995).
GTE S., Inc. v. Morrison, 6 F. Supp. 2d 517 (1998).
Hawaiian Tel. Co. v. FCC, 498 F.2d 771 (1974).
Jefferson Parish Hosp. Dist. No. 2 v. Hyde, 466 U.S. 2 (1984).
Loretto v. Teleprompter Manhattan CATV Corp., 458 U.S. 419 (1982).
MCI Telecomm. Corp. v. Am. Tel. & Tel. Co., 512 U.S. 218 (1994).
MCI v. Bell Atl., 36 F. Supp. 419 (1999).
Mercantile Textile Corp. v. Bd. of Governors of the Fed. Reserve Sys., 638 F.2d 1255 (1981).
Nat'l Broad. Co. v. United States, 319 U.S. 190 (1943).
Nat'l Cable & Telecomm. Ass'n v. Brand X Internet Serv., 545 U.S. 967 (2005).
Ne. Util. Serv. Co. v. FERC, 993 F.2d 937 (1993).

N. Pac. Ry. Co. v. United States, 356 U.S. 1 (1958).
People of the State of California v. FCC, 39 F.3d 919 (1994).
Quest Corp. v. United States, 48 Fed. Cl. 672 (2001).
Reno v. ACLU, 521 U.S. 844 (1997).
SBC Commc'n, Inc. v. FCC, 138 F.3d 410 (1998).
SBC Commc'n, Inc. v. FCC, 56 F.3d 1484 (1995).
Schurz Commc'n, Inc. v. FCC, 982 F.2d 1043 (1992).
Sprint Commc'n Co. v. FCC, 274 F.3d 549 (2001).
Tenneco, Inc. v. FTC, 689 F.2d 346 (1982).
Time Warner Entm't Co. v. FCC, 240 F.3d 1126 (2001).
Time Warner Entm't Co. v. FCC, 93 F.3d 957 (1996).
US West Commc'n, Inc. v. AT&T Commc'n, Inc., 31 F. Supp. 2d 839 (1998).
US West Commc'n, Inc. v. Jennings, 46 F. Supp. 2d 1004 (1999).
US Steel Corp. v. Fortner Enter., Inc., 429 U.S. 610 (1977).
US Telecomm. Ass'n v. FCC, 290 F.3d 415 (2002).
US Telecomm. Ass'n v. FCC, 359 F.3d 554 (2004).
United States v. Am. Tel. & Tel. Co., 552 F. Supp. 131 (1982).
United States v. El Paso Natural Gas Co., 376 U.S. 651 (1964).
United States v. Falstaff Brewing Corp., 410 U.S. 526 (1973).
United States v. FCC, 652 F.2d 72 (1980).
United States v. Gen. Motors Corp., 323 U.S. 373 (1945).
United States v. Loews Inc., 371 U.S. 38 (1962).
United States v. Marine Bancorp., 418 U.S. 602 (1974).
United States v. Nat'l Ass'n of Sec. Dealers, Inc., 422 U.S. 694 (1975).
United States v. Pabst Brewing Co., 384 U.S. 546 (1966).
United States v. Penn-Olin Chem. Co., 378 U.S. 158 (1964).
United States v. Pewee Coal Co., 341 U.S. 114 (1951).
United States v. RCA, 358 U.S. 334 (1959).
United States v. W. Elec. Co., 569 F. Supp. 1057 (1983).
United States v. W. Elec. Co., 797 F.2d 1082 (1986).
United States v. W. Elec. Co., 900 F.2d 283 (1990).
United States v. W. Elec. Co., 900 F.2d 283 (1993).
United States v. W. Elec. Co., 993 F.2d 1572 (1993).
United States v. W. Elec. Co., 46 F.3d 1198 (1995).
United States v. W. Elec. Co., 890 F. Supp. 1 (1995).
Verizon Commc'n Inc. v. FCC, 535 U.S. 467 (2002).
Verizon Commc'n Inc. v. Law Offices of Curtis V. Trinko, 540 U.S. 398 (2004).
W.U. Div., Commercial Telegraphers' Union v. United States, 87 F. Supp. 324 (1949).
WorldCom, Inc. v. FCC, 246 F.3d 690 (2001).
WorldCom, Inc. v. FCC, 308 F.3d 1 (2002).
Yamaha Motor Co. v. FTC, 657 F.2d 971 (1981).
Z-Tel Commc'n, Inc. v. FCC, 333 F.3d 262 (2003).

Agency Decisions

Amendment of the Commission's Rules and Policies Governing Pole Attachments, 13 FCC Rcd 6777 (1998).
Ameritech Corp. & SBC Communications, Inc., 14 FCC Rcd 14 712 (1999).
Ameritech Corp. & GTE Consumer Servs. Inc., 15 FCC Rcd 6667 (2000).
Ameritech Michigan, 12 FCC Rcd 20 543 (1997).

Annual Assessment of the Status of Competition in Markets for the Delivery of Video Programming, 13 FCC Rcd 13 044 (1998).

Appropriate Framework for Broadband Access to the Internet over Wireline Facilities, 20 FCC Rcd 14853 (2005).

AT&T Wireless Servs. & Cingular Wireless Corp., 19 FCC Rcd 21 522 (2004).

Bell Atl. New York, 15 FCC Rcd 3953 (1999).

BellSouth Corp., 13 FCC Rcd 539 (1998).

BellSouth Corp., 13 FCC Rcd 6245 (1998).

BellSouth Corp., 13 FCC Rcd 20 599 (1998).

Comcast Corp., 17 FCC Rcd 23 246 (2002).

Deployment of Wireline Services Offering Advanced Telecommunications Capability, 13 FCC Rcd 24 011 (1998).

Deployment of Wireline Services Offering Advanced Telecommunications Capability, 15 FCC Rcd 385 (1999).

Deployment of Wireline Service Offering Advanced Telecommunications Capability & Implementation of the Local Competition Provisions in the Telecommunications Act of 1996, 14 FCC Rcd 20 912 (1999).

GTE Corp. & Bell Atl. Corp., 15 FCC Rcd 14 032 (2000).

Implementation of Sections 11 & 13 of the Cable Television Consumer Protection and Competition Act of 1992, 8 FCC Rcd 8565 (1993).

Implementation of Section 11(c). of the Cable Television Consumer Protection 7 Competition Act of 1992, 14 FCC Rcd 19 098 (1999).

Implementation of Section 11(c). of the Cable Television Consumer Protection & Competition Act of 1992, 16 FCC Rcd 17 312 (2001).

Implementation of Section 6002(b). of the Omnibus Budget Reconciliation Act of 1993; Annual Report & Analysis of Competitive Market Conditions with Respect to Commercial Mobile Servs., 19 FCC Rcd 20 597 (2004).

Implementation of the Local Competition Provisions in the Telecommunications Act of 1996, 11 FCC Rcd 15 499 (1996).

Inquiry Concerning High-Speed Access to the Internet over Cable and Other Facilities, 15 FCC Rcd 19 287 (1999).

Inquiry Concerning High-Speed Access to the Internet over Cable and Other Facilities, 17 FCC Rcd 4798 (2002).

Inquiry Concerning the Deployment of Wireline Services Offering Advanced Telecommunications Capability to All Americans in a Reasonable & Timely Fashion, 14 FCC Rcd 2398 (1999).

McCaw & Am. Tel. & Tel. Co., 9 FCC Rcd 5836 (1994).

McCaw & Am. Tel. & Tel. Co., 10 FCC Rcd 11 786 (1995).

MediaOne Group, Inc. & AT&T Corp., 15 FCC Rcd 9816 (2000).

MediaOne Group, Inc. & AT&T Corp., 16 FCC Rcd 5835 (2001).

MediaOne Group, Inc. & AT&T Corp., 16 FCC Rcd 20 587 (2001).

NYNEX Corp. & Bell Atlantic Corp., 12 FCC Rcd 19 985 (1997).

OTI Corp., 6 FCC Rcd 1611–13 (1991).

Pacific Telesis Group & SBC Communications, Inc., 12 FCC Rcd 2624 (1997).

Pleading Cycle Established for Comments on Conditions Proposed by SBC Communications Inc. & Ameritech Corp., 14 FCC Rcd 14 592 (1999).

Proceedings for Bell Operating Co. Applications Under New Section 271 of the Communications Act, 11 FCC Rcd 19 708 (1996).

Puerto Rico Tel. Auth. & GTE Holdings, 14 FCC Rcd 3122 (1999).

SBC Communications Inc., 12 FCC Rcd 8685 (1997).

SBC Communications Inc., 15 FCC Rcd 18 354 (2000).
SBC Communications Inc., 16 FCC Rcd 20 719 (2001).
Southeast Tel., Ltd., 12 FCC Rcd 2561 (1996).
Southern New England Tel. Corp. & SBC Communications, Inc., 13 FCC Rcd 21 292 (1998).
Tele-Communications, Inc. & AT&T Corp., 14 FCC Rcd 3160 (1999).
Teleport Communications Group, Inc. & AT&T Corp., 13 FCC Rcd 15 236 (1997).
Teleport Communications Group, Inc. & AT&T Corp., 13 FCC Rcd 3149 (1998).
U.S. West, Inc. & Continental Cablevision, Inc., 11 FCC Rcd 13 260 (1996).
U.S. West, Inc. & Continental Cablevision, Inc., 61 *Fed. Reg.* 58 703 (1996) (proposed final judgment and competitive impact statement).
Verizon Pennsylvania Inc., 16 FCC Rcd 17 419 (2001).
WorldCom Inc. & MCI Communications Corp., 13 FCC Rcd 18 025 (1998).

Statutes

Cable Communications Policy Act of 1984, 98 P.L. 549; 98 Stat. 2779 (1984) (amending the Communications Act of 1934).
Cable Television Consumer Protection and Competition Act of 1992, 102 P.L. 385; 106 Stat. 1460 (1992).
Child Online Protection Act of 1998, 105 P.L. 277; 112 Stat. 2681–736 (1998).
Communications Act of 1934, 73 P.L. 416; 73 Cong. Ch. 652; 48 Stat. 1064 (1934) (codified as amended at 47 U.S.C. §§ 151 et seq).
Communications Decency Act of 1996, 104 P.L. 104; 110 Stat. 133 (1996) (codified as amended at 47 U.S.C. § 223).
Internet Tax Freedom Act of 1998, 105 P.L. 277; 112 Stat. 2681–719 (1998).
Omnibus Budget Reconciliation Act of 1993, 103 P.L. 66; 107 Stat. 312 (1993).
Public Resolution, 74 Pub. Res. 8; 74 Cong. Ch. 31; 49 Stat. 43 (1935) (authorizing and directing the FCC to investigate and report on the Am. Tel. & Tel. Co. and all other cos. engaged directly or indirectly in tel. commc'n in interstate commerce).
Telecommunications Act of 1996, 104 P.L. 104; 110 Stat. 56 (1996).
47 C.F.R. §§ 1.110, 51.505, 76.505 (2005).
15 U.S.C. §§ 1, 18, 21 (2000).
47 U.S.C. §§ 152, 153, 157, 214, 230, 251, 252, 254, 271, 533, 541, 572, 601 (2000).
47 U.S.C. § 221 (1994).

5. Merger analysis in the post-Staggers railroad industry

Curtis M. Grimm[1]

INTRODUCTION

There has been a significant trend towards microeconomic reform world-wide, manifested largely as deregulation in the United States. Traditional regulation in the public utility framework has given way to greater reliance on markets across a number of industries. Substantial merger activity has accompanied deregulation in most industries. This has been the result in some cases of firms unable to merge under regulation exercising their post-deregulation freedom. If regulation had prevented a more efficient or profitable configuration of firms, it is natural to experience a merger wave following deregulation. In other instances, the introduction of competition in conjunction with market reforms prompted multifaceted strategic change, including mergers and other firm reconfigurations to align with the newly competitive environment. Financial pressures from competition may be a factor prompting post-deregulation mergers as well. Finally, the merger waves could, in part, be unrelated to deregulation. Instead, they may be a response to forces such as technological change and globalization, which are prompting mergers to occur in large numbers throughout the economy.

Regardless of the precise antecedent, the United States railroad industry has indeed mirrored the overall trend of substantial merger activity following regulatory reform. The second section of this chapter will review the nature of deregulation in the railroad industry, the institutional structure of merger approval in the deregulated environment and the major mergers which have taken place since 1980. The third section explores how horizontal competitive effects have been evaluated in railroad mergers, including issues of market definition, threshold of harm identification and remedy. The fourth section discusses vertical effects in railroad mergers. Rail-rail mergers, though within a single industry, generally involve both vertical and horizontal effects (*see generally* Grimm, 1984; Grimm and Harris, 1985). Mergers of railroads that are direct competitors, or portions of systems that serve the same city pairs and provide competitive alternatives to customers, are properly viewed through the lens of horizontal mergers. However, mergers of railroads that connect at one or more junction points are best not viewed as horizontal mergers, nor as market extensions as one familiar with antitrust analysis in other industries might infer. Instead, these so-called end-to-end mergers are analogous to vertical mergers in other industries, as railroads connecting at junction points are aligned in an upstream/downstream relationship for customers shipping across both carriers. This chapter concludes with a look to the future.

RAILROAD DEREGULATION AND POST-STAGGERS MERGER ACTIVITY

Somewhat unique among American industries experiencing deregulation, railroads themselves were the primary proponents of deregulation because of their poor performance under regulation. As discussed by Gallamore (1999), rail's ton-mile share of the US intercity surface freight market declined from 65 per cent to 35 per cent with returns on investment consistently in the 2–4 per cent range in the post-WWII decades. Railroad regulation prevented carriers from responding to fundamental changes in their environment during this period. While the rise of automobile and air travel had rendered much of intercity rail passenger service unprofitable, railroads were unable to easily discontinue unprofitable rail passenger trains. Moreover, truck competition had greatly increased. However, railroads were restricted in lowering rates to compete with motor carriers and were also restricted from abandoning rail lines in small towns and rural areas that could now be more economically served by truck. Following a spate of railroad bankruptcies in the early to mid-1970s, including the Penn Central, initial regulatory reform began with the Railroad Revitalization and Regulatory Reform (4R) Act of 1976. The 1980 Staggers Act further deregulated the industry (*see generally* Keeler, 1983). However, the Act maintained the status quo regarding approval of railroad mergers, namely with such authority lodged with the Interstate Commerce Commission (ICC). The Department of Justice (DOJ) Antitrust Division was encouraged to provide evidence within the context of the ICC's proceedings, but it had no authority to challenge a railroad merger. When the Interstate Commerce Commission was eliminated at the end of 1995, rail merger authority continued with its successor, the Surface Transportation Board (STB) (*see generally* Kwoka and White, 1998). This remains an important institutional feature of rail merger policy. The DOJ antitrust division has disagreed with the ICC and the STB regarding appropriate public policy in a number of rail merger cases. The STB's merger statute provides for mergers to be approved if they are consistent with the public interest, so that efficiency and other effects are given more weight than the DOJ's primary emphasis on competition. In addition, while the DOJ conducts a proactive investigation of the impacts of a proposed merger, conducting interviews, investigation and independent analyses of effects, the STB assumes a more reactive posture, relying on interested parties to provide evidence in the form of written statements as the basis for decisions.

US rail deregulation resulted in a greater reliance on free markets to promote railroad profitability and public benefits. By increasing operating freedom and stimulating competition, deregulation spurred the railroad industry to shrink its physical plant and work force to better match available traffic (*see generally* Grimm and Windle, 1999). As discussed by Grimm and Winston (2000):

> The industry abandoned roughly one-third of its track and reduced crew sizes; used contracts to align cars and equipment with shippers' demand and to reduce its vulnerability to problems caused by overcapacity; and expanded the use of intermodal operations, double stack rail cars, and computer systems to provide faster, more reliable service.

Real operating costs per ton-mile have fallen steadily, and, as of 1998, were 60 per cent lower than when deregulation began. Some of the cost decline can be attributed to the long-run trend in rail's traffic mix to include a greater proportion of low-cost bulk traffic, but deregulation's contribution is substantial. Cost reductions and productivity improvements stemmed the long-run erosion in market share. Rail traffic grew. After reaching a post-war low in the mid-1980s, originating rail carloads have grown from 19.5 million in 1985 to 25.7 million in 1998.

All of these factors have boosted profitability. During 1971–80, the industry's return on equity was less than 3 per cent (*see generally* United States General Accounting Office, 1999). During the 1990s, the industry's return on equity averaged 10.7 per cent (ibid). Rail deregulation has clearly been a successful policy. However, deregulation has been accompanied by substantial merger activity, which is discussed next.

Rail mergers since the Staggers Act have been concentrated in two merger waves. Table 5.1 presents information regarding rail merger activity. As discussed by Grimm and Winston (2000), the first occurred in the early 1980s:

> 'Chessie System and Seaboard Coast Line formed CSX, Norfolk and Western and Southern Railroad formed Norfolk Southern, Missouri Pacific and Western Pacific became part of Union Pacific, and the St. Louis–San Francisco Railroad along with Colorado Southern and Fort Worth Denver formed part of Burlington Northern.'

Table 5.1   Class I unification 1980–1998

Effective date of unification	Type of unification	Applicant railroads	Controlling railroad/company
6/2/80	Control	DT&I	GTW
12/1/80	Merger	SLSF	BN
9/23/80	Control	C&O/SCL	CSX
6/3/81	Control	Maine Central	Guilford
1/1/82	Merger	BN/C&S/FW&D	BN
6/1/82	Consolidation	SOU and N&W	NS
12/22/82	Merger	UP/MP/WP	UP
1/1/83	Consolidation	Family Lines/L&N	Seaboard System
7/1/83	Control	Boston & Maine	Guilford
1/5/84	Control	D&H	Guilford
2/19/85	Control	SOO/CMSP&P	SOO
3/26/87	Control	CR-government	CR-private
8/12/88	Merger	UP/MKT	UP
10/13/88	Control	SP/SSW/DRGW	SP
4/27/95	Purchase	UP/C&NW	UP
9/22/95	Merger	BN/ATSF	BNSF
9/11/96	Merger	UP/SP	UP
6/20/98	Control	NS/CSX/CR	NS and CS

Source: Railroad Mergers by Frank N. Wilner and AAR *Railroad Ten-Year Trends.*

Thus, the net result of this merger activity, which was predominantly end-to-end, was a market structure with four large carriers in the West (BN, UP, Santa Fe and Southern Pacific) and three dominant carriers in the East (CSX, NS and Conrail). The Interstate Commerce Commission turned down the one major merger proposed during the 1980s that had significant parallel effects, the Santa Fe/Southern Pacific. US rail structure was relatively stable until the mid-1990s, when the second wave commenced. The starting point was a battle between the UP and BN for control of the Santa Fe; BN was the successful suitor. Union Pacific subsequently merged with Southern Pacific. In the East, NS and CSX vied for acquisition of Conrail; the end result was a joint takeover of Conrail by the two railroads. Thus, the Burlington Northern–Santa Fe and Union Pacific–Southern Pacific mergers left only two major railroads in the western United States while Norfolk Southern's and CSX's joint acquisition of Conrail left only two major railroads in the east. A subsequent merger proposal to consolidate the BN and Canadian National was stymied by the STB with the establishment of an 18-month moratorium on mergers, with a subsequent promulgation of new railroad merger guidelines. Thus, US railroad structure has remained largely stable since the mid-1990s, with two dominant systems in the East and two in the West. Some end-to-end merger activity has taken place since that time, including the purchase by Kansas City Southern of the Texas Mexican Railway and the TFM railroad in Mexico.

US railroad structure now finds the 'Big 4' dwarfing the rest of the US railroad industry. Operating revenues in 2001 for these four were: Union Pacific – $10.6 billion; BN – $9.2 billion; CSX – $6.4 billion and NS – $6.1 billion. All other railroads in the US had 2001 annual revenues well under $1 billion. (Extending the view north of the border, Canadian National has annual revenues of $3.6 billion, while Canadian Pacific has annual revenues of $2.3 billion.) We next turn to the evaluation of horizontal competitive effects.

HORIZONTAL EFFECTS IN RAILROAD MERGERS

The discussion of horizontal effects in railroad mergers will proceed in three sections. First, we discuss the definition of relevant markets, with focus on issues of network complexities and determination of size of origin and destination areas. Second, we discuss the issue of threshold of increase in market concentration as constituting a competitive harm. Third, we discuss the issue of remedy, with the options of divestiture versus trackage rights. In the discussion, we refer to examples from the two prominent post-Staggers horizontal mergers, SP/Santa Fe and UP/SP. We also refer to analyses by the DOJ and the STB, as well as my own, to provide illustrations of the issues.

Definition of Relevant Markets in Rail Mergers

Network complexities
As with any merger analysis, the first step in evaluating horizontal competitive effects in a rail merger is defining the relevant market. The ultimate outcome of a merger case often rests on how the market is defined. A number of problems in defining relevant markets in railroad mergers are analogous to those in manufacturing sector merger cases. For example, the issue of whether or not to include motor carrier market shares along with rail shares in the relevant market is not unlike decisions faced in manufacturing sector definitions of relevant product markets.

However, defining relevant markets in the rail freight industry is especially difficult. This is partially due to the complexity of rail networks. If a starting point for markets is origin–destination pairs (O–D), a given rail link will typically be part of many markets. In addition, between any origin-destination pair, there are a large number of possible routings, with different numbers of competitors involved at different stages of the routings. In such a context, ascertaining market concentration prior to a merger and changes in concentration post-merger is difficult. A reasonable approach to this market definition challenge is to focus on the number of independent alternative routings that exist in the market prior to the merger and the extent that a merger reduces this number. This approach is consistent with the notion long stressed by the Chicago school that a monopolist at one stage of the production process can extract full monopoly profits from successive stages. While empirical evidence reveals limitations to this Chicago view in practice, it is the case that competition is impeded if one firm participates on multiple routings (*see generally* Grimm, Winston and Evans, 1992). The view that independence of routings is critical for effective competition was clearly stated by the ICC: 'Competition between railroads generally requires the presence of two or more independent routes, that is, routes having no carriers in common. When a single carrier is a necessary participant in all available routes, i.e., a bottleneck carrier, it can usually control the overall rate sufficiently to preclude effective competition' (*Consolidated Papers v. Chicago & North Western Trans. Co*. 1991, 338). Accordingly, it is appropriate to focus primary attention in identifying horizontal competitive harms in rail mergers on instances where the number of independent railroad routings is reduced.

Origins/Destinations as Points or Broader Geographic Areas

The second issue in market definition is the size of the origin and destination as end-points of railroad transportation markets. One approach is to only use specific points as O–Ds. This means that railroads are only considered competitors vis à vis a specific customer if they can both physically serve that customer. An alternative is to use a broader geographic area such as a county or BEA, a group of counties delineated by the U.S. Department of Commerce Bureau of Economic Analysis. The rationale for this broader area is that customers can benefit from the presence of a competitor located near to them, even if that railroad does not actually serve their plant. For example, a customer may be able to employ truck transloading over a relatively short distance to access a railroad within its BEA which does not serve the shipper directly. Alternatively, a customer can in some cases threaten to or actually build out a rail spur to access an alternative rail carrier. Further details and examples of how railroads can provide competition in some instances in the absence of actual track access to a shipper can be found in Grimm and Plaistow (1999).

Table 5.2   Memphis to San Antonio market

Current Rail Routes	Market Share for Route
SP DIRECT	17%
UP DIRECT	31%
BN – UP	4%
CSXT – UP	26%
NS – UP	22%

A BEA–BEA market definition also follows that of the Justice Department in the SP/SF and UP/SP cases, in particular that of the DOJ's Pitman in his testimony and academic writings related to the SP/SF case, defining markets as flows between origin and destination BEA's (*see generally* Pitman, 1990). In the SF/SP case, the ICC supported this definition of markets. However, the STB found it too broad in the UP/SP case and relied instead on a point definition of markets.

An example is provided to illustrate market definition based on the number of independent routes between BEA geographic areas as origins/destinations in Table 5.2.

A given customer has five possible rail routings between Memphis and San Antonio. The UP single line routing has the highest market share, with 31 per cent of the volume. Although there are five routings, UP participates in four of these, so that there are only two independent routings in the Memphis–San Antonio market.

Threshold of Determination of Competitive Harm

Once relevant markets are defined, the next step in a horizontal analysis is to determine the degree to which a merger increases concentration and assess what degree of concentration increase constitutes a competitive harm. In the DOJ/FTC horizontal merger guidelines, threshold levels are provided based on initial Herfindahl values and the impact of the merger as measured in a higher Herfindahl level. Common practice in analysis of railroad merger competitive effects has been to discuss thresholds and changes in concentration using numbers of competitors in the market, as opposed to a Herfindahl measure of market structure. Thus, returning to the above example, the Memphis–San Antonio BEA pair constitutes a two-to-one market with regard to the UP/SP merger. Antitrust analyses of railroad mergers have summed up the amount of traffic in such two-to-one markets. For example, in the UP/SP merger case, estimates of the volume of traffic in two-to-one markets ranged from $900 million to $2.5 billion, depending on how markets were defined (*see generally* Grimm and Plaistow, 1999).

While there has been general consensus in horizontal merger cases that two-to-one situations constitute competitive harm, there has been disagreement regarding whether or not reduction of competitors in markets with more than two rivals constitutes a competitive harm. In the UP/SP merger, the STB judged that any markets reduced from three to two competitors did not constitute competitive harm from the merger. In other recent rail merger cases there has, in fact, been a consistent STB policy that there will be no competitive harm from three-to-two situations. This represents an important shift in merger policy between the time of the first major post-Staggers parallel merger brought before the ICC in the mid-1980s (SP/SF) and the second (UP/SP). The ICC denied the SP/SF with strong reference to three-to-two competitive effects as a basis in the decision. The UP/SP had substantially stronger two-to-one and three-to-two competitive effects. The STB acknowledged in the UP/SP decision that its policy had changed regarding three-to-two effects:

> Here, in contrast, applicants presented their plan for addressing competitive harms at the outset . . . [T]he agency also has the benefit of nine years of additional experience with decreasing rates in two-carrier rail market under Staggers Act deregulation. We now believe that rail carriers can and do compete effectively with each other in two-carrier markets. (FD No. 32760, 1996, 116–7)

The change in policy was also suggested in the BN-SF decision:

> We would not necessarily be concerned if GNBC faced a reduction in competitive alternatives from three unrestricted alternatives (BN, Sante Fe, and UP) to two unrestricted alternatives (BN/Sante Fe and UP). Two independent railroads, we think, can provide strong, effective competition provided that, among other things, neither is subject to any artificial restrictions. (Burlington Northern Inc. 1995, 94)

Thus, contrary to the 1980 policy regarding three-to-twos, the STB concluded that there would be no competitive harm in hundreds of markets where the UP/SP reduced the number of rail carriers from three to two. This involved approximately $5 billion in rail freight revenues. In many of these markets UP and SP were the dominant two carriers before the merger. UP and SP had a combined market share of 70 per cent or greater (around $2 billion) of the three-to-two markets. For example, Houston was the originating or terminating point in a significant amount of three-to-two traffic in the UP/SP merger case. Very little of that traffic was intermodal, or automotive, with chemicals accounting for a large percentage of the three-to-two traffic. Thus, the STB ruled out on a blanket basis any competitive harm in three-to-two markets regardless of the market shares of the two merging carriers or the degree to which truck competition might provide a competitive alternative in a particular market (*see generally* Grimm, 1996).

In my view the STB should give greater weight to arguments of competitive harm in situations where the number of rail carrier independent alternatives within a corridor would be reduced by a merger from three to two. Evidence from economic theory and published econometric studies provides a strong consensus that significant competitive harm results in general when reducing rail competitors from three to two. Based on economic theory, there is no basis for a policy dismissing three-to-two competitive effects in rail mergers. As discussed by Kwoka and White (1998), most oligopoly theories suggest that moving from three competitors to two in a market would lead to a diminution of competition and higher rates for shippers. Only the 'Bertrand' theory would support the position of no competitive harms in three-to-two markets. Waldman and Jenson (2007) provide additional details regarding the 'Bertrand' model.

In general, with additional firms, coordination or tacit collusion becomes more difficult, as a greater number of firms increase the probability that the firms will have different notions about what price levels will maximize profits. Therefore as the number of competitors in an industry increases, the intensity of rivalry will also tend to increase. While two firms in any industry will, in most instances, compete to some degree with each other, rivalry will generally be more vigorous when a third firm is present and customers will receive more options, better service and lower prices. With more firms, the chances are greater that any one firm will set off a fierce competitive skirmish or come up with a better way to serve customers. Accordingly, when a third rival is eliminated from a market, prices increase and service quality is diminished.

The existing academic research confirms that rail rates are significantly related to the degree of railroad competition – the number or concentration of railroad carriers which serve given shippers. Rail competition was shown to be important even while pre-Staggers regulation was still present. I conducted a study (published in 1985) based on 1977 data on rail rates and degree of rail competition in 110 rail markets. I defined the rail markets by specific origin-destination pairs. The study found a significant relationship between rates and rail competition at origin and destination, with added competition causing lower rates (*see generally* Grimm, 1985).

Levin (1981) has provided insights through simulations on the social benefits of increasing competition in concentrated rail markets. He has shown that, given various assumptions concerning demand elasticity and revenue/variable cost ratios, the social benefit of adding a second, equal-sized competitor to a monopoly market ranges from 6.8 to 18.9 per cent of the revenues in that market. Adding a third railroad in a two-firm market yields social benefits of from 2.4 to 6.6 per cent of revenues. This suggests that reduction of the number of competing railroads in a market from two to one has a particularly negative effect.

Two studies by MacDonald (1987, 1989) have used post-Staggers data to investigate the impact of rail competition on rates. One study uses 1983 data regarding shipments of corn, soybeans and wheat; and regressions are performed to ascertain the relationship between rates and rail competition. MacDonald concludes: 'The analysis shows an important, statistically significant effect of concentration on prices in an industry with high barriers to entry and large capital commitments' (MacDonald 1987, 162). The second study draws on data from 1981–1985 regarding grain shipments. It concludes:

> Competition among railroads has a statistically significant, fairly strong effect on rates. More competitors, as measured by RRCOMP, are associated with lower rates. The addition or subtraction of a competitor has a larger effect on rates, the fewer the number of competitors in a market. For example, moving from a monopolist to a duopolist in a corn market seventy-five miles from water competition reduces rates by 17.4 percent, while moving further to triopoly reduces rates another 15.2 percent. (MacDonald 1989, 81)

Additionally, a Brookings Institution study in which I participated (*see generally* Winston *et al.*, 1990) supported the importance of railroad competition in reducing rail rates. Using 1985 data drawn over a large number of origin-destination pairs, we found that price-marginal cost margins were significantly lower in markets with a greater degree of railroad competition. Clearly, rail competition is critical. In sum, there is no basis whatsoever for the change in policy providing for sweeping dismissal of three-to-two impacts. Hence, as the industry becomes more concentrated, more emphasis should be placed on preserving the already limited rail service options for shippers.

Remedy for Ameliorating Horizontal Effects

A third key issue in evaluating competitive harms in railroad mergers is the design of conditions to ameliorate competitive harms. The STB has broad powers to condition merger approval, and so can potentially further the public interest through amelioration of competitive harms in the event a merger is otherwise in the public interest. The issue of how best to condition mergers with serious horizontal effects was most salient in the UP/SP merger. The Department of Justice, along with a number of other public agencies and shippers, recommended divestiture in markets where UP and

SP had parallel lines and were the only railroads in these markets. The merger applicants proposed that rival railroad BN be given trackage rights in these two-to-one markets to preserve a second competitor. The STB opted for the trackage rights 'fix' to the merger (*see generally* Kwoka and White, 1998).

VERTICAL COMPETITIVE EFFECTS IN RAIL MERGERS

As discussed in Grimm and Harris (1983) and Grimm *et al.* (1992), a critical issue in rail merger policy has been the resolution of vertical foreclosure concerns. The meaning of vertical foreclosure in the railroad industry can be represented graphically; please refer to Figure 5.1. Carriers 1, 2 and 3 are initially independent, with Carriers 1 and 2 serving the A-B market and Carrier 3 serving the B-C market. Carrier 1 acquires Carrier 3 and a potential vertical foreclosure issue arises with respect to Carrier 2. Carrier 1/3 is now vertically integrated from A to C, while Carrier 2 is not. Thus Carrier 2 is vulnerable to foreclosure, as Carrier 1/3 can refuse to interchange traffic with Carrier 2 on the interline route or can leverage its bottleneck to price squeeze Carrier 2. Carriers 1/3 and 2 have a dual cooperative/competitive relationship following the merger.

In the era of railroad regulation, the Interstate Commerce commission (ICC) took great care in analyzing potential foreclosure effects of end-to-end consolidations, either denying such mergers, or, more commonly, appending to its merger approval conditions designed to mitigate foreclosure impacts. In this sense, the ICC's approach to the foreclosure issue paralleled the DOJ's approach as denoted by DOJ's 1968 merger guidelines. In the late 1970s and early 1980s, there was a wave of end-to-end mergers in the rail industry, as discussed above. The ICC changed its position on foreclosure and adopted the Chicago view, which maintains that an efficient unintegrated firm will never be foreclosed. Revenues would be divided

Figure 5.1   Pre-merger Rail Market

between the integrated and unintegrated carrier such that both would have an incentive to move traffic over the efficient interline route.

The Chicago view can be illustrated with a numerical example. With reference to Figure 5.2, assume that $200 was the maximum rate obtainable for a unit of traffic in the A–C market. Further assume that marginal costs (MC) for the unit of traffic are as follows: Railroad 1's MC for the A–B segment and Railroad 1's MC for the B–C segment are each $50; Railroad 2's MC for the B–C segment are $45. Railroad 2 is therefore the more efficient carrier over the B–C segment. If Railroad 1 handles the traffic over the entire A–C route, it obtains a profit of $100. Railroad 1, however, can obtain a higher profit by interchanging with Railroad 2, so long as Railroad 1 receives a revenue division greater than $150. Railroad 2 would be willing to participate if its revenues were greater than its MC, i.e., at least $45. The two railroads' revenue requirements define a negotiating range such that Railroad 1's division would be between $150–$155 while Railroad 2's would be between $45–$50. As long as Railroad 2's costs are lower on the B–C segment, there will be a division such that both Railroads 1 and 2 have an incentive to interline over the more efficient route. The Chicago view concludes that there is no need for regulatory intervention to prevent Railroad 1 from vertically integrating to obtain this leverage over Railroad 2 and no need for intervention in determining revenue divisions between 1 and 2.

While standard theory argues that efficient interline options will not be foreclosed, in some instances the unintegrated carrier can continue to participate in traffic but finds itself forced down to such low margins that over time it cannot cover its fixed costs. This can lead to erosion of interline competitive options. The STB may also decide to give greater weight to non-economic considerations such as equity or procedural fairness (*see generally* Grimm and Harris, 1983). A third issue regarding the Chicago view is that Railroad 1 may well opt to foreclose the more efficient Railroad 2 rather than exercise a price squeeze. In practice there are restrictions on the execution of price squeezes in the US railroad industry. Revenue divisions over inter-line traffic are typically governed by industry standard

Figure 5.2   Post-merger Rail Market

division rules that set divisions according to mileage or other proxies for relative marginal costs. In the previous example, a standard division rule based on costs would result in Railroad 1 and Railroad 2 each receiving approximately $100 for their interline movement. There is a clear efficiency rationale for establishing such standard divisions, as it eliminates having to negotiate individual divisions over thousands of routings and markets. There also remain legal restrictions on a railroad with a monopoly position to utilize pricing leverage with interline competitors. STB regulatory oversight and, perhaps more importantly, the prospect of antitrust actions for attempted monopolization, provide possible deterrence to exercising full monopoly power. Importantly, Railroad 1 would also have an incentive to refuse to interline with Railroad 2 in order to weaken its direct competitor in the BC market. Thus, I have argued that there may well be an incentive to pursue vertical foreclosure to fully utilize and extend monopoly power (*see generally* Grimm et al., 1992).

Recently, the STB has signaled another policy change indicating a greater concern for vertical foreclosure effects. For example, the STB's most recent merger guidelines discuss the importance of keeping gateways open in end-to-end mergers. Several recent end-to-end mergers have included language in the decisions regarding open gateways. How should the Board proceed in implementing these guidelines, in this or future cases? What framework should the Board use in assessing whether such intervention is necessary as it revisits the vertical foreclosure issue?

The framework I propose is a case-by-case one. The STB should analyse specific facts in assessing the likelihood of foreclosure, the ability of a potentially foreclosed railroad to protect itself and the likelihood that shippers may ultimately pay in higher prices or inferior service. In some cases, I might have concerns in end-to-end mergers if an unintegrated carrier's bargaining position over divisions was substantially weakened and that carrier had no countervailing power (for example, if a short line or small railroad lost a friendly connection in conjunction with a consolidation of two mega-railroads). However, such a circumstance is clearly not present in this case. For vertical foreclosure to be exercised, the integrated carrier must have superior power in the vertical relationship with rival railroads as well as the ability to force shippers to favor its routings.

With reference again to Figure 5.1, Carrier 1 acquires Carrier 3 and a potential vertical foreclosure issue arises with respect to Carrier 2. The key initial question is: Can Carrier 2 protect itself against foreclosure? There are a number of means available in most rail situations. Carrier 2 may have options other than Carrier 3 to reach point C. Carrier 2 may originate or terminate captive traffic on its A–B line. Or, the situation may be reversed in other markets, with a Carrier 2 single-line routing in competition with a

Carrier 1/3 interline routing. The crux of the issue is the relative bargaining power and leverage between Carriers 1 and 2 following the merger. Note that the fact that the merger of Carriers 1 and 3 may alter the leverage between Carriers 1 and 2 is not in itself germane. The key is whether the post-merger leverage between the two carriers allows the unintegrated carrier to protect itself. To summarize, properly evaluating vertical foreclosure concerns from end-to-end aspects of rail mergers will be an essential ingredient of sound rail merger policy in the next merger wave.

CONCLUSION

In the deregulated railroad merger environment, where outcomes are primarily dependent on market forces, sound public policy in evaluating rail mergers is essential. Much of the methodology to evaluate mergers has arisen from analyses and case law of manufacturing industries or retailing. Applying these techniques and precedents to network industries such as railroads presents a host of challenges, such as defining relevant markets. Also, the context with scale economies and lingering regulation raises complexities in how to balance competitive harms with efficiency benefits. It also poses the question whether the numbers of competitors and threshold for competitive harms present in the horizontal merger guidelines are applicable to the railroad industry. Merger activity in the railroad industry has resulted in an industry dominated by four major carriers and has given rise to pressures by customers for new legislation to promote and protect competition. With rumors in the air of new merger activity that would usher in a third and final post-Staggers wave, judicious merger policy will be of paramount importance.

NOTE

1. The author has filed comments with the Surface Transportation Board in a number of railroad merger cases, including the Union Pacific–Southern Pacific merger case on behalf of Kansas City Southern Railway Company.

REFERENCES

Gallamore, R.E. (1999), 'Regulation and Innovation: Lessons from the American Railroad Industry,' in Jose Gomez-Ibanez, William B. Tye, and Clifford Winston, eds, Essays in Transportation Economics and Policy: A Handbook in Honor of John R. Meyer, Washington D.C.: Brookings.

Grimm, C. (1984), 'An Evaluation of Economic Issues in the UP–MP–WP Railroad Merger,' Logistics and Transportation Review 20(3), pp. 239–259.

Grimm, C. (1985), 'Horizontal Competitive Effects in Railroad Mergers,' in Theodore E. Keeler, ed, Research in Transportation Economics, Vol. 2, JAI Press pp. 27–53.

Grimm, C. (1996), 'Verified Statement,' on behalf of the Kansas City Southern Railroad, March 26.

Grimm, C. and R. Harris (1983), 'Vertical Foreclosure in the Rail Freight Industry: Economic Analysis and Policy Prescriptions,' ICC Practitioners' Journal 50(5), July/August, pp. 508–531.

Grimm, C. and R. Harris (1985), 'The Effects of Railroad Mergers on Industry Performance and Productivity,' Transportation Research Record 1029 pp. 9–17.

Grimm, C. and J. Plaistow (1999), 'Competitive Effects of Railroad Mergers,' Journal of the Transportation Research Forum 38(1), pp. 64–75.

Grimm, Curtis M. and Robert Windle (1999), 'The Rationale for Deregulation,' in James Peoples, ed, Regulatory Reform and Labor Markets, Kluwer Press.

Grimm, C. and C. Winston (2000), 'Competition in the Deregulated Railroad Industry: Source, Effect and Policy Issues,' in S. Peltzman and C. Winston, eds, Deregulation of Network Industries: The Next Steps, Brookings, Washington, D.C. pp. 41–72.

Grimm, C., C. Winston and C. Evans (1992), 'Foreclosure of Railroad Markets: A Test of Chicago Leverage Theory,' Journal of Law and Economics 35, pp. 295–310.

Keeler, T.E. (1983), Railroads, Freight, and Public Policy, Brookings, Washington, D.C.

Kwoka, J. and L. White (1998), 'Manifest Destiny? The Union Pacific–Southern Pacific Merger (1996)' in J. Kwoka and L. White, eds, The Antitrust Revolution, 3rd edn, New York: Oxford University Press.

Levin, Richard (1981), 'Railroad Rates, Profitability, and Welfare under Deregulation,' Bell Journal of Economics 12, pp. 1–26.

MacDonald, James M. (1987), 'Competition and Rail Rates for the Shipment of Corn, Soybeans, and Wheat,' Rand Journal of Economics 18.

MacDonald, James M. (1989), 'Railroad Deregulation, Innovation, and Competition: Effects of the Staggers Act on Grain Transportation,' Journal of Law and Economics 32, pp. 63–95.

Pittman, R.W. (1990), 'Railroads and Competition: The Santa Fe/Southern Pacific Merger Proposal,' The Journal of Industrial Economics 39, pp. 25–46.

United States General Accounting Office (1999), Railroad Regulation: Changes in Railroad Rates and Service Quality Since 1990, April.

Waldman, D. and E. Jensen (2007), *Industrial Organization*, Boston: Addison Wesley.

Winston, C., T. Corsi, C. Grimm and C. Evans (1990), The Economic Effects of Surface Freight Deregulation, Brookings Institution, Washington, D.C.

Cases

Consolidated Papers, Inc., *et. al.* v. Chicago and North Western Transportation Co., *et. al.*, 7 ICC 2d 298 (1991).

Union Pacific Corporation, Union Pacific Railroad Company and Missouri Pacific Railroad Company – Control and Merger – Southern Pacific Rail Corporation,

Southern Pacific Transportation Company, St. Louis Southwestern Railway Company, SPCSL Corp. and the Denver and Rio Grande Railroad Company, Finance Docket No. 32760, Surface Transportation Board, served August 6, 1996.

Burlington Northern Inc. & Burlington Northern R.R. – Control and Merger – Santa Fe Pacific Corp. & Atchison, Topeka & Santa Fe Ry., Finance Docket No. 32549, Interstate Commerce Commission, served March 7, 1995.

6. Airline mergers – second-best results in a changed environment

Peter C. Carstensen

INTRODUCTION

'Deregulation' of the commercial airline service was the first major step in the process of limiting or eliminating conventional rate and service regulation in American commercial transportation markets. It is a misnomer to call this process deregulation because that implies that there is no legal oversight or control of industry conduct or structure (*see generally* Carstensen 1989). A more accurate description is that the nature of the legal controls over this industry changed dramatically over the past three decades. Individual airlines were freed to make many more decisions and new entrants were empowered to commence competition provided that they satisfied relevant entry requirements. Overall, most observers have concluded that the changes in regulation improved the quality of service and constrained prices (*see*, e.g., Kahn 1988; Levine 1987).

There has also been a continued stream of critical commentary about the performance of the airline industry. The pricing and service of the leading firms (that some see as being both discriminatory and exclusionary) are among those concerns. In addition, collusive price setting has been a recurrent issue. On the other hand, financial instability has plagued the industry. Major airlines have had to seek protection under the bankruptcy laws repeatedly. New entrants have failed to survive with substantial frequency. The interaction of the patterns of prices and conduct reflecting market specific monopoly power and recurrent financial crises is consistent with the 'hollow core' theory of destructive competition. A market has a hollow core if no stable equilibrium is possible usually because of the necessary size of plants in entry or exit (*see*, e.g., Telser 1978; Sjostrom 1989). However, the dynamics of exogenous demand conditions, including the events of 9/11 that resulted in the grounding of all commercial air services and their slow recovery, the continued evolution of the aircraft employed in the industry and some questionable business strategies may have combined to create these cyclical effects (*see generally Economist* 2005; Wolfe

2005). Hence, the hypothesis that destructive competition is inherent in the industry is not proven.

What is more remarkable in hindsight is that none of the industry policy makers or even their critics, seem to have fully appreciated its network characteristics. Indeed, the concept of networks and their economic analysis is a very recent evolution of competition policy thinking. When air travel is looked at as a network problem, then many of the characteristics that both facilitate and frustrate competition become intelligible. Moreover, it is then possible to explain more systematically the failure of early merger policy and identify the problematic elements of contemporary policy.

In the period immediately following 'deregulation' some high-profile mergers significantly increased market power in some key markets. In subsequent years, the Department of Justice (DOJ) successfully challenged several other major mergers and alliances, e.g., Northwest–Continental and United–US Air, which helped to retain a somewhat less concentrated formal industry structure. However, the DOJ has also allowed other merger-like agreements (i.e., code sharing) that have resulted in increased de facto concentration among the major airline networks. The DOJ has also failed to establish that conduct aimed at excluding new entrants is unlawful (*see generally US v. AMR* 2003). Further, the Department of Transportation (which has concurrent jurisdiction over competitive conduct) has also largely failed to impose market-facilitating constraints on anticompetitive conduct. In this under-regulated context, the impact of the early mergers appears to outweigh the impact of the later, stricter merger policy. However, it is hard to untangle the inherent effects of the significant market power produced by the nature of essential network systems, that airlines necessarily operate from, the consequences of the changes in structure that have resulted from a merger.

This chapter starts with a brief review of the airline industry prior to deregulation. It then describes the conceptual framework that dominated thinking at the time of 'deregulation' and for the period immediately following. This framework had deep and inherent flaws. However, it played a powerful role in rationalizing the questionable merger decisions of that era. The third section provides a revised understanding of network-based competition in airline services. The fourth section then considers the specifics of merger policy and its implementation that have shaped competition in the industry. The final section concludes with a critical review of current policy for airline competition and some suggestions for its improvement.

THE COMMERCIAL AIRLINE INDUSTRY PRIOR TO 1978

Prior to 1978, the government directly regulated entry, routes and prices for commercial airline services. During this period, the regulators followed practices of protecting existing airlines from entry and of balancing route systems as well as fares, in an effort, only fitfully successful, to subsidize short haul travel with the profits of longer hauls (McCraw 1984, 264–265; Carstensen 1989, 111–112). Several rationales justified this system of direct regulation. They included an interest in subsidizing a new industry, ensuring service and safety as well as protection against the perceived risk of 'destructive competition'.

The resulting system of domestic commercial air travel consisted of a group of airlines operating point-to-point routes, often with intermediate stops, protected from new competition by the government. Nevertheless, on those routes where travelers had choices, non-price competition occurred. It consisted of increased frequency of flights as well as extra services such as meals and drinks (Carstensen 1989, 112). In this period, airlines were required to charge set prices and prohibited from giving rebates or discounts. Fares were formulaic and based on average costs. The industry consisted of a group of major air lines that operated 'trunk routes' between major cities and regional carriers that provided service between the major airports and those in small communities. Implicit in this system was a high level of cooperation, because travelers and their luggage often had to move from one airline to another in order to reach their final destination. The regional airlines were the feeder system for the trunk lines. However, the nature of the system was such that the regionals did not have a continuing relationship with any particular trunk line.

Starting in the 1950s, and with increasing strength thereafter, critics looked at the resulting system and found it costly and inefficient (McCraw 1984, 265–270). The central claims were that the market for airline services was not naturally monopolistic nor was it subject to inherent risks of destructive competition. Hence, an open, competitive market was more likely to produce desirable prices and services than would direct regulation. Observations of airline conduct in two intra-state markets where competition existed, Texas and California, supported this contention. Prices were lower and volumes of passengers higher than comparable routes operated under regulation.

By the 1960s, with strong support from the Antitrust Division of the DOJ, there was increasing criticism of direct regulation of transportation markets in general. The airlines were a particular target because of recurring cases of corruption in awarding routes and a general perception that the regulatory agency, the Civil Aeronautics Board (CAB), acted as the protector of the industry in rate and route decisions (Carstensen 1989, 112–114). As a result, President Carter named Alfred Kahn, a well-known and very articulate scholar of regulatory economics, as chair of the CAB (McCraw 1984, 222–299). Kahn in turn started to loosen the regulatory controls over the industry. Powerful legislators, in particular Senator Ted Kennedy of Massachusetts, also took a leading role in criticizing the pricing and service of the airline industry. There was a broad political consensus that the current regulatory system made no sense.

In 1978, Congress approved the Airline Deregulation Act of 1978. The legislation provided for a transition period during which the CAB would be phased out and the Secretary of Transportation would take its place. Initially, the regulatory system still had the authority to pass on mergers. Only in the late 1980s did airline mergers become subject to conventional antitrust law (*see generally* Nannes 2000).

Three important features of the pre-1978 era were the product of the regulatory environment in which this industry had developed and were not inherent to the business, as subsequent experience has demonstrated. Each, however, had significant salience in shaping public policy perspectives. First, fares were regulated and prices were relatively uniform for specific trips. Therefore, the regulations controlled the ability of the airlines to match prices to actual demand (Carstensen 1989, 125–127). This gave the air travel service the appearance of being a commodity like other tangible goods.

Second, the industry operated in a way that offered point-to-point service along linear routes. This structure was not, however, the result of unfettered economic activity. Rather it was a result of the regulatory process that had shaped the industry from its inception. As became evident after deregulation, that configuration of routes was not the way the forces of supply and demand would order airline systems (Carstensen 1989, 121–124).

Third, there was a high level of interchange among the airlines, particularly between regional airlines and the trunk lines. This gave the impression that customers would have choices among airlines for the long hauls while using the regional airlines to get to major airports.

In addition to these features, all of which were artifacts of the way regulation had organized the industry, there was a perception in the mid-1970s that antitrust law was a strong force in controlling concentration in markets through the application of Section 7 of the Clayton Act, which forbade any merger that 'may substantially lessen competition or tend to create a monopoly' (Carstensen 1989, 132–138). Although in fact the Supreme Court had begun to retreat from its strict view of mergers in the mid-1970s (*see US v. General Dynamics*, 1974) and was simultaneously reconsidering many of its other strict standards, this was not yet evident to policy makers.

An additional inherent feature of the market for air travel that was not obvious in the 1970s was that travelers had strong preferences for well-known, established names in the industry (*see generally* Levine 1987). Reputation reflects assurance of safety and reliability. Since prior to deregulation all the major carriers had been in existence for a long period of time without significant new entry, policy makers were perhaps warranted in assuming that any air carrier certified by the FAA, as it must be before starting service, would be seen in the market as an equal substitute for an existing carrier. The limited experience with competition in Texas and California, where the entrants had high-volume markets within which they could focus their efforts at reputation building, did not provide an opportunity to recognize this element of the industry competition.

Conception of the Industry at the Time of Deregulation and its Implications for Merger Analysis

Three assumptions about how deregulated airline markets would operate were both central to the formation of policy and proved highly misleading.

Contestable Markets

The first assumption was that airline markets would be inherently competitive. The basic observations behind this assumption were that airlines seemed to have high variable and low fixed costs. Moreover, airplanes are by definition very mobile and so can be transferred into and out of markets easily – in a physical sense. The experience with actual competition in the intra-state markets showed that fares dropped dramatically when there was competition on a particular route and were relatively uniform. These low fares stood in marked contrast to the high prices charged on comparable high density, interstate routes subject to CAB rate setting (McCraw 1984, 267). In the hypothetical world of policy makers, it was obvious that competition, both actual and potential, would exist for all possible routes once entry was opened up. In consequence, existing airlines would have to bring prices down to a 'competitive' level if they wanted to survive. The great invisible hand of the market would control prices and stimulate more efficient service.

This idea received its most formal statement in the work of Baumol, Panzar and Willig who labeled the concept 'contestable markets' (*see generally* Baumol *et al.*, 1982). The basic argument was hardly novel. It asserted that if entry barriers were low so that a competitor could enter and exit a market without significant costs, then even highly concentrated markets would behave competitively, and commercial airlines were held out as a good example of this model. Drawing on the experience showing that competition drove down prices and the fact that airplanes can be dispatched to serve a market and then withdrawn from it without much cost with respect to the airplanes themselves, the conclusion was that industry structure did not matter in the airline sector. Regardless of concentration, the threat of entry would be sufficient to constrain the ability of the airlines to exploit customers (Levine 1987, 443–444).

The focus of this analysis was almost entirely on the airplane itself. Among the factors that were ignored were the costs of ground services, gates and staffing at each airport being served. These would be sunk costs that an entrant would forfeit if it then left the market. It appears that the theorists were aware that airlines required ground services, but they did not investigate the economic characteristics of those investments.

Uniformity of ticket prices and lack of differentiation of service
In the background of the contestable market model was a second assumption that rested on the past pricing practices of the industry as well as the apparent willingness of consumers to substitute readily among travel providers. This assumption meant that prices for travel would be relatively uniform. If one assumes that there is a creditable threat of competition in the market, the wise incumbent will not try to exploit its customers because that will open the door to competitive entry. The implicit model was that airlines would sell all seats at a set price and if they raised prices, they would raise them across the board.

Secondly, and importantly for contestability, a new entrant, it was assumed, would not face barriers based on the lack of consumer awareness of the airline nor would consumers prefer the established carriers. These assumptions are embedded in the contestable market theory and not made fully explicit as applied to a market in which consumer choice is a key factor.

A 'commodity' approach to the supply of air travel fails to account for the obvious fact that there is no potential for arbitrage by buyers and so the airline may actually have a good deal of discretion to vary prices. Nor does it consider that perceptions of safety and desirability would be important to consumers. While one might have thought these facts were obvious, policy makers at the time completely failed to appreciate the potential for price discrimination. Instead, they imagined that a price increase would apply uniformly to all capacity and so would be likely to invite competition from new entrants who were equally desirable.

Sufficient traffic to sustain competition in all city pairs
Another implicit, but central assumption, was that there was sufficient demand for air travel between specific city pairs to make competitive entry

a viable threat. Again, the analogy to the experience in Texas and California was not examined closely and it was not recognized that those markets involved high demand for travel between the city pairs so that it was economically feasible to commit to multiple trips per day between the points. Demand was sufficient enough that several carriers could operate with relatively high occupancy. Such levels of demand are important to ensure that the markets will be contestable. If total demand is low, then despite the technical feasibility of committing an airplane to provide service between two cities, it is not economically practical.

For an entrant into a mid-sized market to compete it would have to offer access to a number of destinations in order to attract a sufficient number of passengers to sustain its entry (*see generally* Levine 1987). However, this implies a network of service, not merely the entry into a specific market with a flight or flights serving a pair of cities. There were, and are, high-volume city pairs where it is possible to provide service and have sufficient traffic to warrant that service even without travel beyond the city pair, for example, New York and Los Angeles. The capacity of the plane to be used is an important factor that can cause even a city pair with substantial travel to be problematic if the travelers have varied time preferences and if the available planes require relatively large loads to be economically viable.

Indeed, a further complexity of real world of travel is that time of day for arrival and departure is important to many travelers. Hence, one flight a day leaving in the early afternoon is no substitute for many travelers for a plane leaving in the early morning. In order to serve the varied demands of many travelers, it is necessary to offer a choice of departure times. This further fragments demand and reduces the available supply of travelers at any point in time. However, in thinking about the potential competitiveness of airlines, reform advocates and legislators basically ignored these real-world factors.

The Resulting Model Misled Regulators and Investors

The result was a simplistic model of air travel that assumed a commodity-like characteristic for the product, ignored the potential for airlines to impose very different prices for the same basic service (because the buyers could not arbitrage their purchases and were willing to pay different prices for different classes of service) and assumed that the barriers to entry and exit for service between any two locations were very low. If these assumptions had been correct, then the provision of airline services would be highly contestable and market structure would be of marginal significance. However, this model of the airline world lacked reality (*see generally* Levine 1987; Bailey and Williams 1988).

Consistent with the model, however, there was a flurry of new entry and consolidation after the industry was partially deregulated in 1978. The regulatory system still passed on mergers and it embraced the contestable market model so totally that the DOT failed to stop any of the mergers that occurred in this early period. The combination of mergers and the failure or acquisition of almost all of the new entrants in this period resulted in a more concentrated market for airline services than had previously existed (Levine 1987, 478–480). Finally, experience showed that the economists' model of contestable markets was a poor predictor of actual conduct in these markets.

A REVISED UNDERSTANDING OF AIRLINE COMPETITION

In hindsight, one of the most remarkable aspects of airline deregulation was the failure of economists and policy makers looking at the airline business to foresee the kinds of changes that would occur when these businesses were freed to set their own prices and select their own routes. The lack of foresight resulted in a transition that embedded a sub-optimal industry structure and failed to provide any constraints on the pricing discretion of the airlines. The guiding concept in that period was the assumption that all airline markets would be contestable and so the market would work to produce efficient, low-cost air travel without any significant oversight.

Like any transportation or communications system, airlines provide a complex network of connections. A traveler is interested in getting from point A to point B in a timely, safe and affordable fashion. As a result, there are literally tens of thousands of city pairs within the United States and many more globally. This characteristic of travel presents a classic network problem, although the concept was largely or entirely unknown at the time of airline deregulation.[1] All transportation presents a network problem in greater or lesser degree. That is, suppliers have to supply the customer with specific transportation from one identified location to another, and the product is more valuable to consumers if the provider offers service between more locations. In order to compete, therefore, the transportation supplier must have the capacity to serve multiple destinations. When some other entity provides the medium over or through which the service takes place, e.g., highways or waterways, the problem may be reduced because the provider does not have to create its own medium as is the case with railroads. However, the transportation provider must have the means for pickup and delivery of the good or person being transported. Depending on the costs involved, especially the sunk costs, this can be a major barrier to entry by new firms or even expansion by existing firms (*see generally* Levine 1987).

There are several implications of this basic fact for airline competition policy. First, very few travelers will move, on any specific day, between many city pairs. This means that direct flights would be uneconomic even if limited to one trip each way in a day. At the same time, all travelers seeking to get to point A or B in a day might well fill several planes, thus making possible two or more flights a day into each city. This in turn means that some system must exist to collect travelers going to such destinations. Not surprisingly, hub-and-spoke systems emerged to serve most city pairs much as the old trunk-regional system had served earlier (*see generally* Levine 1987).

There are high-density city-pair markets such as those that produced competition in the pre-1978 era. Such pairs generate enough travelers to warrant multiple flights on a point-to-point basis. But even here, an airline that has service to other cities in the region surrounding the major destination will be able to add additional passengers in competition with an airline providing only point-to-point service (*see generally* Levine 1987). The most immediate implication of this insight is that entry by new airlines is going to be costly and difficult in most city pairs. Even in high-density pairs, the entrant will be at a disadvantage, in that without spokes at either end of its system, it can only serve some of the travelers that might use that segment of the route.

A second major competitive problem is that the day and the time of day a flight leaves or arrives is important to some travelers. Hence, loads will vary during the day and during the week, thereby complicating the question of competitive entry. If a new entrant offers a single flight to and from a particular destination, this will serve only a limited segment of travelers who want or need to travel at that time of day. Adding more flights increases the capacity commitment to that market and raises the entrant's costs while flooding the market with potentially unused capacity. Moreover, the fact that entry is necessarily time focused means that an incumbent competitor need respond aggressively only with respect to those of its flights that most directly substitute for that of the entrant both as to time and destination.

A third important factor in the actual operation of air travel markets is that the airlines have great discretion to set prices for each seat. It is impossible to substitute a trip from New York to Fargo, North Dakota for one from New York to Rapid City, South Dakota. Moreover, some travelers will have need to travel despite very high prices (inelastic demand), e.g., a lawyer needing to get to one of those cities to take a deposition, while others are price sensitive. If the airline can distinguish among these classes of customers, for example by imposing a requirement on cheap tickets that the traveler stay over Saturday night before returning, it can charge different prices. Travelers who want to go someplace at the last minute are more likely to be price insensitive. So by changing the price for reserved seats over time, the airline can also distinguish among its customers. With computerized reservation systems airlines became able to price their seats in a highly differentiated way.

In contrast to the mandated, uniform pricing system of the regulated era, this new freedom permits an airline to exploit its power with respect to travelers who want to go to a location where the airline's network is the only or the significantly better option. At the same time, price competition can be highly focused to provide lower prices only with respect to the specific destinations for which there is effective competition. These factors add to the importance of a network. The airline can charge travelers very different prices depending on their destination and the degree of competition the airline faces.

The basis for this pricing freedom is in the nature of the service provided. It is very customer specific. In addition, the legal characterization of the relationship between the traveler and the airline has enhanced the control that the airlines can exercise. Not surprisingly, the airlines as a group have actively sought and supported these characterizations. The ticket is a contract of personal service and can not be transferred or sold. Moreover, and unlike other analogous contracts where the buyer can simply not take the entire service (e.g., patrons can leave a theater or sporting event early; do not have to finish an unsatisfactory meal), the airlines have insisted that customers must take the full service purchased and may not trade, sell, exchange or even abandon any part of that service unless they transact with the airline (*see generally Chase v. Northwest Airlines* 1999).

Two examples illustrate this. First, as single airlines came to dominate hubs, they imposed high prices on tickets for direct travel between spoke cities and the hub city (Dempsey 2002, 130–139). Even when other airlines served the spoke city and the hub city, using such an airline involved a transfer at its own hub. Therefore, that airline had no incentive to engage in price competition when the first airline would always have the advantage of a direct, non-stop flight. At the same time, each airline would usually have discounted travel through its hub to another spoke city where it faced competition. Many airlines diligently policed travelers and travel agents who sold the through ticket to a traveler wanting to deplane in the hub city. If such ticket sales had been permitted, the cheapest available seat through a hub would have provided a cap on the price into the hub city. By actively enforcing rules against travel agents, airlines have sought to block the use of 'hidden city' tickets to cap their monopoly hub prices (*see Chase v. Northwest*, 1999).

A second strategy focused on 'within week' travel where prices were often twice what the airline charged for a ticket with a Saturday stay over. The traveler would buy two of the Saturday roundtrip tickets – one for travel from the origin of the trip and the other from the destination (thus saving the difference between the sum of those prices and the within-week price). The traveler would then use the first half of the first ticket to get to the destination and the first half of the second ticket to return. This 'back to back' ticketing was also a target of airline policing.

The airlines contended that both of these practices mislead them as to the demand for tickets. The counter argument on behalf of consumers was that they had priced the seat and someone had paid the price. The airline has no reason to complain whether the traveler took the seat or not. Of course, if travelers were able to use these strategies, then they would impose modest caps on some dimensions of price discrimination: within-week tickets could not be priced more than twice the price of the cheapest round trip and the price of travel from any spoke city to the hub could not exceed the lowest available price for a round trip through the hub.[2]

The ability to control the use of tickets reinforces and strengthens the capacity of the airline to differentiate its customers. It can offer low prices to end points on its network where it faces strong competition, but insist on higher prices for travel to or from its hub city if it faces little or no effective competition on that service. It can also charge very different prices for service having similar costs depending on the state of competition in the specific city pair. This is a variant of the short haul–long haul problem that was a longstanding issue in railroad service. The railroad would charge very high prices for short hauls where it had a monopoly and lower prices for longer hauls where it faced competition. The legislative solution was to impose a requirement that the railroad not charge more for a short haul than it did for longer hauls. Because the airline deregulation process did not appreciate this issue, no legislative constraint existed to limit the pricing discretion of the airlines.

Two other factors also strongly affect competition in airlines that initial policy makers failed to consider. First, contrary to the theory of contestable markets, there are significant costs of entry and exit (*see generally* Levine 1987). While the planes themselves are by their nature mobile, the airport facilities necessary to support the service are fixed and costly. Airports insist on long-term leases before they will provide gates (and effective competition often requires an entrant to have more than one gate). The entrant must also obtain ground services at each airport it serves as well as provide staffing to handle travelers and their baggage. While contracting with a local service company might provide much of this ground support, even that strategy is costly because the service company now has the fixed investments and the risk of loss if its airline customer abandons the market. In many airports, such services would have relatively few users. This would increase the economic risks for such service and a new entrant would have legitimate concerns that such an operator would favor its existing customers (competitors of the entrant) over the entrant. More often, therefore, the new airline had to make entry through a direct investment in ground facilities and staff.

An additional complication for these entrants is that landing slots and gates are in short supply in some key airports (*see generally* Levine 1987). This makes entry more difficult either because the new entrant has to use a less well-known airport or because it has to provide limited service based on either gate or slot constraints. Such limits make it easier for incumbent airlines to retaliate with selective price cuts and service changes.

`The second factor was the perception of policy makers that airlines were fungible providers of transportation – a perception that turned out to be wrong. However, in the eyes of travelers, new airlines were unproven and presented higher risks. Indeed, all airlines had FAA approval and were subject to FAA inspection; therefore, in an objective sense, all airlines should be equally safe and attractive to travelers. However, in the eyes of travelers, new airlines were unproven and presented higher risks. Thus, a new airline had to invest heavily in promoting itself and its services. This promotion constituted another major entry cost that was necessarily sunk in the particular market (*see generally* Levine 1987). Such investments would be lost if the airline withdrew from that market. In contrast, an established carrier can add an additional destination to its network with much lower costs (*see generally* Levine 1987). Its established customer base is already committed to the use of the airline and so can be expected to use it to get to the added destination. If it is making a new entry into a particular airport, such an airline nevertheless has the benefit of an established name and reputation.

These inherent characteristics of the network nature of the airline business suggest several observations supported by empirical study. First, incumbent airlines have great advantages over new entrants because they have already established networks of hubs while new entrants must enter into multiple markets to offer networks of service to customers (*see generally* Levine 1987; Bailey and Williams 1988). Moreover, the incumbents will have a strong incentive to dominate a hub airport with a substantial customer base because this gives the incumbent a set of travelers – those coming to the hub and those traveling out of the hub – over which it can have significant pricing discretion (*see generally* Werden *et al.*, 1991). Once it has established such a hub, the incumbent can defend it against new entry by selective competition. Other established networks will, on the other hand, have little interest in creating significant price competition into or out of that hub. The resulting price war would only reduce revenues for all concerned (*see generally* Peteraf 1993).

The second observation is that inter-network competition has much greater potential to overcome the costs and barriers of the market process than completely new entry (*see generally* Levine 1987; Willig 1992; Hurdle *et al.* 1989). In non-hub locations, competing networks could offer different combinations of spokes by which the traveler could get to any specific destination. In moderate-sized airports, there would be sufficient numbers of travelers such that each network could fill several planes a day with individuals having diverse destinations. If most of the networks provided service to most of those destinations through different sets of hubs and spokes, competition could be significant. Moreover, a network not offering a particular destination would evaluate entry differently than a new entrant, because the specific destination would be able to draw on the entire network to provide travelers to and from that destination. This does not eliminate the costs of entry, including staffing and ground facilities. However, an established network operator will face lower costs and easier exit if it fails to find a sufficient market for its services.

A third observation is that the varied, physical capacity of airplanes enters into the potential for competition. At the time of deregulation, jet power airplanes were very much the preferred mode of travel, however, those planes had minimum capacities ranging of at least 100 passengers. For lower volumes of passengers, the only available planes were turbo-prop planes that offered a variety of capacity from as few as ten or 12 passengers up to 70 or 80 but travelers generally had a strong preference for jets. This meant that entry into a specific destination required the entrant to generate sufficient volume within a reasonable period of time to cover the costs of a jet. This also made the hub approach more useful because it was easier to get passengers for several destinations together to fill a plane so long as direct flights were not feasible.

In the 1990s, commuter jet aircraft became significant factors in the market. These planes with varying capacities under one hundred passengers and lower operating costs have made it possible to increase the number of direct flights between points. This allows incumbent carriers to redirect some of their traffic to the destination, thus reducing the total volume available for a competing hub-and-spoke service which in turn makes entry more difficult (*see generally* Maynard 2005a). On the other hand, an entrant has a greater range of capacity that it can employ when entering a market. If it expects low volume, it can use a small jet until it has built its business. This also permits new entrants to offer direct service to select destinations where no airline presently has a hub. For example, Alligiant operates a number of flights, usually one a day, between various middle-sized airports such as Madison, Wisconsin and Las Vegas.[3] The central observation with respect to airplanes is that with the evolution of equipment, it is easier to match capacity to demand. However, it is also possible to vary capacity provided to a market. Incumbents can use this ability to flood a market when they wish to challenge a new entrant that offers a directly competing service (*see generally US v. AMR*, 2003; Dempsey 2002; Levine 1987).

Thus, the airline business, once freed from the constraints imposed by the rate and service commands of the CAB, evolved in a pattern similar to other transportation and network systems. It did not take very long for some academic scholars to identify the competitive issues that arise in unregulated networks. In 1981, Almarin Phillips published an article in the Pennsylvania Law Review that identified a number of these issues. In the mid-1980s, Michael Levine, who by then was a professor at Yale's Management School and had worked for the CAB and as an executive on several airlines, wrote at length about the differences between the realities of airline markets and the presumptions that had guided policy at the outset (*see generally* Levine 1987). Indeed, some of the economists who originated the contestable markets model eventually admitted that the model did not work as they had expected in the airline industry (*see generally* Willig 1992).

The constellation of conditions that define potential strategies for airline markets are not inconsistent with those identified in the 'hollow core' model of destructive competition (*see generally* Telser 1978; Sjostrom 1989). That model postulates that there is no stable equilibrium in a market, i.e., the core is hollow, because the quantum changes in capacity resulting from entry produce excess capacity and a cycle of depressed prices until capacity is withdrawn, allowing prices to rise again. However, when prices go up, they reach levels that earn excess profits, inducing entry and thereby continuing the cycle. To achieve stability, such markets require a system of regulation that allows for exclusion of entry and price control to reduce monopolistic exploitation. This model is subject to a number of criticisms because it postulates a very myopic response to increased, pre-entry prices. A rational entrant would consider the likely post-entry price rather than the pre-entry one. In addition, the model rests crucially on the assumption of the lumpy nature of added capacity. One effort to estimate the possible existence of hollow core conditions in European airlines found a statistically significant correlation, but the capacity of the model to explain actual variations in the data was very low (*see generally* Antonia 1998).[4] This suggests that the theory has little explanatory power, at least in that market context, and so provided no justification for regulating entry or even explaining conduct that had exclusionary effect.

The alternative explanation for the observed anticompetitive conduct is that opportunities inherent in the operating conditions of transportation services, and the lack of significant legal constraints on exploiting those options, permit a number of exclusionary strategies targeting new entrants whose services directly overlap those of incumbents in markets with limited demand. Moreover, courts and regulators have difficulty in distinguishing exclusionary conduct that features lower prices and greater capacity from competitive responses to increased competition (*see generally US v. AMR* 2003).

At the same time, as the foregoing analysis has repeatedly emphasized, the capacity of a competing network to make relatively low cost entry (and incur relatively low costs on exit) means that exclusionary conduct is less likely to be effective or to be attempted. Thus, from a competitive perspective, the primary concern ought to be to maintain as many distinct networks as possible. These networks provide actual competition to serve a particular destination and potential competition in all other points that are readily accessible to a hub of that network. It would appear that specific markets are indeed much more contestable if the contestant is a network rather than a new entrant into the business of air travel.

The market power inherent in such networks allows inefficient incumbents to drive more efficient entrants from the market. This is consistent with the existence of price discrimination and other exploitation of travelers by incumbent airlines that still fail or risk bankruptcy. Basically, their costs result from the old protected cartel system in which monopoly profits were distributed among stakeholders in the form of increased compensation and pension rights. There are also significant questions concerning the competency of management of some airlines (*see generally* Dempsey 2002). In contrast, new entrants have much lower operating costs, but often face serious obstacles with respect to entry costs and strategic conduct by incumbents as discussed earlier.

Once the significance of networks and competition among networks is recognized, then the incentive for airlines to enter into code sharing (an agreement that allows one carrier to use services of another carrier as its own) and other strategic alliances becomes clear. Code sharing occurs both within the American market and globally. It now appears that only a few global strategic alliances will exist to link airlines around the world in networks that provide service to a great many more points than any one airline could (*see generally* Schlangan 2000). Similarly in the United States, the code sharing system has allowed airlines with relatively small volumes of traffic to specific destinations to provide better service and easier connections in competition with other networks. These arrangements are a way to share a resource, the network of the partner, which expands the capacity of all participants to serve travelers with specific travel needs. Early work on code sharing suggested that it provided significant economies resulting in lower prices and more efficient service (*see generally* Bamberger, *et al.* 2004).

Code sharing and strategic alliances have an anticompetitive dimension as well. The partners must necessarily agree on the price and the capacity that will be dedicated to the shared parts of the network. This reduces the incentive to compete more directly with the other participants. Thus, the intra-code sharing incentives are such that prices are more likely to be maintained because the threat of potential competition is removed or reduced (*see generally* Hurdle *et al.* 1989). In addition, as the code sharing results in fewer potential networks, this reduces the probability of new competition and makes coordination among networks with respect to price more feasible.

Code sharing and strategic alliances are joint ventures and therefore have a clear structural element to them. Moreover, like other forms of merger, the results can either promote competition or frustrate it. It is also true that because code sharing and other alliances are contractual in character and do not involve consolidated ownership, they are not as durable as complete merger. Once the importance of networks for air travel is appreciated, the central policy problem is to develop standards and criteria for determining the permissible kinds of both mergers and other partial integration of air travel services.

MERGER ANALYSIS AND ENFORCEMENT

With respect to strategic alliances and code sharing, the Secretary has retained the authority to approve or disapprove such transactions. Indeed, prior approval is required. In addition, the Secretary can grant antitrust immunity with respect to international agreements. However, the DOJ has independent authority to challenge such agreements in the domestic market. The DOJ has been an active participant in the proceedings before the Secretary with respect to such requests (*see generally* Schlangen 2000). The treatment of code sharing and strategic alliances has been more complex and it is not clear how well either enforcement agency has conceptualized the issues involved in maintaining a sufficient number of competing or potentially competing networks (*see generally* Hurdle *et al.* 1989; Schlangen 2000).

Conventional merger review has taken place under two distinct modes in the period after 1978. For the first decade, the CAB and then the Secretary of Transportation had exclusive jurisdiction to decide these matters. After 1989, the DOJ had primary authority.

Although in theory the standards for judging the merits of mergers has remained constant since 1978, the response to actual mergers was quite different before and after 1989. In part, this is a result of institutional differences between an industry-oriented regulator and an agency charged with general law enforcement. However, it is also true that by the time the DOJ took over primary merger review, the initial perception that airline markets were easily contestable was largely if not entirely discredited (*see generally* Willig 1992; Kahn 1988; Carstensen 1989). The following discussion examines the two periods of merger review authority separately.

The Early Period – 1978–1988

The period from 1978 to 1988 saw a large number of proposed mergers and acquisitions (*see generally* Mosteller 1999). The Secretary of Transportation did not disapprove any of them (Dempsey 2002, 139). Most were in fact either efficiency enhancing or benign. One group of mergers involved the consolidation of airlines into effective networks. A second category of mergers involved the acquisition of failed new entrants or dying trunk lines. These acquisitions probably had little adverse competitive effect. A third group of mergers involved the vertical integration of trunk lines into regional services that also helped to create and expand their networks. These combinations were more problematic. However, given the incentives in network operations based on hubs, the loss of competitive access was probably unavoidable. Finally, a handful of combinations raised much more serious competitive questions. These were consolidations within a single hub market or combinations of regional carriers serving the same market.

Illustrative of the first type of network building mergers was Republic – the consolidation of North Central (a regional carrier serving the Midwest), Southern (a carrier serving the south) and Hughes Airwest (Dempsey 2002, 141). The combined firm established hubs at Detroit, Memphis and Minneapolis. It competed with Northwest in Minneapolis but was the only airline using Detroit as a hub. Ozark, another example, developed similarly through acquisition of regional carriers and developed a hub in St. Louis, where TWA also had a hub. Among trunk line mergers, the most prominent example of this kind of expansion was the combination of Delta and Western that expanded Delta's network into the western half of the country. These combinations all served to create or expand networks and provided the basis for hubs that created additional competition in the various markets served by the hub.

For travelers, having competing hubs, such as Chicago, Minneapolis, Detroit and St. Louis, meant that unless one was traveling to the hub, there were often two or three choices of carrier. This ensured at least moderate rivalry. The empirical evidence suggests that three competing airlines generated reasonably competitive prices (*see generally* Hurdle *et al.* 1989). Moreover, at this time, competing carriers operated hubs at the same airports. Republic and Northwest used Minneapolis as a hub. TWA and Ozark used St. Louis as a hub. Chicago had both United and American Airlines. In Dallas, Braniff, American and Delta shared the airport. Thus, travelers to such a hub would have the benefit of at least some competition if they departed from an airport with two or more competing networks.

One of the major early new entry successes was Peoples, which developed a major hub at Newark serving the greater New York City area. However, like other entrants, Peoples ran into a variety of economic problems and consolidated with Continental (*see generally* Mosteller 1999). This merger, an illustration of the second category, expanded Continental's network significantly and so had the kind of pro-competitive effect associated with the Delta-Western combination.

The collapse of some of the incumbent trunk lines was a direct result of very dubious business decisions that weakened the capacity of these carriers to compete. Braniff, a conspicuous example, had had a major system serving South America (*see generally* Nance, 1984). It had kept its books in such a way as to charge most of its overhead to that branch of the business and thereby justify high fares on non-competitive routes. Under new management, however, the books suggested that the South American element of the business was unprofitable. Meanwhile American Airlines was engaging in a number of strategic actions to destroy Braniff's domestic business. In what seems a misguided effort to get cash, Braniff leased its South American routes to Eastern. This transaction probably had little or no competitive effect since it substituted one owner for another. However, Braniff's smaller domestic system had to absorb much higher fixed costs. Braniff ultimately failed in its effort to be a major competitor (*see generally* Nance 1984). American Airlines hastened this failure by a number of strategic acts at their Dallas hub including creating false passenger reservations and other comparable acts that cause actual prospective passengers to use other airlines (*see generally US v. American Airlines* 1985).

Of the many mergers in this period, only three raised (at that time and in retrospect) major competitive concerns. In each instance, failure to appreciate the implications of network characteristics contributed to the questionable approvals. Two of these acquisitions involved eliminating competition in hub markets. They were the acquisition of Republic by Northwest and Ozark by TWA. The third problematic merger approved in this period was the merger of Allegheny and Piedmont to form US Air, consolidating two strong regional carriers serving the same area of the country. US Air eventually acquired other airlines including PSA, which had been the pioneer in competition in California, thereby expanding *US Air*'s network significantly.

In both the Ozark and Republic cases, the mergers eliminated hub competition (St. Louis and Minneapolis) as well as directly overlapping networks serving spoke destinations. From the perspective of network competition, these mergers were the most anticompetitive agreements possible. Even if one assumed that Ozark and Republic did not have sufficiently large networks to compete effectively and so were fated to disappear from the market, combination with their most direct competitors would seem to be the least desirable match. Indeed, the DOJ opposed approval of these mergers. Despite this opposition, the Secretary of Transportation granted approval (*see generally* Nannes 2000). Under the law as it stood, no appeal was possible.

The Secretary's rationale for approval rested heavily on the contestable market hypothesis that assumed that competition would arise if the merged airlines raised prices or reduced service, driving prices back down to their competitive levels. Indeed, if the Secretary was correct and all markets were contestable, then these mergers would have had no effect. Of course, this raises the interesting question of why it was rational for the acquiring firms to pay premiums for the acquired assets when they would be unable to exercise their power to raise prices. If the physical assets had more value than the stock market capitalization of the business as a going concern, then a premium might have been rational even if no market power resulted, but based on an objective valuation of the assets, this assumption is unlikely (Levine 1987, 467).

Subsequent empirical work has shown that the effect on travelers in St. Louis and Minneapolis was an increase in prices and a reduction in the number of flights (*see generally* Werden *et al.* 1991). Travelers through Detroit benefited from Northwest's replacing Republic as to the number of flights that were available, but prices also increased. Thus, the contestable market hypothesis was directly falsified as to hub markets themselves. Other empirical work has repeatedly found that single airline hubs have higher prices for comparable routes into the hub than do either hubs with competition or higher volume airports that are not primary hubs (*see generally* Dempsey 2002).

The central failure of merger policy in the first decade following deregulation was the continued adherence to the contestable market model when it was increasingly clear that the realities of the new airline competition made many markets uncontestable. Of course, many of the mergers in this era contributed to the development of larger and more efficient networks. However, the key loss was that more networks could have developed as actual or potential competitors if stricter merger standards had been employed. The fact that merger review remained in an agency that largely identified with the regulated firms, rather than the competitive market, undoubtedly contributed to the impetus to approve these transactions.

The structural changes brought about in this period did a great deal to reinforce the potential for airlines to engage in discriminatory and exclusionary practices. At the same time, the inherent nature of the network character of air travel would have made much of the observed strategic conduct feasible and rational even without mergers. For example, American was successful in driving Braniff from the market and Eastern and Pan American both failed. Hence, while a few key mergers undoubtedly played a role in strengthening the concentration of the market and so made other strategic conduct more attractive, these undesirable practices were likely to have occurred in any event given the underlying conditions under which this industry operates.

Post-1989 Merger Policy

After 1989, the Secretary of Transportation no longer had authority to immunize mergers from antitrust review and the industry came under the same merger review process as applies to the market generally. The late 1980s were also a time when antitrust enforcement was gradually being restored from the very low level it had experienced during the Reagan presidency. Antitrust authorities challenged several merger or merger-like transactions in the 1990s, which helped to retain a somewhat more competitive structure to the networks that had emerged (Willig 1992, 697 lists four cases, none actually litigated). Unfortunately, the analysis of both mergers and code sharing/strategic alliances has focused on measures of impact on specific city pairs (*see generally* Willig 1992; Schlangen 2000) and has ignored the implications of network competition where potential entry is also very important (*see generally* Hurdle *et al.* 1989).

Two key merger challenges, neither of which resulted in a final judgment, involved Northwest's purchase of a controlling interest in Continental (*see US v. Northwest Airlines* 2001) and United's attempt to buy US Air. The Northwest deal was somewhat complicated, but basically the managers of Northwest, who had taken control through a leveraged buyout, were able to buy a controlling interest in Continental. The DOJ Antitrust Division's characterization of the agreement was that this was a consolidation of the two airlines that violated Section 7 of the Clayton Act. While the trial of this claim was proceeding, the case was settled with an agreement that required divestiture of the stock interest in Continental (*see generally* DOJ 2000).

Continental, Northwest and Delta have entered into an extensive code sharing arrangement that allows each to book travelers onto selected flights on the other two airlines. United and US Air have a similar relationship for domestic flights (*see generally* Dept. of Transportation 2003). The efficiency gain of such arrangements comes from the expansion of a network through cooperation. However, the anticompetitive implication is that the members of such a consortium have much less incentive to compete with each other. The modified model of contestability based on network competition suggests that there can be a serious loss of potential competition, the key control over prices, resulting from allowing pervasive code sharing.

United's proposed acquisition of US Airways raised a number of direct competition concerns and the two airlines operated competing hubs in the Washington DC area. United has a hub at Dulles and US Airways has one at National. The proposed deal involved significant divestiture of US Airways' capacity at National Airport to a proposed new entrant that would operate that hub and serve, primarily, the eastern half of the country. After lengthy investigation and significant public outcry, the government finally announced that it would challenge the merger and the parties abandoned it (*see generally* DOJ, 2001b). Shortly thereafter, both companies entered into bankruptcy. However, United and US Air had, and continued to have, code sharing arrangements on some routes and both are members of the same global alliance.

There is an argument that the United-US Air merger would have created an enhanced competitive network in the eastern United States (Chafitz 2002, 224–226). United is largely, this argument claims, an east–west airline with respect to the region while US Airways has many more north–south routes. The result would be a network with greater capacity to compete with Delta and Continental. This analysis highlights the complex nature of the network phenomena in air travel. But ultimately, this merger involves a very high cost to competition in network as well as point-to-point concerns and so its prohibition was undoubtedly in the public interest.

At the same time that the government was preparing to challenge United's proposed acquisition, it did not contest American's acquisition of TWA (*see generally* DOJ 2001a). TWA had been in bankruptcy for some time at that point and was close to collapse. That it needed a new owner seemed evident. It operated a major hub at St. Louis that was a competitive alternative in much of Middle America for the hubs at Chicago, Minneapolis, Detroit and Cincinnati. American already had a major hub at Chicago. Thus, this acquisition resulted in the loss of a significant basis for a competing network for the entire region. At the time of acquisition, American promised to continue to operate a hub at St. Louis (*see generally* Chafitz 2002), but within a couple of years it had cut back the number of flights substantially because it had no incentive to compete with itself. At the same time, by having a minor hub operation at St. Louis, American could reduce the risk that a new entrant or an expanding rival would use that location to develop a competing network.

In 2005, America West, a relatively new entrant, with a route system largely in the southwest, acquired US Air to create a more comprehensive national network without any antitrust objection. America West has also been a price-competitive airline and has indicated that it plans to continue that business strategy. This merger may have a pro-competitive effect because it will create a larger network of service. However, because US Airways has code sharing with United and is a member of the same global alliance as United, there is a risk that if the merged firm retains these relationships, this may temper its incentive to compete.

Indeed, as noted above concerning Delta–Continental–Northwest, both domestic and international alliances and code sharing agreements are an increasingly common form of semi-merger. Internationally, because most countries require that their own nationals own a controlling interest in their flag airlines, standard mergers were not legally possible. Hence, airlines are permitted to engage in strategic alliances that involve not only code sharing, but may also include revenue sharing and collective marketing. As in the domestic air travel markets, the network effects are substantial especially where no other way exists for a traveler to buy a complete ticket from his or her point of origin to destination. Absent such arrangements among airlines, the traveler would need to create his or her own network by changing carriers and purchasing different tickets to complete the journey, at great expense if the carrier has market power on that route. On the other hand, the creation of such global networks can also severely limit the development of competing domestic networks. Since the Secretary of Transportation can immunize international agreements from antitrust review, as a result, such alliances including multiple domestic carriers can be used to eliminate potential network competition.

However, despite the competitive concerns in Northwest–Continental, and the settlement requiring divestiture, major investment groups continue to hold significant stock interests in competing airlines. For example, in 2005, Wellington was the largest institutional investor in Northwest (10.1 per cent) and Continental (13.8 per cent), as well as the second largest such investor in American Airlines (8.33 per cent) and made a major investment in the proposed merger of American West and US Air (Maynard 2005b). This situation should raise serious competitive concerns because Northwest–Continental–Delta constitute one strategic network group while American is in another group and United and US Air are members of the third major network group (*see* www.usairways.com; www.aa.com). When investors hold substantial interests in ostensible competitors, the incentive to compete among such firms or groups of firms is necessarily attenuated.

MERGER AND COMPETITION POLICY FOR THE FUTURE

In the clear light of hindsight, it is now possible to see that the economics of the airline business were more complex and problematic than the early models had revealed. Moreover, it is now possible to identify some policies that might have made for a better transition to a less regulated market with particular reference to the restructuring of airline ownership. At the same time, the evidence, overall, is that travelers are in general much better off with more options and better prices, under a less regulated market system than they had been under comprehensive rate, route and service regulation. But the history of the first 25 years of airline competition is, also, one of sub-optimal competitive structure leading to troublesome conduct and sub-par performance.

Even today, policy makers and law enforcers seem to have an undue focus on specific city pairs in which two airlines presently compete in the analysis of both mergers and code sharing or other strategic alliances (*see generally* Willig 1992; Schlangen 2000). The problem with this narrow view is that it ignores the fact that effective competition involves networks that provide alternative routes for travelers. Moreover, the contestable market theory has more merit with respect to the potential for internetwork competition than the original, and now discredited, theory that applied to city pair markets. Contestability analysis must be applied with care, however, because networks may, or may not, constitute alternatives for specific travel points of origin and destination (*see generally* Hurdle *et al*. 1989). The location of hubs and spokes are the defining characteristics for determining which airline networks can compete effectively for which consumer traffic. This suggests that antitrust policy should focus equally on actual and potential internetwork competition in both merger analysis and the evaluation of code sharing or other strategic alliances. Unfortunately, contemporary policy makers do not yet seem to have grasped fully the implications of this approach. This flaw is most evident in the willingness of antitrust agencies to decline to challenge and courts to approve code sharing among domestic airlines, with the result that there appear to be only three major networks in the United States. Southwest Airlines, alone among the largest airlines, does not participate in any network. This reduces its ability to serve a number of city pairs and compete nationwide. On the other hand, its independence also makes it a potential competitive check on the other three networks.

Finally, merger policy alone cannot solve all of the competitive problems in the airline business. Airlines possess a great deal of market power because most point-to-point volumes are low and there is a capacity to engage in many strategic exclusionary activities. Market facilitating rules that limit the capacity of incumbent airlines to engage in extreme forms of price discrimination and capacity manipulation must complement merger policy. Regulations issued by DOT can also control exclusionary entry and restrictions, such as gate access, that foreclose entry. These hypothetical rules are very difficult to write even in the absence of special interest lobbying and will necessarily impose some limits on conduct that may have legitimate functions in some circumstances. However, restoring some greater standardization to airline pricing and service is likely, on balance, to facilitate both network competition and lower the barriers to new entrants as well as making it easier for smaller airlines to develop their own networks.

CONCLUSION

Looking at the airline industry in the most favorable light, its present state is a 'second-best' approximation of what might have been achieved if better decisions had been made in the formative era. However, it deserves reiteration that the competitive market in air travel has generally served the public interest better than the system it replaced.

NOTES

1. The concept apparently gained currency with the rise of the internet. Neither Levine (1987) nor Carstensen (1989) use the term network although their descriptions of the economic issues in the airline industry involve classic network problems. Willig (1992) does refer to 'network effects'.
2. In addition, passengers would need the right to commence a trip on any leg of a multi-stop ticket. This way, the passenger would get the benefit of a round-trip ticket.
3. Northwest responded in Madison, Wisconsin by initiating a directly competing point-to-point service. Alligent then terminated its service. In the past, Northwest has driven other competing carriers from markets it serves (*see* Dempsey 2002). Other major airlines have employed the same strategy (*see US v. AMR* 2003).
4. The r squared provides a measure of the ability of the model to explain the variation in the data. The reported r squared for different models ranged from .08 to .17. Basically,

while the variables were correlated, they left unexplained almost 85 to 90 per cent of the variation in the data (Antonia 1998, table 6).

REFERENCES

Antonia, Andreas, 1998, 'The State of the Core in the Airline Industry: The Case of the European Market,' *Management and Decision Economics* 19:43–54.

Bailey, Elizabeth and Jeffrey Williams, 1988, 'Sources of Economic Rent in the Deregulated Airline Industries,' *Journal of Law and Economics*, 31:173–202.

Bamberger, Gustavo, Dennis Carlton, and Lynette Neumann, 2004, 'An Empirical Investigation of the Competitive Effects of Domestic Airline Alliances,' *Journal of Law and Economics* 48:195–222.

Baumol, William J., J. Panzar, and R. Willig, 1982, *Contestable Markets and the Theory of Industry Structure*, Harcourt Brace Jovanovich.

Carstensen, Peter, 1989, 'Evaluating "Deregulation" of Commercial Air Travel: False Dichotomization, Untenable Theories, and Unimplemented Premises,' *Washington & Lee Law Review* 46:109–150.

Chafitz, Joel, 2002, 'A Tale of Two Mergers: American/TWA and United/US Air,' *DePaul Business Law Journal* 14:215–230.

Dempsey, Paul, 2002, 'Predatory Practices & Monopolization in the Airline Industry: A Case Study of Minneapolis/St. Paul,' *Transportation Law Journal* 29:127–187.

Department of Justice, 2000, November 6, Press Release: 'Justice Department Announces Tentative Settlement in Northwest–Continental Lawsuit.'

Department of Justice, 2001a, March 16, Press Release: 'Justice Department Announces It Won't Challenge American Airlines/TWA Acquisition.'

Department of Justice, 2001b, July 27, Press Release: 'Department of Justice and Several States Will Sue to Stop United Airlines from Acquiring US Airways.'

Department of Transportation, 2003, January 17, Press Release: 'DOT Conditionally Allows Delta–Northwest–Continental Code-Sharing Agreement.'

Economist, Flying on Empty, May 21, 2005, 65–66.

Hurdle, Gloria, Richard Johnson, Andrew Joskow, Gregory Werden, and Michael Williams, 1989, 'Concentration, Potential Entry and Performance in the Airline Industry,' *Journal of Industrial Economics* 38:119–139.

Kahn, Alfred, 1988, 'Airline Deregulation–a Mixed Bag, but a Clear Success Nevertheless,' *Transportation Law Journal* 16:229–251.

Levine, Michael, 1987, 'Airline Competition in Deregulated Markets: Theory, Firm Stategy and Public Policy,' *Yale Journal on Regulation* 3:393–494.

Maynard, Micheline, 2005a, 'In Airline Shift, More Nonstops Make Schedule,' *New York Times*, May 4, 2005, A1.

Maynard, Micheline, 2005b, '2 Airlines Bring in New Investor on Merger,' *New York Times*, May 30, 2005, C2.

McCraw, Thomas, 1984, *Prophets of Regulation*, Harvard University Press.

Mosteller, Jeff, 1999, 'The Current and Future Climate of Airline Consolidation: The Possible Impact of an Alliance of Two Large Airlines and an Examination of the Proposed American Airlines–British Airways Alliance,' *Journal of Air Law and Commerce* 64:575–603.

Nance, John, 1984, *Splash of Colors*, William Morrow.

Nannes, John, 2000, June 13, Statement before the Committee on Transportation & Infrastructure, U.S. House of Representatives, Antitrust Analysis of Airline Mergers.

Peteraf, Margaret, 1993, 'Intra-Industry Structure and the Response of Rivals, Managerial and Decision Economics,' 14:519–528.

Phillips, Almarin, 1981, 'Airline Mergers in the New Regulatory Environment,' *University of Pennsylvania Law Review* 129:856–881.

Schlangen, Charles, 2000, 'Differing Views of Competition: Antitrust Review of International Airline Alliances,' *University of Chicago Legal Forum*, 2000:413–446.

Sjostrom, W., 1989, 'Collusion in Ocean Shipping: a Test of Monopoly and Empty Core Models,' *Journal of Political Economy* 97:1160–1179.

Telser, Lester, 1978, *Economic Theory and the Core*, University of Chicago Press.

Werden, Gregory, Andrew Josko, and Richard Johnson, 1991, 'The Effect of Mergers on Price and Output: Two Case Studies from the Airline Industry,' Managerial and Decision Economics 12:341–352.

Willig, R.D., 1992, 'Airline Deregulation: DOJ Experience,' *Antitrust Law Journal* 60:695–703.

Wolfe, Kathryn, 2005, 'Rough Skies for the "Big Six",' *CQ Weekly*, April 25, 2005, 1068–1077.

Statutes

Airline Deregulation Act of 1978, 92 Stat. 1705 (1978) codified 49 USC at various places.

Cases

Supreme Court Decisions
US v. General Dynamics, 415 US 486 (1974).

Courts of Appeal Decisions
US v. AMR, 335 F3d 1109 (10th Cir. 2003).
US v. American Airlines, 743 F2d 1114 (5th Cir. 1985).
US v. Northwest Airlines, E.D. Mich., Civ. No. 98-7 4611.

Federal District Court Opinions
Chase v. Northwest Airlines, 49 F.Supp 2d 553 (E.D. Mich. 1999).

7. Hospital mergers

Thomas L. Greaney

INTRODUCTION

If one were to ask a hospital administrator how deregulation had affected his/her institution's operations, the question would be greeted with some surprise, if not outright scorn. To be sure, many regulations have been eliminated over the last twenty years. However, vast areas of administrative oversight persist or have been added during that same period. The extent and nature of deregulation affecting acute care hospitals requires some historical context and an understanding of the complex arrangements that shape today's health care institutions. This chapter will therefore begin with a brief historical account of the changing regulatory landscape. Next, it will provide an analysis of the economic and institutional forces affecting the health care industry today. Then, it will turn to the role of antitrust law in fostering change in an evolving industry.

General acute care hospitals have long been subject to a wide array of federal, state and private regulatory regimes. Although some of the most intrusive, command and control forms of regulation, such as state rate-setting and certificate of need (CON) laws (requiring prior administrative approval for entry and large capital investments) have been removed or modified, a large body of law continues to govern the operations of hospitals. Government-financed payment systems, which include Medicare, Medicaid, TRICARE, the Indian Health Service and a large number of miscellaneous programs, account for more than half of acute care hospital revenues (Mayo 2000, 1267). Not surprisingly, as a condition of payment these programs impose an immense number of regulatory requirements on hospitals.

At the same time, there is no question that over the last 20 years health care policy has shifted dramatically toward reliance on markets and competition to direct the nation's healthcare expenditures. The change, which has been characterized as a move from 'provider driven' health care to 'payer driven' health care (*see generally* Dranove, Shanley and White 1993), was spawned in part by antitrust efforts resulting in elimination of a number of institutional and professional arrangements that formed barriers to competition and insulated both providers and patients from financial responsibility for health care services. As a result of these institutional changes and public policy initiatives, both public and private payment systems demanded that providers engage in active competition for contracts. However, even in the market-driven health care era, the picture is nuanced: a counter-reaction to managed care has somewhat changed the landscape and ushered in some re-regulation and institutional practices inimical to competitive conditions.

THE REGULATORY ERA

States have wide authority to regulate hospitals under the police power. Historically, the prime method of exercising that authority has been licensure pursuant to which state authorities can grant or deny authority to conduct business and impose specific operational and administrative requirements. Although states sometimes penalize deficiencies in quality and safety through civil fines and intermediate sanctions, these have never been important to shaping the competitive dynamics of the industry. As discussed below, most states follow the federal government's lead in deferring to the self-regulatory standards and processes of the Joint Commission on Accreditation of Healthcare Organizations (JCAHO). State CON legislation has been more important. It was a byproduct of the National Health Resources Planning and Development Act (enacted in 1974) which sought to develop standards for controlling the supply, distribution and organization of health resources, especially acute care hospitals. That law created incentives for states to establish State Health Planning and Development Agencies, adopt health planning strategies and enact CON laws to assure an appropriate distribution of resources pursuant to the state plan (Furrow *et al.* 2000, 32–36). Prior approval by a state agency empowered to issue a Certificate of Need was required for all new institutional health services (e.g., hospitals, nursing homes, ambulatory surgery centers) and for all capital expenditures in excess of $150 000. While the federal planning law was repealed in 1986, 37 states continue to operate CON regulatory schemes requiring prior approval for new hospital operation and significant capital investments. CON regulation remains a means for states to control entry or limit expansion by acute care hospitals, although some have weakened or repealed their statutes in recent years. A sizeable economics literature indicates that even in states with vibrant CON regulation, these laws did not succeed in controlling costs. A number of studies and antitrust cases suggest that rivals seeking to thwart entry had used the regulatory process opportunistically.

Another area of state regulation that has been largely replaced is state hospital rate-setting. At one time many states directly controlled the rates charged by hospitals (Harshbarger 1996, 214). Typically, these laws empowered a state commission to set rates (usually employing cost-based standards) and to limit cost shifting. Today, however, only two states, West Virginia and Maryland, regulate hospital rates. However, government payors effect a measure of control over hospital rates. For example, Medicare (which represents approximately 40 per cent of the revenues of the average hospital) reimburses according to an administered price formula.

Other legal regimes, not strictly regulatory, also limited competition during the Regulatory Era. What Havighurst and Blumstein called a 'professional paradigm' dominated the policy and law of health care, giving physicians wide discretion over their professional practice and direct control over most institutional arrangements affecting their practice (*see generally* Havighurst 2000; Blumstein 1998). Antitrust challenges in the early 1980s ended a number of these institutional arrangements – such as physician control over private payment systems, medical ethical rules prohibiting competitive negotiations with health plans and hospital control over Blue Cross plans. These and other antitrust efforts helped usher in the competitive era discussed in the next section.

An important characteristic of hospital economics during the regulatory era was the so-called 'medical arms race' (MAR) (*see generally* Conner, Feldman and Dowd 1998). At this time, both Medicare and private payors like Blue Cross plans (then the dominant form of private insurance) reimbursed hospitals on the basis of their costs or on a fee-for-service basis. In addition, physicians exercised considerable influence over the charitable and community hospitals in which they practiced (*see generally* Pauly and Redisch 1973). As a result of these conditions – the absence of price sensitivity among payers and the strong physician voice in hospital governance – hospitals generally competed for physician affiliation. According to MAR analyses, this led to wasteful expenditures on equipment and facilities that increased costs beyond efficient levels.

The most important change affecting delivery of hospital care during this period came from new regulations affecting government payments to hospitals. In 1983, the federal government adopted a new methodology, a prospective payment system based on diagnostic related groups (PPS/ DRG) for paying hospitals for Medicare services. Abandoning the past practice of paying hospitals for their charges for each product and service rendered to patients, the new system paid a fixed amount for each of over 500 diagnostic treatment groups. Under a theory of 'yardstick competition', these fixed prices might induce hospitals to select the most efficient mix of technology and other inputs and thus roughly mimic competitive results (Dranove and Satterthwaite 2000, 1118). The move to PPS payment had profound implications because it put hospitals at risk for the costs of their services and in turn created incentives to impose cost controls and adopt arrangements with staff physicians to economize care.

Another important source of regulation of hospitals comes from laws directed at nonprofit organizations. The nonprofit form has long dominated acute care hospitals in America. Although hospital consolidation in the 1980s changed the picture somewhat, as large proprietary chains acquired or joint ventured with nonprofit hospitals in many markets, the proportion of nonprofit hospitals has remained relatively constant (at 60 per cent) (Sloan 2000, 1144). With nonprofit hospitals also obtaining tax exempt status under IRC 501(c)(3), the Internal Revenue Service began to play an important regulatory role in the business conduct of such hospitals. For example, IRS rules limited the extent to which exempt organizations could partner with physicians and require some community benefit. While requiring that exempt hospitals provide 'community benefits', the IRS did not impose quantitative requirements on the amount of charitable care that exempt hospitals were required to provide. However, a handful of states have done so.

THE COMPETITIVE ERA

Beginning in the 1980s as professional restraints and regulatory barriers were removed, competitive norms and institutional arrangements emerged, spurred generally by the rapid growth of managed care. Preferred Provider Organizations, Health Maintenance Organizations and other intermediary organizations were formed to facilitate competitive contracting by providers for the business of employers and insurers. Hospitals were forced to compete on price and other variables under the threat of loss of preferred status in managed care networks. In addition, payers insisted that hospitals and physicians accept risk, usually in the form of global or capitated payments for treatments of patients.

A byproduct of competitive pressures was increasing consolidation. Many hospitals (both for profit and nonprofit) pursued aggressive acquisition strategies, merging with local rivals to create multi-hospital systems that assured them prominent, if not dominant, positions in their local markets. While only 31 per cent of hospitals were part of a hospital system in 1979, by 2001 that number had increased to 54 per cent and another 17 per cent participated in looser health care networks (FTC/DOJ 2004, ch. 4, 10–11). During this period of consolidation, the nation's antitrust enforcement agencies (the United States Department of Justice, the Federal Trade Commission and, to a lesser extent, state Attorneys General) recognized that mergers of rival hospitals held the prospect of having both pro- and anti-competitive impacts. On the one hand, an increasingly competitive market-place spurred by managed care was insisting that hospitals not only deliver services at lower cost, but in groups or bundles that enabled managed care intermediaries to offer 'preferred provider' hospitals that could adequately serve the needs of an entire geographic area. Mergers of once-rival hospitals seemed a logical path toward rationalizing an industry regarded as wasteful. Hospitals were seen as engaged in the 'medical arms race' and more solici-tous of doctors' interests than community service or cost-effective patient care.

Yet many of the mergers were taking place in already-concentrated markets and communities saw consolidation reduce the number of choices to three, two and sometimes one hospital system. Antitrust enforcers viewed this degree of concentration as threatening to undermine the entire premise of a competition-based policy in health care. Managed care buyers could hardly be expected to fulfill the promise that competitive, selective contracting would serve to rationalize care delivery and lower costs if they faced dominant or oligopolistic sellers of hospital services. Federal antitrust authorities under the Carter, Reagan and Bush Administrations, as well as several state Attorneys General, responded with lawsuits chal-lenging a number of hospital acquisitions – the government brought 18 cases in federal court or in administrative proceedings before the FTC between 1980 and 2001 (Table 7.1, Greaney 2004). As detailed below, after several important victories in the 1980s, things went sour for the govern-ment in hospital merger litigation. Losing seven consecutive decisions in the federal courts, the government confronted accreting judicial precedent drawing hospital markets far broader than the local boundaries they had alleged in their complaints.

The final chapter of this account begins in the late 1990s with growing public dissatisfaction with limitations of choice and second-guessing by insurance companies regarding medical decision making. This so-called 'managed care backlash' resulted in the enactment of a large number of state laws regulating health insurers and imposing requirements such as mandated benefits and that health plans admit any willing provider to their networks. These laws and growing public resistance to restrictions on choice resulted in a substantial erosion of plans' capacity to control costs through selective contracting and utilization controls (*see generally* Havighurst 2000). The impact on health insurance costs was also signifi-cant. Health costs, which had stabilized during the years when the managed care model was at its zenith, began to rise again as health insurers took a more passive role vis-à-vis providers. The current era, which might be called the post-managed care era, finds managed care unable or unwilling to exercise control over utilization. 'Consumer directed health care' embraces a variety of health plan arrangements that put responsibility on insureds to make decisions about the locus of care and to accept a share of the cost of incremental service.

HOSPITAL MERGER ACTIVITY AND ANTITRUST ENFORCEMENT

As conditions conducive to competition began to evolve in the 1980s the federal government took an active role in policing hospital mergers. Most of the early antitrust challenges to hospital mergers involved market shares reaching near-monopoly levels. In seven of the nine cases brought during this period, the post-merger HHI exceeded 5000; in eight of these cases the merged firm had market shares of at least 54 per cent (Table 7.1). The government was successful in five of the six merger challenges decided on the merits by federal court or FTC adjudicatory decisions between 1984 and 1994. A number of other mergers were voluntarily abandoned after the government indicated its intention to initiate a legal challenge.

These early successes are also notable for the fact that they were brought during the era in which fee-for-service payment still predominated. This form of payment, which was the norm in both the private and public sectors, permitted hospitals to bill on a cost basis. Not surprisingly, this produced incentives for overuse of services, as hospitals had no reason to equate marginal costs with marginal benefits of additional increments of care. Economists theorized that the incentives to overuse care were most pronounced where hospitals faced competition, as rivalry to recruit staff physicians led to greater expenditures on costly equipment. Empirical studies also indicated that this 'medical arms race' occurred where hospitals lacked sufficient market clout to counteract physician demands for equipment (*see generally* Dranove and Satterthwaite 2000). If, as these studies suggested, price and costs varied *inversely* with hospital market concentration conditions, mergers in even highly concentrated markets arguably would not lessen competition. Thus, it was argued that increased hospital market concentration would improve economic welfare by reducing expenditures on marginally useful equipment and amenities. A number of hospital pricing studies of the era preceding managed care competition, indicating hospitals were able to charge supracompetitive prices regardless of market structure, lent support to this view (Connor *et al.* 1998). Finally, cartel theory buttressed the argument that hospital market concentration

Table 7.1   Hospital merger cases filed by government antitrust agencies: alleged market concentration and outcomes[1]

Case	Post-merger Share	Post-merger HHI	Change in HHI	Winner (Basis)
In re Evanston Northwestern Healthcare Corp.[2]	N/A	N/A	N/A	Gov't
State of California v. Sutter Health Sys.[3]	50%	N/A	N/A	Hospital (Geog. Mkt)
FTC v. Tenet Healthcare Corp.[4]	84%	6000–7000	2700–3200	Hospital (Geog. Mkt)
United States v. Long Island Jewish Medical Center[5]	100%	N/A	N/A	Hospital (Prod. Mkt)
FTC v. Butterworth Health Corp.[6]	65–70%	4506–5079	1675–2021	Hospital (Comp. Effects)
FTC v. Freeman Hospital[7]	24.4%	1624	222	Hospital (Geog. Mkt)
United States v. Mercy Health Servs.[8]	78%	N/A	N/A	Hospital (Geog. Mkt)
Columbia/HCA Healthcare Corp.[9]	70%	6400	2400	Settled
FTC v. Hospital Bd.[10]	67%	N/A	N/A	Hospital (State Action Immunity)
Dominican Santa Cruz Hosp.[11]	76%	6350	1700	Settled
United States v. Morton Plant Health System[12]	50–60%	3100–4400	1100–1900	Settled
FTC v. University Health[13]	43%	3200	630	Gov't
Adventist Health System/ West[14]	94%	8900	4300	Settled
Reading Hospital[15]	77%	6500	1700	Settled
United States v. Rockford Memorial Corp.[16]	64–72%	5647	2621	Gov't
United States v. Carilion Health Sys.[17]	70%	N/A	N/A	Hospital (Prod. And Geog. Mkts)
Hospital Corporation of America (Norfolk, VA Market)[18]	45%	2590	890	Settled

Table 7.1 (continued)

Case	Post-merger Share	Post-merger HHI	Change in HHI	Winner (Basis)
Hospital Corporation of America (Odessa, TX Market)[19]	58%	4350	820	Settled
United States v. National Medical Enterprises[20]	54%	3847	1187	Hospital
American Medical International[21]	76%	6025	2207	Gov't
American Medical I International (2nd Market)[22]	87%	7775	3405	Gov't
Hospital Corporation of America (Chattanooga)[23]	22.9%	2242	310	Gov't
Hospital Corporation of America (Chattanooga) (2nd acquisition)[24]	26.7%	2416	174	Gov't
United States v. Hospital Affiliates International, Inc.[25]	72.9%	N/A	N/A	Gov't

did not lead to harmful welfare effects. Given the absence of mechanisms for price-shopping (before the advent of managed care), the heterogeneity of hospital products and the enormous number of individual prices charged by each hospital, it was unlikely that a merger would enhance the merged hospital's ability to collude explicitly or tacitly.

The FTC took the position that it was important to protect price competition, however minimal, and that preserving market structures in order to preserve the opportunity for increased rivalry in the future would enhance consumer welfare. In two influential opinions, *Hospital Corporation of America v. FTC* and *United States v. Rockford Memorial Corp.*, Judge Richard Posner of the Seventh Circuit Court of Appeals agreed with the government and brushed aside allegations that conventional merger principles should not apply. While acknowledging the literature questioning the structure-conduct-performance paradigm in hospital markets, he found the state of economic learning was 'at an early and inconclusive stage,' not yet sufficient to abandon traditional presumptions (*United States v. Rockford Memorial Corp.*, 898 F.2d 1278, 1286 (7th Cir. 1990)). The court's position is notable for its willingness to minimize the significance of the economic questions raised about hospital competition and its disregard for the lack of significant mechanisms for price competition at the time. In addition, Judge Posner analyzed the HCA merger using a collusion model that seems a poor fit given the facts prevailing in the early 1980s. The court's analysis proceeds rather mechanically through classic indicia of potential collusion (e.g., barriers to expansion, cooperation among sellers, inelasticity of demand). Analyzing the propensity of the acquisitions to increase the risk of collusion, the HCA opinion describes six factors militating in favor of possible collusion and six factors militating against. However, it offers no weighting of those factors or qualitative analysis to explain its conclusion that the evidence was sufficient to support the FTC's conclusion that the merger threatened competition.

The *Rockford* opinion and several subsequent cases also examined and ultimately rejected the contention that risks of anticompetitive harm were mitigated by the fact that nonprofit hospitals were involved. The contention was that the nondistribution constraint inherent in the nonprofit form and the community orientation of those entities reduced the likelihood that the merged hospital would exercise its new-found market power. However Judge Posner issued a notable dictum (dubbed 'Posner's lament'), which, as we will see, spurred future inquiry into this question:

> It is regrettable that antitrust cases are decided on the basis of theoretical guesses as to what particular market-structure characteristics portend for competition. We would like to see more effort put into studying the actual effect of concentration on price in the hospital industry . . . This is a studiable hypothesis, by modern methods of multivariate statistical analysis . . . *Rockford Memorial Corp.*, 898 F.2d at p. 1286 (1990).

Given the incipient state of managed care in the market at that time, the possibility that hospitals might collude on a large number of prices and other competitive variables seemed remote under conventional cartel analysis. In glossing over market peculiarities that cast considerable doubt over the applicability of traditional presumptions, the FTC and the courts were content to rely on Section 7's focus on propensities and future effects to find that the merger might inhibit future competitive conditions, even though competition was at an underdeveloped stage at the time of litigation.

Other issues common in merger litigation have proven less controversial. For example, entry barriers have never been an important mitigating factor in hospital merger analysis. Even in markets in which CON regulation does not pose a significant obstacle to entry, scale economies and other impediments to entry have obviated the importance of this issue. Likewise, although defendants have routinely invoked an efficiencies defense in the litigated cases, it has never been outcome-determinative. The claim that the merger will result in substantial efficiencies that offset any adverse effects from increased concentration has met judicial resistance in most cases, due in part to the complexity and confusion surrounding the issues involved (indeed, courts and commentators have branded the efficiencies defense an 'intractable subject for litigation', 'inherently difficult' and 'easier to assert than to prove'). Following the standards set forth in Department of Justice/FTC Horizontal Merger Guidelines, most courts have found efficiencies claims lacking for failing to establish that the claimed savings were 'merger specific' (i.e., that the merger was necessary to achieve the efficiencies) or that they were verifiable, likely to occur and not 'speculative' (Department of Justice/FTC Merger Guidelines § 4.0). Two cases held that defendants must demonstrate that efficiency benefits will be passed on to consumers. Although several courts have cited efficiencies as additional reasons for approving the merger, they have done so as part of the overall balancing of the merger's likely effects and probability of its substantially lessening competition.

Courts have almost uniformly defined the product market in hospital merger cases as a grouping of acute care inpatient services offered by non-government hospitals. This approach recognizes that patients consume a variety of related products and services in hospital stays. A person admitted for surgery, for example, would typically need laboratory and diagnostic services, 24-hour nursing care, use of surgical facilities, consumable products and biologicals and so on. The prevailing approach goes further and also groups unrelated services offered by the hospital, such as neo-natal care, general surgery, vascular surgery, etc. as a distinct relevant product market. This analysis follows the 'cluster market' theory adopted in banking and other markets in which demand-side transaction cost savings dictate consumer preferences for one-stop shopping. It is generally appropriate in hospital markets because managed care entities usually seek to purchase a full complement of primary and secondary inpatient services from each hospital (Furrow 2000 vol 2, 223–225). This analysis also explains why certain services such as complex 'tertiary care' (e.g., organ transplants) and other specialty services (e.g., in-patient psychiatric care), are not included in the product market definition in most merger cases. Managed care buyers are likely to 'carve out' such services and contract separately for them with hospitals specializing in such services.

Here again, however, it may be noted that changing market conditions may alter the contours of product market definitions in the future. As services move to outpatient settings such as physician offices or stand-alone surgi-centers they may no longer be included in the 'inpatient acute care market' and a broader market will be appropriate for those services. In addition, the recent development of inpatient specialty hospitals (e.g., heart hospitals that perform heart surgeries and other procedures on an inpatient basis, but do not offer other services in the conventional cluster market) suggests that the cluster market concept may not hold for these services where state regulation permits them to operate. In markets where such hospitals have flourished, payers are increasingly willing to carve out segments of the inpatient care market and contract with specialty providers for them.

THE TIDE TURNS: HOSPITAL MERGER ANALYSIS IN THE 1990s

Following the initial series of successful merger challenges described above, the tide turned rather abruptly, with the government losing all seven cases litigated in federal court since 1995 (*see* Table 7.1). By some accounts, these decisions emboldened others to undertake highly concentrative mergers and chilled the willingness of government enforcers to pursue a vigorous merger enforcement agenda. In addition, recent studies have concluded that increasing concentration among acute care hospitals has led to price increases without offsetting benefits in quality, efficiency or charity care (*see generally* Cuellar and Gertler 2005; Strunk 2001). A close examination of the courts' reasoning in these cases reveals a tendency to neglect the subtleties of health care markets and to apply ill-fitting 'Chicago School' principles to circumstances that require more nuanced analysis. This chapter will first consider several doctrines that have been sharply disputed in these cases and will next examine some of the issues underlying those disputes.

Failure to prove the relevant geographic market alleged in the complaint has been a decisive or important factor in five of the seven government defeats in litigation. Accepting defendants' contention that a sufficient number of patients may switch to more distant hospitals in the event of a 'small but significant increase in price,' several courts have implicitly drawn markets as large as 70–100 miles – thereby including more distant hospitals in the relevant market so as to obviate competitive concerns with the mergers under examination. Several courts have been persuaded by the fact that a minority of inhabitants of the local market alleged by the government were willing to travel outside the area and that no significant physical or other obstacles impeded travel. These decisions also tended to downplay testimony of market participants, including insurers and employers, who had supported the government's contention that the hospital market was local and that insureds would not respond to price changes by traveling to more distant hospitals.

There are empirical and intuitive reasons to question these results and the analytic approach of the courts in these cases. Most observers and a number of courts agree that patients strongly prefer local hospitals for primary and secondary inpatient care. Physician staff privilege patterns, managed care contracting practices and, in some cases, state regulations reinforce this preference. Empirical studies of distances actually traveled confirm that 'migration' for hospital care is geographically narrow across the entire range of payers (*see generally* Mobley and Frech 2000). This data suggests that managed care does not significantly impact the extent of the geographic market for hospital care. Hence, there has been little observed 'steering' of insureds to distant hospitals. Likewise, simulations and empirical studies suggest that most patients strongly prefer local hospitals and that the willingness of a few to travel greater distances does not reflect the likely demand responses to increased prices post merger. Finally, a key analytic tool, 'critical loss analysis', has been misapplied in some decisions (*see generally* Langenfeld and Li 2001; Frech *et al.* 2004).

The courts' erroneous reasoning in these cases can be traced to a series of mistakes, all stemming from a tendency to apply simplifying economic models to markets that do not fit the mold. A principal flaw in the case law rests with judges' tendency to ignore the highly idiosyncratic nature of decision making by health care consumers. For example, courts have accepted economic testimony that the mere presence of some patients on the fringe of the market, willing to travel to more distant locales for non-emergency hospital services, suggests the willingness of others to do so in response to higher prices. This approach ignores the fact that a myriad of factors other than price – i.e., personal, logistical and other considerations – shape purchasing decisions for highly differentiated services. Ignoring the differentiated demand for hospital services, courts have been susceptible to what has been called the 'silent majority fallacy' – the assumption that the willingness of some to travel greater distances for routine services implies that others will respond similarly in the event of increased prices (*see generally* Capps *et al.* 2001).

A second flaw in the courts' approach to geographic markets is a propensity to overlook the importance of agency relationships in determining consumers' responses. For example, in evaluating consumer demand, courts have failed to appreciate that the selection of hospitals occurs in two distinct phases. First, hospitals vie for inclusion in networks selected for beneficiaries by MCOs and employers. Next, hospitals also compete at a second stage for the business of insured persons who choose among hospitals both in and out of network. Patients' migration patterns might be very different at each of these two stages. Economic analysis demonstrates that anticompetitive effects may be realized at either stage, even though considerable migration might occur across tentative market boundaries (*see generally* Vistnes 2000).

Finally, many of the decided cases fail to take into account that hospital services are highly differentiated. For example, buyers' perceptions of qualitative differences among hospitals and of certain hospitals that occupy a special niche position (such as those affiliated with teaching institutions) may change the competitive dynamic in a given market. Consequently, some hospitals may constitute a separate market or be able to exercise 'unilateral' market power despite the presence of numerous less sophisticated or prestigious rivals. However, the single litigated case in which a plaintiff attempted to demonstrate a market for 'anchor hospitals' (those which managed care hospitals deemed essential to successfully market their networks) was unsuccessful. Perhaps gun shy from this defeat and failures in more conventional cases, the government did not assay a second case based on unilateral effects analysis in the hospital market until its challenge to a consummated merger in Evanston, Illinois in 2004.

Controversy also surrounds court decisions rejecting challenges to hospital mergers on grounds other than the market definition issue. In a widely noted case, *FTC v. Butterworth Health Corp.* (1996), a federal district court invoked the nonprofit status of the merging hospitals and their voluntary commitments to restrain future pricing to approve a merger creating a monopoly in acute care hospital services in Grand Rapids, Michigan. The court found that after the merger, the merged entity would control up to 65 per cent of the relevant markets, that new entry was highly unlikely due to regulatory and minimum efficient scale constraints and that the vigorous bargaining with managed care that marked the market before the merger would be likely to diminish. Supported by evidence from employers, third-party payers and the parties' own concession that they sought to 'level the managed care organization playing field' by reducing certain discounts, the link to future exercise of market power could not have been stronger. Indeed, the court conceded that there was 'no question but that . . . the merged entity would have substantial market power' (*Federal Trade Commission v. Butterworth Health Corp.*, 946 F.Supp. 1285, 1302 (W.D. Mich. 1996)).

Despite prior case law to the contrary, the court relied on limited economic evidence and expert testimony that not-for-profit hospitals operate differently in highly concentrated markets than do profit-maximizing firms. The court went on to find that the defendants had successfully rebutted both the FTC's prima facie case and the additional evidence of likely harm. Several factors other than nonprofit status contributed to the conclusion that the proposed merger was not likely to cause anticompetitive effects. These factors included the governance structure of the hospital, a 'community commitment' undertaken by the merged entity to freeze prices and profit margins for a specified period and to provide certain amounts of charity care, and efficiencies resulting from the merger. Unfortunately, the court did not explain what weight it accorded to each consideration or state whether one would be sufficient to remove the transaction from condemnation under merger law. While this precedent does not stand for the proposition that nonprofit status by itself will immunize hospital mergers or even suffice to rebut a presumptive showing of illegality (the court inserted a caveat that its conclusions regarding the nonprofit status of hospitals were 'not a dispositive consideration'), the practical effect of the opinion should not be underestimated. It probably echoes judicial sentiment that, holding everything else constant, nonprofit hospitals are less likely to exercise market power than their for-profit counterparts and that nonprofit status should be accorded some weight in the mix of considerations. Indeed, the FTC/Department of Justice hearings and report on competition in health care markets took great pains to dispute the empirical basis for the *Butterworth* court's findings (*see generally* FTC/DOJ Report 2004; Greaney 2006).

Perhaps responding to Judge Posner's 'lament', the *Butterworth* court's decision relied on empirical support on the question of nonprofits' competitive role in health care. The court's finding on this issue cited two studies prepared by William Lynk, one published in the Journal of Law and Economics examining the post-merger pricing behavior of California hospitals that acquired significant market shares by their mergers (*see* Lynk 1995); and a 'replication' of that study using data on Michigan hospitals prepared by Dr. Lynk for the Butterworth-Blodgett litigation. The court deemed the reports' finding that 'on balance increased nonprofit market share is associated with lower, not higher, prices', to provide 'material' support for defendant's claim that the merger would not result in a lessening of competition. (*Butterworth* 1996, p. 1297). Closely linked in the analysis was the court's assessment of the governance structure of the merged entity. Relying on a rather rudimental institutional economics assessment, it ventured the view that the hospital was also likely to operate benignly because of its community-based governance. Noting that the merged hospital would be 'comprised of community business leaders who have a direct stake in maintaining high quality, low cost hospital services', it apparently accepted a claim based largely on a theoretical argument by Dr. Lynk that, as seen in consumer cooperatives, local board membership would help check any price-elevating tendencies attributable to the hospitals' dominant market position (*see generally* Lynk 1994). As additional support for this proposition, the court relied on the subjective intentions of the parties, noting that community representatives testified 'convincingly' that the merger was motivated 'by a common desire to lower health care costs and improve the quality of care' (*Butterworth* 1996, p. 1298).

Another persuasive factor was a 'Community Commitment' made by the merging hospitals, pledging to freeze prices and margins while maintaining certain levels of charity care. For the court, this undertaking to 'refrain from exercising market power in ways injurious to the consuming public' served both to 'corroborate other evidence that nonprofit hospitals may be treated differently under the antitrust laws' and to 'undermine the predictive value of the FTC's prima facie case' (*Butterworth* 1996, p. 1296). Finally, the court interpreted the peculiarities of health care financing to militate in favor of deference to health care providers. It disparaged managed care as a vehicle for 'cost shifting' from one set of consumers to another and thus of dubious benefit, concluding: 'Viewing the managed care discounts in light of their impact on the welfare of consumers as a whole exposes them as illusory. Such selective price advantages are hardly the sort of benefit the antitrust laws are designed to protect' (*Butterworth* 1996, p. 1299). In a startling reversal of the way most health economists viewed the market, the merger's propensity 'to stem the growing influence of managed care organizations' and 'level the playing field' was seen as *promoting* consumer welfare by curbing the undesirable side effects of an unchecked marketplace. Beyond opening itself to the problems associated with rate regulation inherent in this approach, the court was apparently oblivious to the dynamics of markets in which differential pricing is the mechanism by which price is ratcheted down (*see generally* Greaney 1997, 218; Jacobs 1998).

Academic criticisms of the *Butterworth* decision have been manifold: many finding its evaluations of the empirical record before it suspect, questioning its normative biases, rejecting its assumptions about nonprofit corporate governance and doubting the wisdom and efficacy of its remedies (Blumstein 1998; Greaney 1997; Jacobs 1998). Indeed, several studies, including one replicating the empirical record, have disputed Dr. Lynk's conclusions (Dranove and Ludwig 1999; Keeler *et al.* 1999). The practical significance of the case should not be overstated, however. The government's failure to aggressively challenge consolidation in the health care industry is primarily the product of the enormous obstacles created by court decisions on geographic market issues. At most, *Butterworth* and the several other opinions expressing reluctance to find nonprofits susceptible to exercising market power may have contributed at the margin to the government's passivity in health care (Greaney 2006).

The *Butterworth* case is one of several resulting in a quasi-regulatory approach to resolving antitrust disputes. The presence of a 'community commitment' enforced by judicial decree binding the merged hospitals to freeze their list prices and managed care rates at pre-merger levels and to limit their profit margins was central to the court's approval of the merger.

Several state Attorneys General have entered into settlements of cases challenging hospital mergers on similar terms, accepting price concessions as well as commitments to offer specified amounts of charity care or other community benefits in return for permitting the merger to go forward. (Greaney 2002, 188.) This approach can be questioned on several grounds. First, it substitutes a crude form of rate regulation for competition, relying on a necessarily slim evidentiary record about future market conditions and entrusting the decision to a judiciary lacking expertise in the health care industry or in rate setting. Moreover, the process is likely to be deficient inasmuch as it is extraordinarily difficult to control nonprice adjustments such as changes in inputs and quality and cost shifting to governmental payers and because no ongoing administrative supervision is provided.

Another source of difficulty in the case law involving hospital mergers was the failure to account for the heterogeneity of hospitals in many markets. The most important judicial decision involving this issue, the *Long Island Jewish Medical Center* (LIJ) case, involved the merger of two prestigious hospitals offering sophisticated services (North Shore Hospital and LIJ Medical Center) that the Department of Justice claimed would eliminate competition to serve as 'anchor hospitals in a managed care plan's network'. As 'anchor hospitals', the merged entities allegedly possessed characteristics that distinguished them from all others in the area and made each the next-best substitute for the other. Under the government's theory, the hospitals were distinguishable by virtue of 'their premier reputations, their comparably full range of high-quality services, and their strategic location for serving Queens and Nassau counties'. In addition on the demand side, consumers 'strongly desire[d] the up-front option to be able to use these two premier hospitals' (*United States v. Long Island Jewish Med. Ctr.*, No. 97-3412 (E.D. N.Y. 1997) (Complaint, ¶ 2)). Together, these attributes made the two hospitals essential to managed care buyers and hence could be seen as constituting either a separate product market or could imply that the merger could give rise to adverse consequences under a 'unilateral effects' theory.

First, the district court rather mechanically rejected the anchor hospital concept as inconsistent with precedent in hospital merger cases. The court apparently concluded that case precedent precluded alternative market definitions, such as 'general acute patient service'. The court held in the alternative that the government had failed to establish that the services offered by the merging hospitals were unique. This holding is of dubious relevance inasmuch as it does not address the core contention that managed care companies and their insureds viewed the two hospitals as distinct from others due to their excellence, sophistication and reputation. These perceptions arguably created an 'option demand' for those hospitals by consumers who had to pre-commit to networks when purchasing health insurance (*see generally* Vistnes 2000.) Indeed, the perceptions of market participants imbued the merging hospitals with special attributes that were unduplicated, thus making them indispensable to managed care entities. As such, separate treatment for product market purposes might have been appropriate. In addition, the court was unmoved by exceptionally strong evidence of the parties' own perceptions and intent. The LIJ case may have had an important impact on the trajectory of government merger enforcement. Perhaps chilling government challenges to mergers involving unilateral effects, the case may have deterred enforcement that would have explained the significance of a differentiated product market for hospital care.

Responding to its string of defeats in litigation and seeking to 'reinvigorate the Commission's hospital merger program' by challenging 'consummated transactions that might have resulted in anticompetitive price increases', the FTC undertook in 2002 a 'retrospective review' of completed hospital mergers. It subsequently filed an administrative complaint challenging an acquisition that had occurred two years earlier by Evanston Northwestern Healthcare Corporation of Highland Park Hospital. In July 2007, some seven years after the merger had been consummated, the FTC concluded that the acquisition violated Section 7 of the Clayton Act. In a highly unusual and controversial step, the Commission declined to order divestiture and required instead that ENH establish two separate and independent negotiating teams to allow managed care organizations to negotiate separately with the newly acquired hospital on the one hand and ENH's two other hospitals (*In the Matter of Evanston Northwestern Healthcare Corporation* (2007)).

The case is unusual and significant in several respects. An important feature of the case is that it was the first since the *Long Island Jewish Medical Center* to deal squarely with unilateral effects in a market of differentiated products. Central to the Commission's conclusion that the merger violated the Clayton Act were its findings that it actually resulted in higher prices in the market. The record, the Commission found:

> shows that senior officials at Evanston and Highland Park anticipated that the merger would give them greater leverage to raise prices, that the merged firm did in fact raise its prices immediately and substantially after completion of the transaction, and that the same senior officials attributed the price increases in part to increased bargaining leverage produced by the merger.

Significantly, the FTC concluded that the econometric analyses performed by the parties – including that of ENH's own economic expert – demonstrated unequivocally that prices to managed care organizations had risen substantially more than other hospitals' prices post-merger, and that it was very unlikely that these increases resulted from causes other than the merged entity's ability to exercise its market power. These price increases not only established anticompetitive effects, but they were also used by the Commission to define the relevant geographic market, because they demonstrated that hospitals in other geographic areas did not constrain price increases. This evidence was backed up by a number of pre-merger documents of the merging parties in which ENH and Highland Park officials indicated that they anticipated that the merger would give them greater leverage to raise prices. For example, Evanston board minutes revealed that hospital executives viewed the merger as a chance to '[i]ncrease our leverage, limited as it might be, with the managed care players and help our negotiating posture'.

Merely showing post-merger price increases is not in itself sufficient to establish that those increases were causally related to enhanced market power. The FTC thus undertook to examine and reject alternative explanations advanced by ENH to explain the sharp post-merger price increases. For example, in response to ENH contention that its significant post-merger improvements at Highland Park Hospital partly explained its ability to raise prices to payers, the Commission found that the vast majority of these quality improvements could have been made without the merger and that, in many cases, Highland Park already had plans in place pre-merger to make such improvements. Notably, the decision was also unsympathetic to respondents' attempts to bring quality improvements into the competitive calculus, finding that the record did not support the contention that price increases reflected increased demand generated by enhanced quality. Finally, the opinion dismissed the ENH's 'learning about demand' argument which held that its post-merger price increases for Evanston Hospital were caused by ENH obtaining information about Highland Park's historical pricing rather than by the exercise of market power.

The Evanston decision is perhaps most notable for several things the FTC elected *not* to do. The decision avoided the issue raised by Count II of the complaint, which alleged that the proof of actual anticompetitive effects obviated the need to define a relevant product and geographic market under Section 7. While recognizing that 'market definition is not an end in itself but rather an indirect means to assist in determining the presence or the likelihood of the exercise of market power', the Commission nevertheless found it unnecessary to decide the issue in this case in light of its findings of liability on traditional grounds. Second, the Commission declined to rely on patient flow data in determining the contours of the geographic market. It noted the severe theoretical problems in applying tests to service industries and concluded 'we should view patient flow data with a high degree of caution . . . and at best, we should use it as one potentially very rough benchmark in the context of evaluating other types of evidence'. Finally in choosing to rely on the highly unusual remedy of ordering separate negotiating units, the Commission may have opened itself to considerable criticism. It is far from clear, for example, how this remedy will restore the benefits of competition when the parties are allowed to fully integrate their operations and planning in all respects except contracting with payers. In short, one must ask in the context of a fully consummated merger, 'what is left to negotiate?' In addition, supervising the arrangements necessary to ensure meaningful separation between the bargaining units may enmesh the Commission in cumbersome and detailed regulatory oversight of a kind antitrust authorities usually abhor.

AN ANALYTICAL PERSPECTIVE ON THE HOSPITAL MERGER CASES

The preceding discussion reveals that hospital merger law enforcement has received a mixed reception in the courts and suggests that judicial appraisals have not been adequately attuned to the unique economics of health care markets. This section addresses several questions arising out of this experience: What role has antitrust law played in promoting competition and has that involvement helped consumers? What explains the turnabout in the cases addressing hospital mergers? What does the future hold for antitrust analyses of hospital mergers?

Antitrust has long been a powerful instrument for competitive reform in health care. By helping to remove barriers to competition such as professional ethical guidelines and control over hospitals and payment systems, the law set the stage for the rapid rise in competitive financing and delivery systems that evolved in the 1980s. Merger enforcement played an important role in securing the conditions necessary for the development of competition by preserving market structures conducive to competitive bidding and negotiation by payers. Somewhat paradoxically, the litigated cases that initially set limits on horizontal mergers did so by relying on the prospect for future competitive interactions, finding mergers violated the Clayton Act even though there was scant price competition at the time and the risks of collusion were at best speculative. However, relying on Section 7's prospective orientation and the need to prevent structural impediments to increasing price rivalry, early court decisions credited nonprice competition in the market and did not demand rigorous proof that collusive conduct was likely to occur. These decisions helped foster development of competitive conditions for future bargaining between hospitals and managed care entities.

The available economic evidence supports the thesis that application of antitrust merger principles in the hospital context benefited consumers. Empirical studies of the relationship between concentration and performance (measured by prices, margins and costs) since competition took hold in the late 1980s are consistent with the conventional structure-conduct-performance paradigm (*see generally* Dranove and Satterthwaite 2000; FTC/DOJ Report 2004). Further, some analysts assert that the concentration in hospital markets resulting from lax merger enforcement in the 1990s is one cause of the steep escalation of health care costs in recent years (*see generally* Cuellar and Gertler 2005, Strunk 2001.)

The government's sharp reversal of fortune in court can be traced to a number of factors. From an economic standpoint, the cases failed to take into account the myriad of market imperfections that make interpreting facts and applying conventional economic principles a complex undertaking. Agency relationships pervade the health care marketplace and accurate assessments of 'buyer' preferences for particular hospitals or their responses to potential price hikes must take into account those relationships. A number of evaluations of these cases point to failures to include careful assessments of agency, product differentiation and buyer heterogeneity in reaching findings regarding geographic and product markets for hospital services (*see generally* Greaney 2004; Vistnes 2000; Capps *et al.* 2001). From a doctrinal perspective, one may discern in these decisions a tendency among the courts to apply Chicago School assumptions uncritically in health care markets with results that are predictably unsatisfactory given the myriad of market imperfections that beset health care markets (*see generally* Greaney 2004).

Another explanation for the outcomes in the hospital merger cases is that courts may have implicitly internalized the skepticism about health care markets characterized in the popular press as a 'managed care backlash'. Betraying a strong undercurrent of suspicion about the role of managed care and perhaps competition in general in health care markets, one federal circuit court of appeals decision quoted Judge Richard Posner's hyperbolic dictum that 'the HMO's incentive is to keep you healthy if it can but if you get very sick, and are unlikely to recover to a healthy state involving few medical expenses, to let you die as quickly and cheaply as possible' (*Federal Trade Commission v. Tenet Health Care Corp.*, 186 F.3d 1045, 1054 (8th Cir. 1999)). Other courts have gone further, explicitly downplaying testimony from managed care buyers or suggesting that competition resulting from rivalry among such entities was not in consumers' interest. Further, the *Butterworth* court and some state Attorneys General have turned to explicitly regulatory mechanisms to control monopoly power, adopting judicial decrees fixing price and profit levels in lieu of enjoining mergers that create anticompetitively structured markets.

What can one predict regarding antitrust appraisals of hospital mergers in the current era of consumer directed health care? With a relatively toothless managed care sector having far less bargaining leverage vis-à-vis providers, and capitation models of payment in sharp decline, courts may be even more reluctant to assume that a hospital merger will harm consumers. At the same time, the consumer directed approach, which leaves price/quality judgements to patients (who will be asked to pay out of pocket for treatments at more expensive hospitals), also depends on the existence of competitive hospitals and, therefore, competitive norms may still prevail. While a careful economic appraisal may question whether consumers, unaided by third-party intermediaries, can make informed, welfare-enhancing choices, it is unlikely that antitrust courts will second-guess the wisdom of the prevailing marketplace. Hence, one may venture the prediction that antitrust standards will remain relatively oblivious to the changing managed care marketplace when evaluating hospital mergers.

CONCLUSION

Some years ago, in an article entitled, 'Night Landings on an Aircraft Carrier', I suggested that appraisals of hospital mergers were especially difficulty because, 'like pilots landing at night aboard an aircraft carrier, courts are aiming for a target that is small, shifting and poorly illuminated' (Greaney 1997). Today it appears that a number of federal judges have missed their mark, though perhaps understandably so, given the task at hand. With health care markets moving into markets in which third-party payers are disabled from mitigating market imperfections, one cannot confidently predict that competitive markets will improve consumer welfare. However, in all likelihood, antitrust law will muddle along, choosing to take the economic market as it finds it.

NOTES

1. Sources: Vol. 2, Miles, Health Care & Antitrust Law, Furrow 2000 at §12–13 and complaints and consent decrees. Data in table is based on market allegations contained in government's complaints. The accompanying footnotes describe courts' holdings on markets alleged by the government. Where no judicial opinion resulted, the market alleged in the government's complaint is provided.
2. FTC Docket No. 9315, 2007 WL 2286195 (August 6, 2007), *available at* http://www. ftc.gov/os/adjpro/d9315/index.shtm.
3. *130 F. Supp 2d 1109 (N.D. Cal 2001)*. Product market: acute inpatient care hospital services. Geographic market: court found the market extended beyond the State's alleged 'Inner East [Oakland] Bay' area to include at least San Francisco and eastern portions

of Oakland. The market share of merging parties under the alleged geographic market is found in Langenfeld and Li, note 59, at 329.

4. 17 F. Supp. 2d 937, 946 (E.D. Mo. 1998); rev'd 186 F.3d 1045, 1052-54 (8th Cir. 1999). Product market: primary and secondary inpatient hospital care services. Geographic market: 65 mile radius from location of merging hospitals plus a large hospital in St. Louis, approximately 145 miles away.
5. 983 F. Supp. 121, 137 (E.D. N.Y. 1997). Product market: general acute care inpatient hospital services. Geographic market: one relevant market that included hospitals in that county as well as hospitals in two other Long Island counties and Manhattan.
6. 946 F. Supp. 1285, 1294 (W.D. Mich. 1996). Product market: all general acute care inpatient hospital services and primary care inpatient hospital services. Geographic market: greater Kent County, including approximately 106 zip code areas and nine hospitals.
7. 911 F. Supp. 1213, 1222 (W.D. Mo. 1995). Product market: acute care inpatient hospital services. Geographic market: hospitals in a 13-county area.
8. 902 F. Supp. 968 (N.D. Iowa 1995) (vacated as moot). Product market: acute care inpatient services. Geographic market: the court did not make a specific finding of geographic market, but held the geographic market was neither county in which hospitals were located and half-circle within 15-mile radius extending from county's edge, nor city in which hospitals were located. The court indicated that the market included hospitals between 70 and 100 miles from the merging hospitals.
9. 120 F.T.C. 949, 952 (1995). Product market: psychiatric hospital services. Geographic market: tri-city area of south-central Virginia.
10. 38 F.3d 1184, 1187 (11th Cir. 1994). Product market: acute care inpatient hospital services. Geographic market: county where hospital was located.
11. 118 F.T.C. 382, 386 (1994). Product market: acute care inpatient hospital services. Geographic market: Santa Cruz county area.
12. No. 94-748-CIV-T-23E (M.D. Fla. Filed May 5, 1994) (declaration of Gregory S. Vistnes, Ph.D., Economist, Antitrust Division, May 12, 1994). No findings as to product or geographic markets.
13. 938 F.2d 1206, 1211 & n.12 (11th Cir. 1991). Product market: acute care inpatient hospital services. Geographic market: two counties in Georgia and one in South Carolina.
14. 117 F.T.C. 224, 306 (1989) (*Owen and Yao, Comm'rs*, concurring). Product market: acute care inpatient hospital services. Geographic market: southeastern Mendocino/western Lake County area, the southeastern Mendocino County area, and/or portions of these areas.
15. 113 F.T.C. 224, 285, 288 (1990). Product market: general acute care hospital services. Geographic market: Berks County, Pennsylvania.
16. 717 F. Supp. 1251, 1280 (N.D. Ill. 1989). Product market: acute care inpatient hospital services. Geographic market: one entire county, almost all of another and several zip code zones in four others.
17. 707 F. Supp. 840, 848 (W.D. Va. 1989). Product market: acute care inpatient hospital services. Geographic market: all counties and cities from which the acquiring hospital drew at least 100 patients a year, which included 16 counties and three cities in Virginia and three counties in West Virginia.
18. 106 F.T.C. 298, 301, 303 (1985). Product market: psychiatric services. Geographic market: Norfolk-Virginia Beach-Newport News, Virginia Metropolitan Statistical Area.
19. Ibid. Product market: general acute care hospital services. Geographic market: Midland/Odessa area in Texas.
20. No. F-83-481-EDP (E.D. Cal. filed Oct. 31, 1983) (complaint). No findings as to product or geographic markets.
21. 104 F.T.C. 1, 201 (1984). Product market: general acute care hospital services. Geographic market: city and county where merging hospitals were located (San Luis Obispo County and the City of San Luis Obispo).

22. Ibid. Product market: general acute care hospital services. Geographic market: City of San Luis Obispo.
23. 106 F.T.C. 298, 301, 303 (1985). Product market: psychiatric services. Geographic market: Norfolk-Virginia Beach-Newport News, Virginia Metropolitan Statistical Area.
24. Ibid. Product market: general acute care hospital services. Geographic market: Midland/Odessa area in Texas.
25. 1980–81 Trade Cas. (CCH) 63, 721, 77, 853 (E.D. La. 1980). Product market: in-patient psychiatric care. Geographic market: hospitals in New Orleans and its surrounding areas.

REFERENCES

Blumstein, James F. (1998), 'The Application of Antitrust Doctrine to the Healthcare Industry: the interweaving of empirical and normative issues', Indiana Law Review 31 (1), 91–117.

Brooks, J. M., A. Dor, and H.S. Wong (1997), 'Hospital-Insurer Bargaining: an empirical investigation of appendectomy pricing,' Journal of Health Economics, 16 (4), 417–434.

Capps, C. et al. (2001), 'The Silent Majority Fallacy of the Elzinga-Hogarty Criteria: a critique and new approach to analyzing hospital mergers,' National Bureau of Economic Research 8216.

Connor, R., R.D. Feldman, and B.E. Dowd (1998), 'The Effects of Market Concentration and Horizontal Mergers on Hospital Costs and Prices', International Journal of the Economics of Business, 5 (2), 159–180.

Cuellar, Allison Evan and Paul J. Gertler (2005), 'How the Expansion of Hospital Systems Has Affected Consumers', Health Affairs, 24 (1), 213–219.

Danger, Kenneth and H.E. Frech (2001), 'Critical Thinking About "Critical Loss" in Antitrust', Antitrust Bulletin, 46 (2), 339–355.

Dranove, David and R. Ludwig (1999), 'Competition and Pricing by Nonprofit Hospitals: a reassessment of Lynk's analysis', Journal of Health Economics, 18 (1), 87–98.

Dranove, David, M. Shanley, and W. White (1993), 'Price and Concentration in Hospital Markets: the switch from patient driven to payer driven competition', Journal of Law and Economics 36 (1), 179–204.

Dranove, D. and M.A. Satterthwaite (2000), 'The Industrial Organization of Health Care Markets', in Anthony J. Culyer and Joseph P. Newhouse (eds), The Handbook of Health Economics 1B, 1093–1139.

Federal Trade Commission and United States Department of Justice (2004), Improving Health Care: A Dose of Competition.

Frech, H.E., James Langenfeld and R. Forrest McCluer (2004), 'Elzinga-Hogarty Tests and Alternative Approaches for Market Share Calculations in Hospital Markets', Antitrust Law Journal, 71 (3), 921–947.

Furrow, Barry R., Thomas L. Greaney, Sandra H. Hohnson, Timothy S. Jost, and Robert L. Schwartz (2000), Health Law, vol 2, St. Paul, Minn.: West Group.

Gift, T.L., R. Arnould, and L. Debrook (2002), 'Is Healthy Competition Healthy? New Evidence on the Impact of Hospital Consolidation', Inquiry (Spring), 45–55.

Greaney, Thomas (2002), 'Whither antitrust? The uncertain future of antitrust in health care', *Health Affairs*, 21 (March/April), 185–201.

Greaney, Thomas (1997), 'Night Landings on an Aircraft Carrier: Hospital Mergers and Antitrust Law', American Journal of Law & Medicine, 23 (2), 191–220.

Greaney, Thomas L. (2004), 'Chicago's Procrustean Bed: Applying Antitrust Law in Health Care', Antitrust Law Journal, 71 (3), 857–920.

Greaney, Thomas L. (2006) 'Antitrust and Hospitals Mergers: Does the Nonprofit Form Affect the Competitive Substance?', Journal of Health Politics, Policy & Law 31, 511–535.

Harshbarger, Laura J. (1996), 'ERISA Preemption Meets the Age of Managed Care: Toward a Comprehensive Social Policy', Syracuse Law Review, 47 (1), 191–224.

Havighurst, Clark C. (2000), 'The Backlash Against Managed Care: Hard Politics Makes Bad Policy', Indiana Law Review, 34 (2), 395–417.

Jacobs, Michael S. (1998), 'Presumptions, Damn Presumptions and Economic Theory: the Role of Empirical Evidence in Hospital Merger Analysis', Indiana Law Review, 31 (1), 125–142.

Keeler, E., G. Melnick, and J. Zwanziger (1999), 'The Changing Effects of Competition on Non-Profit and For-Profit Hospital Pricing Behavior', Journal of Health Economics, 18 (1), 69–86.

Kopit, William G. (1999), 'Can the Nonprofit Status of the Merging Facilities Change the Proper Analysis of a Hospital Merger Under the Antitrust Laws?', in Antitrust in the Healthcare Field, American Health Lawyers Association.

Langenfeld, James and Wenqing Li (2001), 'Critical Loss in Evaluating Mergers', Antitrust Bulletin, 46 (2), 299–337.

Lynk, William J. (1995), 'Nonprofit Hospital Mergers and the Exercise of Market Power', Journal of Law and Economics, 38 (2), 437–461.

Lynk, William J. (1994), 'Property Rights and the Presumptions of Merger Analysis', Antitrust Bulletin, 39 (2), 363–383.

Melnick, G.A., E. Keeler, and J. Zwanziger (1999), 'Market Power and Hospital Pricing: Are Nonprofits Different?', Health Affairs, 18 (3), 167–173.

Mayo, Thomas Wm. (2000), 'The First Fifty Years: Health Law's Greatest Hit', Syracuse Law Review, 50 (4), 1261–1277.

Mobley, Lee R. and H.E. Frech (2000), 'Managed Care, Distance Traveled, and Hospital Market Definition', Inquiry, 37 (1), 91–107.

Pauly, Mark and Michael Redisch (1973), 'The Not-For Profit Hospital as Physicians' Cooperative', American Economic Review, 63 (1), 87–99.

Sloan, F.A. (2000), 'Not-For-Profit Ownership and Hospital Behavior', in Anthony J. Culyer and Joseph P. Newhouse (eds.), The Handbook of Health Economics 1B, 1140–74.

Strunk, Bradley C., Paul B. Ginsburg and John R. Gabel (2002), 'Tracking health care costs: growth accelerates again in 2001', Health Affairs, http://content.healthaffairs.org/cgi/reprint/25/3/w141.

Vistnes, Gregory (2000), 'Hospitals, Mergers, and Two-Stage Competition', Antitrust Law Journal, 67 (3), 671–692.

United States Department of Justice and Federal Trade Commission (1992), Horizontal Merger Guidelines.

Cases

In Re Evanston Northwestern Healthcare Corp., FTC Docket No. 9315, 2007 WL 2286195 (August 6, 2007), *available at* http://www.ftc.gov/os/adjpro/d9315/index.shtm.

FTC v. Butterworth Health Corp., 946 F.Supp. 1285 (W.D. Mich. 1996).
Hospital Corporation of America v. FTC, 807 F.2d 1381 (7th Cir. 1986).
United States v. Rockford Memorial Corp., 898 F.2d 1278 (7th Cir. 1990).
United States v. Long Island Jewish Med. Ctr., 983 F.Supp.121 (E.D. N.Y. 1997).

8. Mergers and competition policy in the banking industry

Bernard Shull

INTRODUCTION

The transformation of commercial banking in the United States over the last 25 years has been characterized by a merger movement of immense proportions. These mergers have substantially reduced the number of independent institutions, produced a handful of very large banking firms that operate in markets throughout the country (and the world) and have increased national (aggregate) concentration substantially. It has involved bank entry into newly permissible financial and non-financial activities, and bank-like powers for other financial institutions. It has converted the old 'commercial banking industry' into what many now label 'the financial services industry'. The transformation has been generated by market developments, new legislation and revised regulation that have swept away long-existing restraints.

The next section briefly reviews the history of bank competition policy in the United States. The following section examines the legal and market changes that initiated new policies in the recent past. The subsequent sections examine policy implementation at the Federal banking agencies that has facilitated bank mergers and activity expansion, describe the size and scope of the resulting structural changes, review relevant information on the economic impact of the changes and present some proposals for further modifications in policy.

While uncertainty remains as to costs and benefits, there is little evidence that the structural changes that have developed to this point have created any net benefit. Further, the likely long-run outcome of the changes underway raises important questions independent of the issues typically raised in merger and activity expansion proposals. A full review of the policies that have facilitated mergers and activity expansion and induced the ongoing transformation is in order.

COMPETITION POLICY IN PERSPECTIVE[1]

Commercial banking was centuries old when the first commercial banks were established in this country (during and immediately following the Revolutionary War). The early banks received legislative grants of corporate charters and states foreclosed opportunities for others to enter the business by passing restraining laws that overrode the common law rights of individuals to issue notes that would circulate as currency. (Hurst, 1973, 152–153). Public policy did not envision free competitive markets for banking.

Even when procompetitive policies were adopted, e.g., through the establishment of 'free banking laws' in the late 1830s and thereafter, unique restraints on geographic and product expansion were sustained. In the decades following the Civil War and into the twentieth century, the numbers of small banks, encouraged by restrictions on branching, multiplied rapidly. In 1921, there existed close to 30 000. Influential legislators viewed unit (one-office) banking as a competitive ideal (*Changes in the Banking and Currency System of the United States* 1913, 13).

Banks were excepted from procompetitive policies established for industry in general. Court decisions indicating that 'money transactions' were not interstate commerce made the Sherman Act inapplicable. The only relevant section of the Clayton Act was Section 8 (imposing restraints on interlocking directorates) which the Federal Reserve Board (Board) reluctantly enforced based on the authority given it by Section 11 of the Clayton Act (Shull, 1996, 262ff).

A high rate of bank failure, particularly in the farm sector in the 1920s, and the massive failures of the early 1930s that accompanied the Great Depression, persuaded Congress to impose additional limitations on competition in banking. The Banking Act of 1933 included provisions that restricted entry by new charter (in the course of establishing provisions for deposit insurance) and set maximums on deposit rates of interest (a prohibition of interest on demand deposits and Regulation Q). The long-existing policy of separating banking from other forms of commercial enterprise was fortified in the name of safety and soundness by drawing a firm legislative line between commercial and investment banking (Glass-Steagall provisions of Banking Act of 1933). In addition to new laws and regulations, bank supervisors, aiming to curb bank runs and failures, urged banks in local areas to cooperate with one another rather than compete (Berle, 1949, 595). In general, all banks were viewed as 'too important to fail'. In merger cases, the principal aim of bank regulators was the elimination of floundering banks.

From the 1940s through the 1960s, bank failures dropped sharply, with no more than a handful occurring each year. How much of this reduction was due to anticompetitive policies, how much to federal deposit insurance and how much to a stable and growing economy supported by an anti-cyclical monetary and fiscal policies seemed, for a time, irrelevant.

In 1946, there were about 14 000 commercial banks in the United States, and a few multiple bank holding companies (such as Transamerica). They were largely unregulated and relatively unrestricted in their geographic reach and in the activities of their subsidiaries. Nationally-chartered banks could branch only to the extent state law allowed state chartered banks to branch. Consequently, branch banking was limited in about one-third of the states and prohibited in another third. Federal and state banking agencies, whose prior approval was required, did not evaluate mergers on the basis of their competitive effects. Their evaluations were largely confined to 'banking factors', including effects on management and the convenience and needs of communities (Shull, 1996, 265ff). Looking back in 1949, Adolph Berle observed that '[t]he Congress of the United States has determined to deal with banking in a manner different from other forms of "commerce"' (Berle, 1949, 590).

LEGISLATIVE AND MARKET CHANGES

The modification of anticompetitive banking policies began shortly after the end of World War II. Experience after the war suggested that the massive bank failures of the 1920s and 1930s were a unique phenomenon caused by factors other than excessive competition. Even so, bank failure, as a general matter, remained unacceptable and banks continued to be highly regulated and closely supervised firms. However, new legislation, the newly discerned applicability of the antitrust laws, the emergence of new competitors and fervor for deregulation produced new competition policy in banking.

HOLDING COMPANY ACQUISITIONS AND BANK MERGERS

The Bank Holding Company Act of 1956 focused on the activities of largely unregulated bank holding companies (Transamerica, being the model) that increased concentration by the acquisition of banks across state lines and that had combined commercial activities with banking. The Act required holding companies, defined as firms controlling two or more banks, to refrain from the acquisition of banks in states other than their home states, unless authorized by specific legislation in the other state

(Douglas Amendment). The Act also required holding companies to divest almost all their non-traditional banking business. It also modified the way in which holding company acquisitions were to be evaluated. For the first time, it required the Board, the sole Federal supervisor of holding companies, to consider not only 'banking factors' in reviewing acquisition proposals, but also 'the preservation of competition' (Sec. 3(c)).

The Bank Merger Act (passed in 1960) took a similar approach to the evaluation of bank mergers. In this case, prior approval authority was divided at the Federal level, in accordance with the regulatory status of the resulting bank, among the Office of the Comptroller of the Currency (OCC), the Board and the Federal Deposit Insurance Corporation (FDIC). In addition to assessing 'banking factors', these agencies, were to consider the 'effect of the transaction on competition'. Neither the Holding Company nor Merger acts, however, provided any instruction on how competitive effects were to be measured or weighed relative to other factors.

APPLICATION OF ANTITRUST LAWS TO BANKING

In *U.S. v. South-Eastern Underwriters Association* (1944) the Supreme Court held that insurance was 'in commerce' and, therefore, subject to the Sherman Act. This implied that commercial banking was also covered. The Supreme Court's decisions in *Philadelphia National Bank-Girard Trust* (1963) and *First National Bank & Trust of Lexington* (1963) made it clear that Section 7 of the Clayton Act applied to bank mergers, as did the Sherman Act.

In its *Philadelphia* decision, the Court established a framework for competitive evaluations. The geographic market was established as 'the area in which the seller operates and the purchaser can practicably turn for supplies', typically identified as the merging banks' 'service areas'. The product market was established as 'commercial banking', that is, 'the cluster of products . . . and services . . . denoted by the term commercial banking', excluding other financial institutions that competed in one or more of the product lines. A 'substantial lessening of competition' was defined in terms of levels and changes in market concentration resulting from a proposed bank merger. Amendments to the Merger and Holding Company acts in 1966 integrated the prior approval authority of the Federal banking agencies and the Justice Department's authority to sue under the antitrust laws.[2]

From the mid-1960s through the 1970s, the Federal banking agencies and notably the Board periodically denied merger proposals. Litigation clarified the scope and limits of the laws (Shull, 1996). By the mid-1970s, the reach of the new integrated approach had been delineated. Among other things, the courts made it more difficult for the federal banking agencies to deny mergers on the basis of adverse effects on potential competition. The courts also determined that it was not within the power of the agencies to deny mergers whose anticompetitive effects did not reach Section 7 standards.

EMERGENCE OF NEW COMPETITORS

The legal wall erected between commercial banks and other competitors began to erode in the post-war housing boom when savings and loans (S&Ls), an institution resuscitated by the federal government in the 1930s and unrestricted by deposit rate maximums, found it profitable to compete with commercial banks for deposits. Thereafter, in a period of rising interest rates and inflation, other relatively unregulated competitors for particular banking services emerged, including money market funds (for deposits), finance companies (for some kinds of loans) and, subsequently, savings institutions and credit unions (for both deposits and loans).

DEREGULATION

The unintended consequences of regulatory restrictions in a period of inflation and rising interest rates made a number of constraints on banking untenable. Therefore, they were substantially modified or eliminated in the 1980s and thereafter. 'Deregulation' not only rescinded the anticompetitive restrictions of the 1930s, but a number of those that were much older.

Passing of Depression-Borne Restrictions

Passage of the Depository Institutions Deregulation and Monetary Control Act of 1980 (DIDMCA) initiated a phase-out of deposit rate maximums. It also expanded the powers of savings institutions and credit unions, making them more comprehensive providers of financial services and, thereby, more competitive with commercial banks. Reinterpretation of regulations by the OCC (first attempted in the 1960s) and the other banking agencies softened the severe restrictions on new bank charters that had been established in the 1930s.

Relaxation of Older Restrictions

Commercial banks in the United States had long been restricted in the geographic area in which they could establish offices (both within states and across state lines) and also in the activities in which they could engage. Constraints on multiple-office banking began to erode in the 1980s as states began to change their laws. Some entered into interstate compacts, permitting reciprocal interstate holding company expansion.

The Riegle-Neal Interstate Banking and Branching Efficiency Act of 1994 established a national standard. It overrode the reciprocal banking provisions of 30 state laws and permitted bank holding companies to acquire banks in any state, to convert their banks to branches of interstate banks and to establish de novo or newly chartered interstate branches in accordance with state law.

Seeking profitable opportunities in new activities, such as insurance, securities, real estate brokerage, leasing, travel agencies and a variety of others, commercial banks had searched from the early 1960s for legal avenues that would permit entry. The one-bank holding company, exempted from regulation under the 1956 Act, provided a lawful avenue that was exploited by large banking organizations in the late 1960s. In 1970, Congress amended the Bank Holding Company Act to eliminate this exception and, simultaneously, authorized the Board to establish a list of permissible activities that were 'closely related to banking' and 'a proper incident thereto' (Section 4(c)(8)).

Beginning in the 1980s, the Board, the OCC and the FDIC all relaxed important restrictions. The Board permitted bank holding companies to engage in the securities business through so-called 'Section 20 subsidiaries'. The FDIC held that the Glass-Steagall Act did not apply to non-member insured banks and permitted less restrictive state law to prevail. The OCC permitted national banks to expand their insurance activities and, in doing so, was supported by Supreme Court decisions.[3] In 1994, the OCC proposed and in 1996 adopted a revised rule permitting national banks through operating subsidiaries to engage in a variety of activities not permitted the bank itself. (12 C.F.R. part 5).[4]

Pressure for comprehensive reform with respect to expanded activities, termed 'financial modernization', heightened with the Board's approval in 1998 of the Citicorp-Travelers merger. The approval was conditioned on Travelers' agreement to conform its activities within two years, by divestiture if necessary, to those permitted by the Bank Holding Company Act.[5]

Congressional passage of the Gramm-Leach-Bliley Act in 1999 (GLB) expanded the universe of activities in which commercial banks could be involved through affiliates and subsidiaries, provided a new organizational and regulatory framework and averted any need for a Citigroup divestiture.[6] In general, GLB permitted the integration of commercial banking, securities and insurance firms, and their expansion into other financial and nonfinancial businesses. The newly permissible activities were designated as 'financial in nature', or 'incidental' to financial activities or 'complementary' to financial activities.[7] They were to be undertaken in a new kind of bank holding company termed a 'financial holding company' (FHC) and, with some important exceptions, through a new kind of bank subsidiary termed a 'financial subsidiary'.[8] The Board, in consultation with the Secretary of the Treasury, was given authority to determine whether or not an activity was 'financial in nature or incidental' to financial activities.[9] It was given sole authority for determining whether an activity is 'complementary'.[10] 'Merchant banking', involving investments in any kind of firm without the intention to control or manage the firm, was included in the law as a financial activity.[11] The Board and the Secretary of the Treasury were authorized to issue regulations jointly to implement merchant banking authority.

POLICY IMPLEMENTATION AT THE FEDERAL REGULATORY AGENCIES

Legislation that relaxed restrictions on banks, aimed at creating a more competitive environment, was accompanied and elaborated on by changes in policy at the federal banking agencies. The changes are reflected in procedures, proposals, rules and regulations relating to both mergers and new activities.

Mergers

In 1982, the Justice Department's revised Horizontal Merger Guidelines initially prompted changes in merger policy. The Guidelines suggested that the DOJ should consider a larger typical local geographic market when determining customer response to differential pricing.[12] The Guidelines also recommend an enlargement of the product market to include other depository institutions. The Board, the principal banking agency decision-maker in large merger cases, had already considered the nature and scope of the geographic market expansion, along the cross-elasticity lines suggested by the Guidelines. It altered its calculation of market concentration to include the deposits of 'thrifts', weighing them at 50 per cent (other agencies have included 100 per cent of thrift deposits). Under the Guidelines, the Justice Department defined concentration thresholds in terms of levels and changes in the Herfindahl-Hirschman Index (HHI). Justice also modified the thresholds for banking to accommodate what was perceived as an intensification of competition from outside the industry.[13]

The effects of these modifications on merger analysis were to reduce market concentration in the typical merger case and increase the likelihood of approval. Further, the liberalization of multiple-office banking restrictions created opportunities for market-extension mergers that would not directly affect local market concentration and, therefore, were not typically deemed objectionable.

In addition, the Board made clear that it would not always adhere to the Justice Department's concentration thresholds.[14] It introduced a set of 'mitigating factors' that would permit merger approval even if concentration thresholds were violated. These included the continued presence of potential competition, the existence of a substantial number of remaining banks in the market, improvements in efficiency and related 'convenience and needs' considerations.[15] It did not establish any symmetrical set of aggravating factors that would permit denial of a merger if concentration levels were not violated. Based on experience, there is a question as to whether there is, at present, any level of concentration that would preclude a merger approval by the Board or for that matter any federal banking agency.[16]

Even in cases where neither concentration effects nor mitigating factors justify approval, there remains a way to avoid denial. Divestitures of competing branch offices to reduce objectionable increases in concentration, negotiated by the staffs of the Fed and/or Justice, have largely extinguished any probability that a large bank merger will be denied.[17]

The result of these modifications has been a substantially reduced denial rate for competitive reasons. For example, the Board, by far the most conservative of the federal banking agencies in the 1960s and 1970s, denied only eight merger proposals on competitive grounds between 1983 and 1994.[18] This compares to its denial of 63 proposed mergers between 1972 and 1982, in far fewer cases (Holder, 1993, 34). In recent years, there have been no denials at all. The elimination of denials by the federal banking agencies and suits by the Justice Department meant the end of litigation and court decisions that, for the first 15 years or so after the *Philadelphia National Bank case*, dominated bank merger evaluations.[19]

Activity Expansion

As noted, GLB authorizes the Board, in consultation with the Secretary of the Treasury, to determine activities not specified in the statute to be 'financial in nature or incidental'. It authorizes the Board to determine that an activity is 'complementary' to a financial activity. Financial holding companies and financial subsidiaries are not required to secure prior approval for entry into activities that have been determined to be 'financial in nature or incidental'. However, they must provide the Board with post-entry notification. Therefore, no net public benefits test is required for entry into new financial activities.

Over the past several years, the Board, either by itself or jointly with the Secretary of the Treasury, has implemented the merchant banking provisions of GLB. The Board authorized FHCs to engage in 'finder' activities and indicated it will consider proposals by FHCs to engage in, or acquire companies involved in, nonfinancial data processing as 'complementary' to financial activities on a case-by-case basis. Additionally, the Board proposed to establish 'real estate brokerage and management' as a 'financial in nature or incidental' activity.' A rule has been adopted that permits all bank holding companies to engage in an expanded range of commodity derivative activities. Citigroup has been authorized to engage in commodity transactions as a 'complementary' activity.

In 2001, the Board/Treasury proposed to establish real estate brokerage and management as activities that are 'financial in nature or incidental to a financial activity.' The proposal outlined an analytical framework for interpreting the provisions of the law that suggest a potential for bootstrapping regulatory determinations of permissible activities.[20] The Board/Treasury analysis begins with the idea that activities that are 'closely related to banking,' under the 1970 Amendments to the Bank Holding Company Act, are a subset of activities that are 'financial in nature or incidental' under GLB. The 'closely related' standard has, for the past 30 years, been based on supply-side characteristics specified by the circuit court decision in *National Courier Association v. Board of Governors of Federal Reserve* (1975). The question, the court said, was whether the proposed service was generally provided by banks, or operationally or functionally so similar to services provided by banks already that banks are particularly well equipped to provide it and the proposed service is 'so integrally related' to services already provided as to require their provision in a specialized form (ibid. 1237). The Board/Treasury proposal argued that real estate brokerage and management are 'closely related to banking' because, among other things, some depository institutions in some regulatory domains are engaged in the activities and because they are functionally similar to acting as a 'finder', an activity recently ruled permissible for FHCs. In banking, finding comparable product and production processes is invariably linked to earlier regulatory decisions by one or more of the multiple agencies that make such decisions.

The supply-side exploration under Section 4(c)(8) of the Bank Holding Company Act is augmented under GLB by the determination of whether a service is 'financial in nature or incidental.' Under the new law, the inquiry partially turns on the question of whether the activity is '. . . necessary and appropriate to allow an FHC . . . to compete effectively with any company seeking to provide financial services . . .'. This is a demand-side standard that is conceptually measurable by cross-elasticity of demand or some variant.

The interaction of the old supply-side standard with the new demand-side standard makes for a potentially explosive expansion of permissible activities. If it is finally determined that real estate brokerage and management are 'closely related to banking' because they are functionally similar to services banks already provide, it would be a small step to a finding that the ownership of real estate and real estate development (e.g., home construction) have become 'necessary and appropriate'. It is not unusual for real estate brokers and management firms, which provide some financial services, to also own and develop properties for sale or lease. Then, for competitive reasons, real estate ownership and development can be found to be 'financial in nature or incidental'. Once ownership and development are deemed permissible, other real estate-intensive activities may, because of functional similarities, become 'closely related to banking'; e.g., oil exploration and agriculture. If not closely related, such activities might be classified as 'complementary'. This suggestion may seem an exaggeration. But the American Bankers Association has argued that real estate itself is a financial asset. Construction, agriculture, mining and oil exploration were precisely the types of activities in which Transamerica was engaged prior to passage of the Bank Holding Company Act of 1956.

More generally, under the 'closely related' and 'necessary and appropriate' standards, the regulatory decisions that expand the set of closely related activities are likely to expose banks to new rivals whose services become reasonably close substitutes for the services offered by banks and, therefore, are, arguably, 'financial in nature or incidental'. As a result, no logical limit exists to the kinds of activities that could become permissible.

STRUCTURAL EFFECTS

Modifications of bank merger policy beginning in the early 1980s, along with deregulation, generated the current bank merger movement and activity expansion. The scope of these changes and their effects are examined below.

Mergers

The current bank merger movement in the United States began in the early 1980s, with many of the mergers in the early years a product of imminent or actual bank failure.[21] From 1980 through 1999, there were

Table 8.1   Number of mergers, new charters and failures* 1999–2003

Year	Depository institution mergers	Bank mergers	New bank charters	Bank failures
1994	475	359	48	11
1995	475	354	110	6
1996	446	310	148	5
1997	422	304	207	1
1998	493	370	193	3
1999	333	245	237	7
2000	255	179	192	6
2001	231	177	132	3
2002	203	146	81	10
2003	184	127	116	2
Totals:	3517	2571	1464	54

*Note: 'Depository institutions' are defined as commercial banks, savings banks, savings & loan associations and industrial banks. The last three institutions are, in combination, termed 'thrifts'. Mergers are limited to combinations of separately owned and controlled firms. New charters and failures are for commercial banks only. Because new charters may be obtained by established banking organizations, they need not constitute new entry into banking, but could constitute new entry into a specific market.

Source: Merger data from Stephen J. Pilloff, *Bank Merger Activity in the United States*, 1994–2003, Table 1, 3. Charter and Failure Data from Financial Structure Section, Board of Governors of the Federal Reserve System and Federal Deposit Insurance Corporation.

about 8000 commercial bank mergers. The rate fell over the next several years, but remained high (see Table 8.1).[22] The colossal magnitude of the merger movement is apparent.

The most striking feature of the bank merger movement has been the size of the banking firms merging. Between 1991 and 1998, there were 29 so-called 'mega-mergers' in which both the acquiring and acquired bank had more than $10 billion in assets (Shull and Hanweck, 2001, Table 5.1, 120–121). From 1999 to 2003, there were at least another 19 that fell into this class (Pilloff, 2004, Table 7, p. 9).

The large combinations have been well publicized. These have included the mergers of both Chase Manhattan and Manufacturers Hanover with Chemical Banking Corporation, Security Pacific and Continental Bank with BankAmerica Corporation, C&S/Sovran with NCNB Corporation, Barnett with Nations Bank, Core State with First Union, NationsBank with Bank of America, and First Union with Wachovia. The combination of Deutsche Bank and Bankers Trust in 1999 created the world's largest banking organization at the time with over $830 billion in assets.

In 2004, BNP Paribus with $1.2 trillion in assets, acquired BancWest with assets of $24 billion. Wachovia Corporation, a banking organization with over $400 billion in assets, announced a merger with South Trust, with about $53 billion. Thereafter, Bank of America announced it was merging with Fleet Boston. JPMorgan Chase announced a merger with Bank One. The combinations of recent years heralded the return of the mega-merger, after a brief respite during the recession, stock market crash and sluggish growth of the early years of the new century. The merger lineage of the current five largest banking organizations in the United States is traced in Table 8.2.

Effects of Mergers on Structure: Numbers and Concentration

The combinations of the last 25 years have conspicuously altered banking structure in the United States. The number of independent commercial banking organizations has been roughly cut in half since 1980 – from 12 342 to about 6371 in 2004 (see Table 8.3).[23] As might be expected, the decline in the numbers along with the mega-bank mergers has raised concentration at the national level. The share of the ten largest banking organizations in the United States increased from 18.6 per cent in 1980 to about 48.1 per cent at the end of June 2004; over this same period, the share of the top five has risen from 13.5 per cent to 35.7 per cent (Table 8.3).

National concentration, however, has not been a focal point for merger policy. Since the *Philadelphia National Bank* case, the focus has been on 'local areas' to which small and intermediate-sized customers appeared limited in obtaining banking services. In general, Metropolitan statistical areas (MSAs) and non-urban counties have been accepted as a starting point in defining the geographic locus of relevant competitive relationships.

In contrast to the national levels, concentration in local areas has not changed very much (*see* Table 8.4). In 1984, the average three-bank concentration ratio (the percentage of bank deposits held by the three largest banks) for commercial banks in MSAs was 66.3 per cent. In 2003, it was 62.8 per cent. In non-metropolitan area counties, the change over the same time period was from 89.4 per cent to 86.2 per cent. When 'thrifts' (savings and loans and savings banks) are combined with commercial banks (weighted at 50 per cent in accordance with Fed practice in merger analysis), the concentration increases slightly rather than decreasing, albeit from a lower level. From 1984, the first year for which such data is available, to 2003, the three-bank ratio in MSAs increased from 53.2 per cent to 58.1. Over this same period, the ratio in non-MSAs counties increased from 83.5 per cent to 84.1 per cent (*see* Table 8.4).

This relative stability at the local level does not warrant the conclusion that nothing of importance has happened where it really counts. First, there

*Table 8.2   Merger lineage of five largest domestic banking organizations,
2004*: Principal mergers: 1991–2004***

Banking Organization	Total Assets 12/31/04 (Billions of $)	Acquisitions (Billions of $ in Assets)
Citigroup	$1484.1	1998: Travelers ($420.0) a. Citicorp ($331) (CitiGroup)
		2001: CitiGroup a. European American ($15 billion)
		2002: CitiGroup a. Golden State Bancorp ($50.7)
JPMorgan Chase Co.	$1157.3	1991: Chase Manhattan a. Manufacturers Hanover
		1993: Bank One a. Valley National ($11.5)
		1996: Chemical a. Chase Manhattan ($121)
		2000: Chase Man. a. Morgan & Co. ($73.8) (JPMorgan)
		2004: JPMorgan a. Bank One
Bank of America Corp.	$1112.0	1991: Nations Bank a. C&S/Sovereign (51.4)
		1991: Fleet Financial Group a. Bank of New England
		1992: BankAmerica a. Security Pacific ($76.4)
		1993: Nations Bank a. MNC ($17.0)
		1994: BankAmerica a. Continental (($22.6)
		1995: Fleet Financial a. Shawmut ($32.7)
		1996: Fleet Financial a. National Westminster (430.1)
		1996: Bank of Boston a. BayBanks ($12.1)
		1997: Nations Bank a. Barnett ($44.7)
		1997: Nations Bank a. Boatmen's ($41.8)
		1998: Nations Bank a. BankAmerica ($265) (Bank of America)
		1999: Fleet Boston a. Bank Boston Corp ($50.7)
		2002: Fleet Boston a. Summit Bancorp ($39.9)
		2004: Bank of America a. Fleet Boston
Wachovia Corp.	$493.3	1991: First Union a. Southeast ($13 390)
		1995: First Union a. First Fidelity ($36.2)
		1996: CoreStates a. Meridian ($14.7)
		1998: First Union a. Core States ($48.5)
		2001: First Union a. Wachovia ($75.6) (Wachovia)
		2004: Wachovia a. South Trust ($53.0)
Wells Fargo & Co.	$427.9	1996: Wells Fargo a. First Interstate ($58.1)
		1998: Norwest a. Wells Fargo ($93.2) (Wells Fargo)
		2000: Wells Fargo a. First Security Corp ($21.4)

Note: * In 1991, the largest five domestic banking organizations in US held 16 per cent of commercial banking assets in US. In 2004 (6/30/04) they held close to 36 per cent (35.7). ** All acquisitions are of organizations with $10 billion or more in assets.

Source: Board of Governors, Federal Reserve System (Financial Structure Section). *See also* Stephen Pilloff, *Bank Merger Activity in the United States, 1994–2003*, p. 9, Table 7.

Table 8.3   Industry-wide banking structure: 1980–2004

Structural characteristic	Year			
	1980	1990	1997	2004*
No. of insured US commercial banks	14 407	12 194	9 604	7 623
No. of banking organizations	12 342	9 221	7 122	6 371
No. of banking offices	52 710	63 392	71 080	75 827
Concentration (per cent of deposits)				
Held by top 5	13.5	13.1	22.5	35.7
Held by top 10	18.6	20.0	29.9	48.1
Held by top 25	29.1	34.9	47.0	62.2
Held by top 100	46.8	61.4	69.1	78.6

* As of June 30, 2004.

Source: Adapted from data in Stephen A. Rhoades (1996), 'Bank Mergers and Industry-wide Structure, 1980–94.' Updated and revised data have been obtained from the Financial Structure Section Board of Governors of the Federal Reserve System. Concentration data is consolidated for banking organizations.

has been no significant decrease in average concentration in local areas. In the litany of the Justice's Guidelines, the HHIs in local banking markets typically range from 'moderately concentrated' to 'highly concentrated'. Secondly, the changes in concentration ratios over the last 25 years are *averages*. There is some evidence that concentration has increased in a substantial number of areas.[24] Finally, the mega-mergers of recent years have produced a small group of very large banking organizations that confront different sets of small local banks and one another in an increasing number of markets.[25] It is reasonable to believe that these developing market and cross-market structures are bound to affect the significance of local market concentration.

Activity Expansion

There is no detailed time-series data indicating the extent to which the banking system has expanded into the new activities that the GLB has made possible. The Board and the Treasury, in accordance with the requirements of GLB, did submit a joint report to Congress on FHCs four years after the law was enacted.[26] Among other things, the report indicated that:

(1)   More than 600 companies operate as FHCs. These include 49 of the 71 US-based bank holding companies with assets of $10 billion or

Table 8.4   Local market concentration: 1980–2004

Structural characteristic	Year		
	1984	1990	2003
Concentration ratios – Top 3			
MSAs			
Commercial banks	66.3	67.5	62.8
Plus Thrift Deposits (50%)	53.2	56.1	58.1
Non-MSAs			
Commercial banks	89.4	89.6	86.2
Plus Thrift Deposits (50%)	83.5	84.2	84.1
Herfindahl-Hirschman Index (HHI)			
MSAs			
Commercial banks	1958	2010	1846
Plus Thrift Deposits (50%)	1366	1466	1608
Non-MSAs			
Commercial banks	4358	4291	3946
Plus Thrift Deposits (50%)	3781	3788	3725
No. of markets	2736	2681	2585*

* For end of year, 2002.

Note: 'MSA' is 'Metropolitan Statistical Area' as defined by the Department of Commerce. 'Non-MSAs' are counties not included within MSAs. 'HHI' is the Herfindahl-Hirschman Index as used by the Justice Department and the Federal bank regulatory agencies to measure concentration.

Sources: This table is adapted from data in Stephen A. Rhoades (1996), 'Bank Mergers and Industry-wide Structure, 1980–94.' Updated and revised data have been obtained from the Financial Structure Section, Board of Governors of the Federal Reserve System. 1997. Concentration data is consolidated for banking organizations. For slightly different data, see Stephen Pilloff, 'Commercial Banking,' at p. 239, Table 9.6.

more and 473 US-based bank holding companies with assets of less than $1 billion. FHCs represent 78 per cent of the total assets of all bank holding companies. By acquiring banks, some prominent non-banking companies have become FHCs, including Charles Schwab MetLife, and Franklin Resources.

(2)   Over 50 FHCs engage in security underwriting and dealing. The assets of securities subsidiaries of FHCs have increased from $877 billion at the end of 1999 to $1.62 trillion at the end of March 2003.

(3)   Around 26 FHCs are engaged in insurance underwriting. Their underwriting assets have increased from $116.1 billion at the end of 2000 to $356.2 billion at the end of March 2003.

(4)   A total of 26 FHCs engaged in merchant banking. Their assets were about $9.5 billion at the end of 2000 and did not change materially over the reporting period.
(5)   Citigroup is currently the only domestic FHC engaged in clearly non-financial activities – trading oil and gas, although the extent of this trading constitutes only a small proportion of Citigroup's business.

The report leaves a number of gaps. Because it covers only FHCs and does not include financial subsidiaries, it does not provide comprehensive data on the volume and distribution of each type of new activity undertaken. Moreover, the information provided has not been updated since 2003.

The available data does not permit definitive conclusions. However, it suggests that GLB has not, as yet, had a major impact on banking/financial structure. There has yet to be any combination comparable to the Citicorp-Travelers merger in 1998. Furthermore, in January 2005, Citigroup announced that it was selling Travelers Life and Annuity business to MetLife because life insurance, a business it termed 'manufacturing', had a lower return than the distribution of financial products (Lenzer, 2005). Further, the intention of the Board and the Treasury announced in 2001 to establish real estate brokerage and management as a 'financial or incidental activity' has been becalmed pending congressional review and possible new legislation.[27]

While bank entry into commerce under GLB appears to have progressed slowly, commercial firms found a new way into banking through the acquisition of industrial loan companies (ILCs). ILC acquisitions have been the most recent in a line of seemingly minor exceptions permitted by law that have opened a door for wide-ranging combination, and prompted regulatory and congressional responses. The Bank Holding Company Act of 1956 (BHCA) imposed severe activity restrictions on regulated holding companies, but exempted those with only one bank holding. Amendments to the BHCA in 1970 closed the door on one-bank companies; but it exempted those that didn't offer both demand deposits *and* business loans. It thus allowed commercial and non-bank financial firms to acquire so-called 'non-bank banks'. The Competitive Equality Banking Act of 1987, shut the door on 'non-bank banks', but excluded from BHCA reach the ILC, a long-obscure financial institution that had emerged in the early twentieth century to provide loans to workers; in more recent years, the ILC had, in a number of western states, developed into a more general banking firm, offering a variety of loans and insured deposits. ILCs have been acquired by Merrill Lynch, Morgan Stanley, American Express and other financial firms, as well as by General Motors, General Electric, BMW, Target, and Toyota. Wal-Mart and Home Depot have sought ILC charters.

Wal-Mart's 2005 deposit insurance application for a Utah ILC sparked national controversy. In addition to the potential breakdown in the barrier between banking and commerce, it intensified a dispute between the FDIC and the Federal Reserve as to the kind of supervision such combinations require. Under existing law, the FDIC constitutes the sole Federal authority for ILC. Its 'bank-centric' approach focuses on risk-based capital requirements and deposit insurance premiums, coupled with existing 'firewalls' to insulate the ILC from damaging transactions with its affiliates. Under GLB, such affiliations are supervised on a consolidated basis by the Federal Reserve. Congress established consolidated supervision in part because of the doubt about the efficacy of 'firewalls'.

Given continuing concerns about bank safety, the efficacy of 'firewalls' raises questions about 'bank-centric' supervision. On the other hand, 'consolidated supervision' raises questions because it portends the introduction of bank regulation into wide areas of the private sector. The Hobson's choice between 'bank-centric' and 'consolidated supervision' provides one reasonable justification for closing the ILC 'loophole' and sustaining a separation between banking and commerce.

In 2006, the FDIC placed a six-month moratorium on ILC applications by commercial firms, which it extended in 2007. Wal-Mart subsequently withdrew its application. Congress is currently considering the elimination of the ILC exception.

COMPETITIVE ISSUES

Bank mergers and activity expansion have been heralded as the progenitor of improvements in efficiency and competition, to say nothing of risk reduction through diversification and macro-financial stability. Improvements in efficiency and risk reduction, to the extent they develop, should yield lower prices and improved quality if the banks are subject to the pressure of more intense competition.[28]

A large body of research exists on the relationship between bank performance and local market concentration.[29] Modern bank merger policy was founded on the presumption that such a relationship existed. Recent observations comparing the pricing behavior of large or multimarket banking organizations with small or single-market banks illuminate differences in behavior between the latter and the former. Experience suggests that some modification of the present conventional view may be in order.

(1) Single-market banks offer interest rates on deposits that appear to be related to local market conditions that consequently vary substantially

from one MSA to another (*see, e.g.*, Heitfield, 1999; Biehl, 2002). In contrast, multimarket banks establish uniform deposit rates across local market areas, at least through geographic areas as extensive as states (*see, e.g.*, Radecki, 1998; Heitfield, 1999).

(2) The uniform deposit rates offered by multimarket banks are lower, on average, than the rates offered by single-market banks (*see, e.g.*, Biehl, 2002; Hannan and Praeger, 2004).

(3) Fees on a variety of retail accounts and services imposed by banks with multistate operations have been consistently higher than fees at banks that operate within one state (*see, e.g.*, Hannan, 1996).[30]

(4) Both surveys and anecdotal information have suggested a developing commercial banking practice of linking the provision of credit to the purchase of other financial services, in particular underwriting services. There has been some evidence that large borrowers, in particular, have been subjected to tying activity.[31]

(5) Accounting statements and other public information reveal that large banking firms have a substantial funding cost advantage over small banks (Shull and Hanweck, 2001, 162–164).

These results suggest a number of questions. Why do large, multimarket banks post uniform deposit rates over broad geographic areas, seemingly forgoing the profit opportunities of geographic price discrimination? Why are the fees at large, multistate banks higher and the deposit rates at multimarket banks lower than at single-state and single-market banks? Do the competitive relationships that exist (or are developing) between large, multimarket banks and small, local banks differ from the relationships that existed earlier between large and small local banks? Will higher fees and lower deposit rates result in loss of market share for large, multistate, multimarket banks? Are the ties that large borrowers have reported truly 'voluntary' and indicative of a more efficient production process and/or greater customer convenience in linking related services at one-stop shops? Or do they reflect an expansion of market power? Is the funding advantage of large banking firms related to increased efficiency of one kind or another or lower risk attributable to greater diversification? Or is it attributable to lower risk associated with the market perception that they are too-big-to-fail?

Recent research has focused on some of these questions, but has found few definitive answers. Among the speculations are the following:[32]

(1) Uniform rates set by multimarket banks reflect a weighted average of the conditions prevailing in the local markets in which they operate (*see* Park and Pennacchi, 2004).

(2)   Local market concentration is still relevant for local banks, but not for multimarket banks that appear to be affected by concentration at the state level (*see, e.g.*, Hannan and Praeger, 2004, Heitfield and Praeger, 2004).

(3)   The greater the importance of multimarket banks in a local area, the lower the deposit rates of single-market banks. The implication is that over time, as multimarket bank shares of local markets expand, local market concentration will become less important (*see, e.g.*, Hannan and Praeger, 2004).

(4)   Lower deposit rates offered by large, multimarket banks reflect greater access to wholesale funds that are cheaper than retail sources of funds (*see, e.g.*, Hannan and Praeger, 2005; Kiser, 2004).

(5)   Greater access to cheaper, wholesale funds exerts downward pressure on loan rates as well as lower deposit rates, thus is beneficial to loan customers (*see generally* Park and Pennacchi, 2004; Hannan and Praeger, 2005).

(6)   Lower deposit rates offered by large, multimarket banks are offset by the provision of higher-quality service (*see* Dick, 2003).[33]

While much about the impact of the structural changes in local areas, independent of concentration, remains uncertain, the available evidence does not provide strong support for the supposition that mergers have intensified competition. Further, the emergence of a relatively few, very large banks operating in increasing numbers of markets raises new competitive issues that merit attention. There is evidence from other industries that mutual forbearance in such circumstances is to be expected. In banking, it is plausible that regulatory forbearance for very large organizations ('too-big-to-fail') provides a motive for merger and a unifying bond for very large organizations, as well as a funding advantage that modifies rivalry in local areas.[34]

POLICY PROPOSALS

The relaxation of geographic and activity restrictions, aimed at establishing a more competitive banking system, has generated mergers and activity expansion that continue to alter banking/financial structure. To date, the near-term benefits have not been obvious.

Near-term benefits aside, there has been, for some time now, a plausible consensus about where bank mergers and activity expansion are leading. The long-term result is likely to be a small number of very large banking organizations, present in most MSAs, along with a large number of relatively small, local community or regional institutions.[35] The large organizations will combine traditional banking services with a variety of other financial products and are likely to engage in a widening area of what can reasonably be termed nonfinancial and commercial activities. These few large organizations will have a dominant share of the banking and related financial business in many local areas and will face one another in large numbers of separate geographic and product markets.

Through most of US history, this is precisely the kind of structure (common in many other countries) that was deliberately avoided. There has been no public debate on the desirability of this changed structure and no explicit congressional decision to alter the traditional aim. In fact, in liberalizing branching and activity restrictions, Congress has given lip service to its desire to avert such structural consequences. In passing the Riegle-Neal Act in 1994, Congress imposed national and statewide concentration limits resulting from interstate bank mergers. In passing the Gramm-Leech-Bliley Act in 1999, Congress explicitly affirmed its intention to maintain a separation between banking and commerce. Well-known experts, including Henry Kaufman, Robert Rubin, Alan Greenspan and Paul Volker testified to their intense concerns about the creation of dominant industrial-financial conglomerates (*Financial Services Modernization Act of 1999*, 70–76). A review of the current policy framework is in order, if for no other reason than because it facilitates such structural results.

In considering both near-term and long-term effects, it should be recognized that even if each merger and new activity decision made by a federal agency were 'right' within the existing policy framework, and was not injurious to competition, the end result of the accumulated decisions could still be 'wrong' by producing a less competitive financial/commercial structure. Such contradictions are familiar in economic analysis; e.g., in what Alfred Kahn once termed 'the tyranny of small decisions' (*see* Kahn, 1966).

The proposals outlined below are moderate, reflecting the uncertainties that continue to exist.[36] However, it is believed that little would be lost by slowing down the continued expansion of the relatively few very large banking organizations that have emerged.

Evaluation of Large Bank Mergers

The federal banking agencies and the Justice Department should undertake a more complete competitive analysis of proposed mergers involving banking organizations with assets of $20 billion or more. In all such mergers, the agencies need to consider not only the effects of the merger on local area concentration, but also the effect on the market position of the resulting firm relative to other banks in the market (i.e., its 'dominance'). The agencies should also consider the likely impact on the competitive behavior of the remaining banks, the likelihood of intermarket coordination among large, multimarket organizations of similar size and scope and the establishment or augmentation of a banking organization that is 'too-big-to-fail', i.e., a bank whose failure would threaten the entire financial system and is thereby guaranteed government assistance if it faces a high risk of insolvency.[37]

Evaluation of Aggregate Concentration

In general, Congress has been aware of the issues raised by the growth of a small group of large banking organizations through interstate expansion by merger. The Riegle-Neal Interstate Banking and Branching Efficiency Act of 1994 established concentration limits for merging institutions of 10 per cent of nationwide deposits and 30 per cent of state deposits.[38] However, if national or statewide banking concentration has anticompetitive significance as a proxy for market dominance and/or mutual forbearance, these effects are likely to develop in a incremental manner, not suddenly above a specific limit.

The federal banking agencies and the Justice Department should evaluate large bank merger proposals by imposing increasing negative weights as an absolute aggregate concentration limit is approached. For example, an acquisition that would give the merged banks an 8 per cent share of national deposits (or some more appropriate measure of concentration) should be evaluated as raising more significant competitive issues than an acquisition that would result in a 4 per cent share. This proposal is aimed at making the limit(s) effective by recognizing and avoiding the argument that absolute limits alone invariably appear arbitrary and invite evasion when they become binding.

'Too-Big-to-Fail' and Negotiated Divestitures

The likelihood of regulatory support for very large banks, by reducing the risk of default, tends to reduce their funding costs and expand their borrowing capacity. This creates an incentive for greater risk taking that confers a competitive advantage over smaller banks. In this context, the practice of negotiating divestitures to facilitate the merger of such banks should be reconsidered.

There remains uncertainty as to whether divestiture agreements have successfully eliminated the likely anticompetitive (high concentration) effects that motivate them.[39] The sale of branch offices can affect deposit concentration, without affecting loan concentration because loans, unlike deposits, are frequently booked at central locations. Moreover, because of the likely migration of at least some borrowers and depositors to other banks after a merger has eliminated their first choice, the immediate impact of the sale of branch offices can overstate longer-run effects.

Whatever their immediate and even longer-term effects on local market concentration, divestiture does not provide an appropriate remedy for permitting mergers that produce or augment the size of banks that become too-big-to-fail. The federal banking agencies and the Justice Department should abstain from negotiating divestitures for the purpose of approving a merger where the banks involved have become too-big-to-fail.

It is recognized that the Federal banking agencies are not disposed to making such determinations public prior to an imminent failure. However, FDICIA does contain a systemic risk exception. The problem should not be ignored. Federal bank regulatory agencies need to make determinations as to whether the insolvency of a very large banking organization is likely to meet the FDICIA exception. Given that 'too-big-to-fail', based on public concerns about systemic risk is a long-existing and probably irrevocable fact-of-life, it behooves the agencies to rethink their views. Agencies should not augment the problem through their merger and activity expansion decisions.

'TOO-BIG-TO-FAIL', CAPITAL REQUIREMENTS AND INSURANCE PREMIUMS

The existence of banks that are too-big-to-fail produces a funding cost and, therefore, a competitive advantage over smaller banks. Increasing the capital requirements and deposit insurance premiums of very large banks can moderate this advantage. Higher capital requirements would also tend to discourage mega-mergers by eliminating the growth incentive to achieve 'too-big-to-fail' status.

It is understood that it is no simple matter to disentangle reduced funding costs attributable to likely federal support in exigent circumstances from other factors related to possible economic advantages of size and diversification. However, a calculation can be made that would tend to make the capital costs of very large banks about the same as the capital costs of comparable unregulated firms that do not have the benefit of federal banking agency support. A similar approach can be taken with respect to deposit insurance premiums.[40]

Review of GLB

Given the statements of US representatives and senators instrumental in passing GLB about their intention to maintain separation between banking and commerce, it is not clear that the potentially explosive possibilities for expansion in the law were fully considered. While these possibilities do not, as yet, seem to have been exploited, Congress should revisit the issue before they are.

Congressional and Public Oversight

As a means of keeping the public abreast of the state of competition in the financial services industries and to facilitate congressional oversight, the Board, Treasury and the other relevant federal agencies should report to Congress annually. They should report both on their policies of promoting competition and on the state and trends of competition and concentration in banking and financial services markets. Such a report on competition and concentration would be comparable to the Board's semi-annual reports to Congress on monetary policy.

CONCLUSIONS

While banking remains a highly regulated and supervised industry in the United States, over the last quarter-of-a-century, both depression-generated and older restrictions have been eliminated. The liberalization of multiple-office banking has generated a massive merger movement. The liberalization of permissible activities promises to further contribute to the expansion of large banking organizations. Thus far, the effects on competition have been mixed at best. Aside from immediate effects, the structural reorganization is producing a relatively small number of very large banking organizations that confront one another in numerous geographic and product markets. It is also producing much smaller fringe banks in local areas. The competitive effects of the developing structure are problematic and warrant serious reconsideration of current law, regulation and policy.

NOTES

1. For a detailed discussion of early competition policies toward banking in the United States, on which this section and the next draws, *see* Shull and Hanweck (2001), Ch. 3.
2. The amendments required the banking agencies to deny proposed mergers that violated Section 2 of the Sherman Act and also Section 7 of the Clayton Act, except where 'the

anticompetitive effects of the proposed transaction are clearly outweighed in the public interest on the probable effect . . . in meeting the convenience and needs of the community. . . .'. The Justice Department was authorized to challenge any Federal banking agency approval by obtaining an automatic injunction to stay the merger on entering suit within 30 days.

3. *See NationsBank v. Variable Annuity Life Insurance Co.*, 115 S.Ct. 810 (1995) and *Barnett Bank of Marion County N.A. v. Nelson*, 517 U.S. 25 (1996).

4. For a detailed review of these developments, *see* Shull and White (1998).

5. Travelers' activities which the Board found impermissible under the Bank Holding Company Act included underwriting property and casualty, life, and commercial insurance, distributing shares of mutual funds and investments in commercial companies, trading in physical commodities, and oil and gas exploration. The Fed's decision also required Traveler to conform its subsidiaries controlling mutual funds and underwriting securities to the requirements of Section 20 of the Glass-Steagall Act, and related regulations and orders.

6. GLB repealed two of the four sections of the Banking Act of 1933 known as the Glass-Steagall Act: Section 20, that prohibited banks from having affiliates principally engaged in dealing in securities, and Section 32, that prohibited interlocks of directors and officers of securities firms and banks. By not repealing Section 16 that limits banks that deal in and underwrite securities to specified types (Federal government and municipal securities) and Section 21, that prohibits firms dealing in securities from accepting deposits, it precluded the kind of 'universal banking' in which all securities activities could be conducted within the bank itself.

7. Section [4(k)] of the Act lists a number of permissible financial activities: 'lending, exchanging, transferring, investing for others, or safeguarding money or securities, insuring, guaranteeing, or indemnifying against loss, harm, damage, illness, disability, or death, or providing and issuing annuities, and acting as principal, agent, or broker for purposes of the foregoing in any State.' The Section also includes securities underwriting, dealing and market making, sponsoring all kinds of mutual funds and other investment companies, any activity the FRB has found, under 4(c)(8) to be permissible, merchant banking, insurance company portfolio investments, and health insurance. Also identified are 'complementary activities' that, by exclusion, must be 'commercial activities' that are determined to be related, in some way, to financial activities.

8. For FHCs and subsidiaries, affiliated banks must be well capitalized and well managed and have a satisfactory CRA rating. 'Financial subsidiaries' of national and insured state-chartered banks are more limited than FHCs. Activities not permitted include: 1) insurance or annuity underwriting (except for underwriting permitted prior to January 1, 1999); (2) insurance company portfolio investments; (3) real estate investment and development (except as authorized by law); and (4) merchant banking. With exceptions, national banks are also prohibited from underwriting or selling title insurance. GLB requires the Board and the Treasury to jointly reconsider the merchant banking prohibition after five years. The decision to permit financial subsidiaries to engage in merchant banking could have been made as early as November 2004. As of this writing, the Board and the Treasury have not lifted the merchant banking prohibition.

9. The Board must notify the Secretary of the Treasury of applications or requests to engage in new activities.

10. Determinations are made on a case-by-case basis. In determining that an activity is complementary, the Board must find that the activity poses no risk to the safety and soundness of insured depository institutions or the financial system in general.

11. Under the GLB, merchant banking investments may be retained as long as necessary to permit disposal on a reasonable basis consistent with the financial viability of the activity. However, an FHC may not routinely manage or operate a company held as a merchant banking investment, except as necessary to obtain a reasonable return on the investment. Congress also recognized that insurance companies and securities firms may have equity interests in businesses engaged in 'commercial activities' not authorized by the Act. GLB provides for their retention indefinitely, or for some period of time,

depending on the dates on which the equity interests were acquired and the proportion of a company's revenue they provide.

12. For an analysis of this approach for determining the geographic market in a bank merger case, *see* Shull 1989.

13. Justice informed the Federal banking agencies that it would generally not challenge a merger unless the post-merger HHI was at least 1800 and the merger raised the HHI by more than 200 points (100 points for industry in general), *see* Rule, 1985.

14. *See*, for example, First Bank Systems (1993) 51 n.10. For a description of the Federal Reserve's approach, *see* Meyer 1998, 438.

15. For a discussion of the kinds of mitigating factors used by the Board, *see* Holder (1993).

16. In a 1997 decision, for example, the Fed permitted the leading bank in the local Columbus, Ohio market, with about 61 per cent of market deposits, to acquire the second-largest bank in the market with about 19 per cent. *See* Southern National Corporation (1997). It did require divestitures that notably restrained the increase in the leading bank's market share to about 64 per cent. The approval, nevertheless, permitted the market HHI, which was more than double the level which the Justice Department viewed as 'highly concentrated' before the merger, to increase further. The Board's approval of the merger of NationsBank Corp and Barnett Banks, Inc. in 1997 raised similar questions in several Florida markets, *see* NationsBank (1998).

17. There have been numerous cases of divestitures in recent large bank mergers. For an early example, *see* 'BankAmerica Corporation', (1992).

18. Between 1980 and 1994, the Board decided over 70 per cent of the bank acquisition cases reviewed by the Federal banking agencies.

19. From 1974 to the last lower court decision in a banking case in 1985, neither the Justice Department nor any Federal banking agency has won a case. For a review of the early litigation and court decisions, *see* Shull and Hanweck, 2001, Ch. 4.

20. Board of Governors of the Federal Reserve System and U.S. Department of the Treasury (2003). For an analysis of this proposal, *see* Shull, 2002, 52ff.

21. For a discussion of the differences between the early and later mergers, *see* Shull and Hanweck, 2001, 6.

22. The data from 1980 to 1999 is for all commercial banks, including those commonly-owned. The more recent data is for independently-owned firms only, but also includes combinations of 'thrifts' (principally savings institutions) and 'thrifts' with commercial banks. For four separate merger reports by economists at the Fed, *see* Rhoades, 1996, Rhoades, 2000, Pilloff, 2001, and Pilloff, 2004. Pilloff (2004) relies on private information, and describes the differences in his and earlier numbers.

23. Numbers and concentration data are from the Financial Structure Section, Research Division, Board of Governors of the Federal Reserve System. Data is for end-of-year (December 31) except 2004 which is for June 30.

24. The average HHI for MSAs, including thrifts weighted at 50 per cent, increased substantially between 1985 and 1997. More than three times as many MSAs had increases as had decreases. For relevant sources, *see* Shull and Hanweck, 2001, 148.

25. For data on the growth of multimarket linkages between 1986 and 1994, *see* Shull, 2000, 63–65.

26. Board of Governors of the Federal Reserve System and U.S. Department of the Treasury 2003.

27. *See* National Association of Realtors (2004). There is another notable event with respect to GLB that has not yet occurred. As noted, the new law authorized the Fed/Treasury to permit financial subsidiaries of national and state banks to engage in merchant banking as of November 2004.

28. A review of research findings on bank efficiency and diversification can be found in Shull and Hanweck, 2001, 151ff. *See* Berger and Humphrey, 1997 and Rhoades, 1998.

29. For a recent review of the range of research in this area, *see* Berger *et al.*, 2004.

30. *See also* the Fed's *Annual Report to the Congress on Retail Fees and Services of Depository Institutions* beginning in 1989 through 2003. Board of Governors of the Federal Reserve

System (1989–2003). For example, an early report noted that bank revenues from service charges on all deposits (consumer and business) rose substantially between 1989 and 1993, with the increase being more pronounced at larger banks. The fees that have increased are associated with the maintenance and use of retail deposit accounts and with specialized services, such as money orders, stop payment orders and overdrawn accounts.

31. *See*, for example, Association for Financial Professionals (2003) and Sapsford (June 9, 2004). Neither the Federal banking agencies nor the General Accounting Office has found any substantial evidence of unlawful tying arrangements under Section 106 of the Bank Holding Company Act. See U.S. GAO (2003). At least some of the 'ties' that have been alleged can be viewed as 'voluntary' and, therefore, not in violation of Section 106. The distinction between 'voluntary' and 'coercive' tie-ins was addressed by the Conference Committee in its Report on the proposed amendments to the Bank Holding Company Act in 1970. The Committee indicated that Section 106 was aimed at 'coercive' tie-ins, while the Fed, in evaluating acquisition proposals under Section 4(c)(8), would deal with 'voluntary' tie-ins; i.e., by rejecting acquisitions that created the market power necessary to 'encourage' voluntary acquiescence. *Bank Holding Company Act Amendments* (1970), 18.

32. Reviews of the developing literature can be found in Hannan and Praeger, 2004 and 2005.

33. The 'quality' of bank services is not easily measured. Dick's measure included branch density, number of employees per branch, salary per employee, geographic diversification and the age of a bank (as a proxy for experience). There is some survey evidence indicating customers have experienced reductions in quality of service as a result of mergers. *See* Chu, June 2, 2004.

34. These characteristics suggest a dominant firm-price leadership model (dynamic limit pricing) modified by both mutual forbearance and regulatory forbearance. A model along these lines has been developed by Shull and Hanweck, 2001, 166ff. They found its implications consistent with a number of puzzling observations and recent research findings.

35. In the early and mid-1990s, there were a number of studies that projected the likely effects of the merger movement on 'numbers' and 'concentration' over time. Linear extrapolations of trends suggested various outcomes, depending on starting and ending dates, and the methodology adopted. For a review of these studies and an additional study using somewhat different methodology, *see* Shull and Hanweck, 2001, 172–173.

36. A fuller description of similar proposals can be found in Shull and Hanweck, 2001, 190–197.

37. As an alternative, the Federal banking agencies might decide large bank merger cases on the basis of a net public benefits; i.e., they would be required to balance gains in efficiency, stability through diversification, etc. against potentially adverse effects, including increases in concentration and other factors such as the extent of local market dominance, inter-market cooperation, and growth to a size 'too-big-to-fail'.

38. The use of deposits to measure the significance of aggregate concentration is moot. Other measures are preferable. *See* Shull and Hanweck, 2001, 195–196.

39. There is some evidence that divestiture policy has had a procompetitive effects, *see* Pilloff, 2002, Burke, 1998. But, as discussed, questions about long-run competitive consequences remain.

40. For a fuller discussion of this proposal, *see* Shull and Hanweck, 2001, 196–97. Capital requirements should be raised to approximate the capital cost of otherwise comparable banks and unregulated firms that do not enjoy the likelihood of Federal support. Correspondingly, federal deposit insurance premiums paid by these banks should be set to reflect both expected and unexpected losses to the insurance fund(s) if they were to fail.

REFERENCES

Association for Financial Professionals (2003), *Credit Access Survey: Linking Corporate Credit to the Awarding of Other Financial Services*, Bethesda, MD.

Bank Holding Company Act Amendments (1970), Conference Report to Accompany H.R. 6778, No. 1747, 91st Cong., 2d Sess., Washington, D.C.

Biehl, A. (2002), 'The Extent of the Market for Retail Banking Deposits,' *The Antitrust Bulletin*, 47, 91–106.

Berger, Allen N. and David B. Humphrey (1997), 'Efficiency of Financial Institutions: International Survey and Directions for Future Research,' *European Journal of Operations Research*.

Berger, Allen N. *et al.* (2004), 'Introduction: Bank Concentration and Competition: An Evolution in the Making,' *Journal of Money, Credit and Banking*, 36 (3, Part 2), 433–451.

Berle, A.A. (1949), 'Banking under the Antitrust Laws,' *Columbia Law Review*, 589–606.

Board of Governors of the Federal Reserve System and U.S. Department of the Treasury (2003), *Report to Congress on Financial Holding Companies under the Gramm-Leach-Bliley Act*, Washington, D.C.

Board of Governors of the Federal Reserve System (1989–2003), *Annual Report to the Congress on Retail Fees and Services of Depository Institutions*, Washington, D.C.

Burke, Jim (1998), 'Divestitures as an Antitrust Remedy in Bank Mergers,' No. 1998–14, Financial and Economic Discussion Series, Board of Governors of the Federal Reserve System, Washington, D.C.

Changes in the Banking and Currency System of the United States (Sept. 9, 1913), Report of the House Committee on Banking and Currency, Report No. 69, 63rd Cong., 1st Sess, Washington, D.C.

Chu, Kathy (June 2, 2004), 'Bank Mergers Don't All Win Raves: A Fifth of Customers Say They Are Worse Off, Citing High Fees, Decline in Service,' *The Wall Street Journal*, D2.

Dick, Astrid A. (2003), 'Market Structure and Quality: An Application to the Banking Industry,' *Finance and Economics Discussion Series*, 2003–14, Board of Governors of the Federal Reserve System, Washington D.C.

Financial Services Modernization Act of 1999, Sen. Report No. 106–44, 106th Cong., 1st Sess., Washington, D.C.

Hannan, Timothy H. (1996), 'Bank Fees and Their Variation Across Banks and Locations,' unpublished paper.

Hannan, Timothy H. and Robin A. Praeger (2004), 'The Competitive Implications of Multimarket Bank Branching,' *Journal of Banking & Finance*, 28, 1889–1914.

Hannan, Timothy H. and Robin A. Praeger (2005), 'Multimarket Bank Pricing: An Empirical Investigation of Deposit Interest Rates,' unpublished paper.

Heitfield, E.A. (1999), 'What Do Interest Rate Data Say about the Geography of Retail Banking Markets?' *The Antitrust Bulletin*, 333–347.

Heitfield, Erik A. and Robin A. Praeger (2004), 'The Geographic Scope of Retail Deposit Markets,' *Journal of Financial Services Research*, 25, 37–55.

Holder, Christopher (1993), 'The Use of Mitigating Factors in Bank Mergers and Acquisitions: A Decade of Antitrust at the Fed,' *Economic Review*, Federal Reserve Bank of Atlanta, 78.

Hurst, Willard (1973), *A Legal History of Money, 1774–1970*, Lincoln, N.E., University of Nebraska Press.

Kahn, Alfred E. (1966), 'The Tyranny of Small Decisions: Market Failures, Imperfections and the limits of the Economy', *Kylos*, 19, 1, 23–47.

Kiser, Elizabeth K. (2004), 'Modeling the Whole Firm: The Effects of Multiple Inputs and Financial Intermediation on Bank Deposit Rates,' Working Paper No. 2004-07, Federal Reserve Board, Washington D.C.

Lenzer, Robert (2005), 'Citi's Rainy Day Strategy,' forbes.com, January 31, 2005.

Meyer, Lawrence H. (1998), 'Statement' before Committee on Banking and Financial Services, U.S. House of Representatives, April 29, 1998 as reprinted in *Federal Reserve Bulletin*, (1998) 84, 438–451.

National Association of Realtors (2004), 'Banks in Real Estate,' Briefing Paper, www.realtor.org

Park, Kwangwoo and George Pennacchi (2004), 'Harming Depositors and Helping Borrowers: The Disparate Impact of Bank Consolidation,' unpublished paper.

Pilloff, Stephen J. (2001), 'Commercial Banking,' in Walter Adams and James W. Brock (eds.), *The Structure of American Industry*, Upper Saddle River, NJ, Prentice Hall, 224–254.

Pilloff, Steven J. (2002), 'What Happened at Divested Bank Offices? An Empirical Analysis of Antitrust Divestitures in Bank Mergers,' Finance and Economic Discussion Series, No. 2002–60, Board of Governors of the Federal Reserve System, Washington D.C.

Pilloff, Stephen J. (2004), *Bank Merger Activity in the United States*, 1994–2003, Staff Study No. 176, Washington, D.C., Board of Governors of the Federal Reserve System.

Radecki, Lawrence J. (1998), 'The Expanding Geographic Reach of Retail Banking Markets,' *Economic Policy Review*, (4), Federal Reserve Bank of New York, 15–34.

Radecki, Lawrence J. (2000), 'Competition in Shifting Product and Geographic Markets,' *The Antitrust Bulletin*, (45), 571–613.

Rhoades, Stephen A. (1996), *Bank Mergers and Industry-wide Structure, 1980–94*, Staff Study, No. 169, Washington, D.C., Board of Governors of the Federal Reserve System.

Rhoades, Stephen A. (1998), 'The Efficiency Effects of Bank Mergers: An Overview of Case Studies in Nine Mergers,' *The Journal of Banking and Finance*, 22, 273–291.

Rhoades, Stephen A. (2000), *Bank Mergers and Banking Structure in the United States: 1980–98*, Staff Study, No. 174, Washington D.C., Board of Governors of the Federal Reserve System.

Rule, Charles (1985) 'Letter to the Honorable C. Todd Conover, Comptroller of the Currency,' February 8, 1985.

Sapsford, Jathon (June 9, 2004), 'Executives See Rise in "Tying" Loans to Other Fees,' *Wall Street Journal*, A1.

Shull, Bernard (1989), 'Provisional Markets, Relevant Markets and Banking Markets: The Justice Department's Merger Guidelines in Wise County, Virginia,' *The Antitrust Bulletin*, 34(2), 411–428.

Shull, Bernard (1996), 'The Origins of Antitrust in Banking: An Historical Perspective,' *The Antitrust Bulletin*, 41(2), 255–288.

Shull, Bernard (2000), 'Merger Policy in the U.S.A.: Is There Need for a Change,' in D.B. Papadimitriou (ed.), *Modernizing Financial Systems*, New York, St. Martin's Press, Inc., 54–75.

Shull, Bernard (2002), 'Banking, Commerce and Competition under the Gramm-Leach-Bliley Act,' *The Antitrust Bulletin*, 47(1), 25–62.

Shull, Bernard and Gerald Hanweck (2001), *Bank Mergers in a Deregulated Environment: Promise and Peril*, Westport, C.T., Quorum Books.

Shull, Bernard and Lawrence White (1998), 'The Right Corporate Structure for Expanded Bank Activities,' *The Banking Law Journal*, 115(5), 446–476.

U.S. Department of Justice (1982), Horizontal Merger Guidelines, 47 Fed. Reg. 28493.

U.S. General Accounting Office (2003), *Bank Tying: Additional Steps Needed to Ensure Effective Enforcement of Tying Prohibitions*, GAO-04-03, Washington, D.C.

Cases

Supreme Court Decisions

U.S. v. South-Eastern Underwriters Association, 322 U.S. 533 (1944).

Philadelphia National Bank-Girard Trust, 374 U.S. 321 (1963).

First National Bank & Trust of Lexington, 376 U.S. 665 (1963).

NationsBank v. Variable Annuity Life Insurance Co., 513 U.S. 251 (1995).

Barnett Bank of Marion County N.A. v. Nelson, 517 U.S. 25 (1996).

Court of Appeals Decisions

National Courier Association v. Board of Governors of Federal Reserve, 516 F.2d 1229 (D.C. Cir. 1975).

Federal Reserve Board Decisions

BankAmerica Corporation, 78 Fed. Res. Bull. 338 (1992).

First Bank Systems, 79 Fed. Res. Bull. 50 (1993).

Southern National Corporation, 83 Fed. Res. Bull 597 (1997).

NationsBank, 84 Fed. Res. Bull. 129 (1998).

9. The European experience with merger and deregulation

Susan Beth Farmer

INTRODUCTION

The modern European Union, now comprising 27 Member States, provides a useful example of a supra-national effort to simultaneously integrate previously independent nations and their respective legal systems and break down trade barriers among these states while promoting free market economic conditions and economic competition. The European project is proceeding primarily in a highly regulatory, top-down fashion directed by the executive and administrative bodies of the Community, which enforce European statutory law and jawbone national governments to bring competition to previously regulated industries and to eliminate subsidies that benefit their national champion industries. In key sectors of the economy, including such important industries as gas and electric utilities and banking, the goals of competition on the one hand, and national protectionism, on the other, continue to clash despite the best hopes of the original architects and modern leaders of the European Union (Norris 2006, p. C1). By comparison, the market for airline transportation has become increasingly competitive since deregulation, reflected in increasingly substantive review and ultimate approval of a series of mergers in the industry.

The policy of deregulation in the European Union was a deliberate choice. The European project offers an illuminating contrast to deregulation in American industries described in previous chapters for four reasons: (1) it is the result of conscious economic policy choice adopted from the outset of the Union, (2) it paints with a broad brush, encompassing many industries, (3) issues of federalism are more acute as the regulators in Brussels seek to impose market competition, referred to as 'liberalization', and limit protectionism, referred to as 'State Aid', on the sovereign Member States, and (4) all three functions are bundled in the Directorate General for Competition except for State Aid in the transportation sector. Though the European strategy of deregulation and competition seeks to be organized and deliberate, it has proceeded unevenly and has been more successful in some industries, and some countries, than others. The agricultural and financial industries, for example, are still characterized by important national protections while sectors including energy, both gas and electricity, and airline transportation have shaken off the chains of regulation and leapt ahead into growing European competition.

Several conclusions follow from a review of the European experience with deregulation and subsequent mergers that provide a contrast with the similar deregulation undertakings in the same industries in the United States.

First, enforcement and regulatory authority are largely bundled at the supra-national level with the Competition Directorate of the Commission (DG Comp) responsible for enforcing European Union antitrust law, investigating and directing national deregulation (liberalization) of markets, and finally, enforcing the rules against discriminatory state support and preferences (State Aid) in most industries. Individual European States also have responsibility for antitrust enforcement in some cases and for deregulating their markets and eliminating State Aid. Assigning responsibility for competition enforcement, deregulation and reduction of government protection to a single supra-national entity is not the American model, which is more fragmented. Centralizing the authority within the Commission allows it to develop and enforce a consistent plan to promote competition in Europe, but runs the risk that one prong or another will be neglected. Indeed, the complexity of the Community organization increases the likelihood that deregulation will not take place evenly in all sectors of the economy. There are more than three dozen Directorates General within the Commission. DG Comp shares the responsibility for breaking down barriers to Europe-wide commerce. DG Energy and Transport oversees those sectors while DG for the Internal Market and Services coordinates the overall progress towards a single European market and implementation of the single market for the free movement of goods, labor and capital throughout the Community.

Second, deregulation has proceeded more quickly and smoothly in some industries than in others. This chapter will discuss the energy, airline transportation and financial services sectors, which provide an overview of the varying Community approach to deregulation and a good comparison with United States' legal developments discussed in other chapters. To briefly summarize: energy and financial services are officially deregulated but are not yet fully competitive while competition in transportation markets is proceeding in airline services and access to airports, but railroads remain highly regulated in much of Europe.

Third, the barriers to Europe-wide competition depend, in part, on characteristics peculiar to each industry. In general, the industries discussed below arose in local markets, in most cases before the founding of the European Community, and some of the geographic markets are still largely national. Gas and electric utilities markets suffer from two barriers to European competition: state or municipal ownership and the need to access the transmission lines or pipelines to move the product geographically. Cross-border competition in transportation depends on the mode: railroads face interconnection technology and State Aid issues while national airlines may benefit from state protection and aid but are less limited by technical bottlenecks. Financial institutions are subject to regulation by national banking agencies, which may not view competition as an important goal. In addition, the legal barriers to branching to another country are low, but the psychological barriers appear to be high as consumers are reluctant to trust a foreign bank with their assets. Finally, national officials have granted preferences to national firms, most recently in a cross-border merger of electric and gas utility firms. By comparison, although this chapter will not discuss telecommunications in detail, European competition in some aspects of mobile telephony is well established because consumers have adopted high-technology products that seamlessly cross national borders unless there are technical bottlenecks. Sophisticated consumers take advantage of advances in telecommunications technology and they are not loyal to a national provider (Martin *et al.* 2005).

The growing group of Member States have agreed to certain fundamental principles, enunciated in the Treaty of Rome and subsequent treaty documents, which reserve certain powers to the States while requiring them to take proactive action to adopt and enforce new laws. The Treaty structure attempts to bring free market competition by incremental steps to the traditionally regulated industries: transportation including airlines, financial markets including banking, the energy sector including gas and electricity, telecommunications. First, Member States are permitted to continue to regulate these market sectors, with important exceptions described below, but the Treaty also mandates a specific program of 'liberalization' or deregulation, enforced by the Commission. Government support, called State Aid, to sectors of the market is designed to be similarly limited in time and scope, with Commission oversight. Finally, and somewhat at odds with the commitment to deregulation and market competition, the EU also embraces universal availability of certain necessities of life, including transportation, energy and communications services. The Commission affirmed that:

> [t]he basic concept of universal service is to ensure the provision of high-quality service to all at prices everyone can afford. Universal service is defined in terms of principles: equality, universality, continuity and adaptability; and in terms of

sound practices: openness in management, price-setting and funding and scrutiny by bodies independent of those operating the services . . . Universal service is, none the less, a flexible concept, which evolves gradually in line with specific structural and technical features and sector-specific requirements. It is also evolutionary in the way it has to adapt to technological change, new general interest requirements and users' needs. (Communication from the Commission (1996), Services of General Interest in Europe, p. 3.)

At first glance, the European image may appear orderly, proceeding directly from inefficient regulation to market competition, but the actual experience has been less orderly, slower than originally anticipated, and perhaps more contested than expected. However, the European experience with deregulation provides a vivid and illuminating comparison with the American one described in this volume.

European Union Legislative Framework

Founding principles

The European approach to mergers in deregulated or newly competitive industries has been fundamentally different from the American story described in the other chapters in this book for several reasons. First, the independent existence of the European Union as a political entity is a relatively recent phenomenon and the legislative history that underlies the Union's founding documents reflect substantive competition law theories that differ in important ways from the American justifications. Secondly, anti-merger legislation in the EU is very recent, especially as compared to the United States' history of nearly a century of merger litigation under the Clayton Act. The first European merger regulation was adopted in 1989 (Merger Reg. 4064/89 (1989)) and, due in part to important decisions of the Court of First Instance a decade later (Case No. T-342/99, Airtours v. Commission (2002); Case No. T-5/02, Tetra Laval BV v. Commission (2002); Case No. T-310/01, Schneider Electric SA v. Commission (2002)), the regulation was substantially amended in 2004 (Merger Reg. 139/2004 (2004)). Finally, the European Union is an evolving entity that imperfectly mirrors the American federal system.

The European Commission is empowered to administer and enforce the EU competition statutes, reviewed by the Court of First Instance and European Court of Justice. In addition, the 27 Member States have their own competition statutes and enforcement agencies, which apply EU competition law as well as the laws of the individual Member State. Various sectors of State economies were and are government-regulated monopolies, including energy, telecommunications, transportation and postal services. The Commission has the authority to direct the Member States to deregulate and introduce competition, but this power is limited and applied with caution (EC Treaty Arts. 3, 10, 86, 226; European Commission (1996) *XXV Report on Competition Policy*, COM(96) 126). Accordingly, the Commission is at once the enforcer of competition law in economic sectors over which it exercises competence and a watchdog and cheerleader over *potentially* competitive sectors. The United States' experience in promoting competition and enforcing the antitrust law will likely serve as a model for the European system with important limitations because the Member States retain significant sovereignty.

The now 27-member European Union was a post-World War II creation motivated by entirely different concerns than the American experiment:

> In post-war Europe, administered economies faced development needs and state monopolies. The institutions of the European Union were created in a context of state intervention through ownership and control over trade and prices, as Europe was rebuilding after depression and war. The designers of the new post-war political economy framework, seeking to expand and integrate markets and sustain development, concluded that competition policy would be a necessary element of the new structure, principally to curb the abuses of national monopolies. (Wise 2005, p. 9)

The Treaty of Rome established the Common Market in 1957, under circumstances and economic conditions that were vastly different from the founding of the United States in the eighteenth century. From the outset, the power of the central government to act was limited to 'the powers conferred upon it by this Treaty and of the objectives assigned to it therein . . . Any actions by the Community shall not go beyond what is necessary to achieve the objectives of this Treaty' (Art. 5). The purposes of the Community, and the competition laws enacted as part of the original Treaty, differ from the goals of United States antitrust law:

> [t]he Community shall have as its task, by establishing a common market and an economic and monetary union and by implementing common policies or activities referred to in Articles 3 and 4, to promote throughout the Community a harmonious, balanced and sustainable development of economic activities, a high level of employment and of social protection, equality between men and women, sustainable and non-inflationary growth, a high degree of competitiveness and convergence of economic performance, a high level of protection and improvement of the quality of the environment, the raising of the standard of living and quality of life, and economic and social cohesion and solidarity among Member States (Art. 2).

Specific objectives recognized by Treaty include 'an internal market characterized by the abolition, as between Member States, of obstacles to the free movement of goods, persons, services and capital' (Art. 3(c)), 'a common policy in the sphere of agriculture and fisheries' (Art. 3(e)), 'a common policy in the sphere of transport' (Art. 3(f)), 'a system insuring that competition in the internal markets is not distorted' (Art. 3(g)), 'the strengthening of the competitiveness of Community industry' (Art. 3(m)), 'encouragement for the establishment and development of trans-European networks' (Art. 3(o)), and 'measures in the spheres of energy, civil protection and tourism' (Art. 3(u)). Thus, there is plain tension between the goals of competition, reduction of barriers to the free movement of goods among the member countries, and the promotion of a single market. The EU has dealt with these diverse goals by both requiring competition and allowing the member states to regulate specific industrial sectors of their economies.

Competition law
Competition was so important to the goals of creating a supra-national Community that two fundamental antitrust principles were written into the original Treaty: prohibitions on collusion, Article 81 (formerly Art. 85), and anti-monopoly prescriptions, Article 82 (formerly Art. 86). The European Commission was initially empowered to enforce the competition Articles by Regulation 17, adopted by the Council in 1962. In 1997, the Commission adopted a program to modernize EU competition law, apply economic principles in case analysis, and announced a simplified one-stop-shop for firms subject to the competition Articles, noting that:

> [C]ompetition policy must adapt to the economic realities of the contemporary world, including such factors as the single market, technological progress, and globalisation. . . . in a single market, with fifteen Member States, a market that is moving towards an economic and monetary union which will increase the comparability of prices and intensify trade, and preparing for enlargement towards central and eastern Europe. (1997 Report on Competition Policy)

Additional candidate countries including Croatia, the former Yugoslav Republic of Macedonia, and Turkey are now seeking accession to the EU.

The Commission is responsible both for enforcing the European Union antitrust articles and merger regulation and also for monitoring and enforcing the provisions promoting liberalization and prohibiting State Aid. On the one hand, gathering all of these related issues together within the jurisdiction of one enforcement agency allows the agency to take a broad view of competition and strive to coordinate all three facets of its enforcement obligations to achieve more competitive markets. On the other hand, there is a serious risk of fragmentation and preference for one or another of the three legs of competition enforcement by the agency or its appointed Commissioners.

The Community adopted legislation specifically dealing with mergers in 1989, and the first Commission challenge to a proposed merger occurred in 1991 (Wise 2005; Merger Reg. 4064/89 (1989)). The current Merger Regulation was revised in 2004, after important changes in the operation and scope of the European Union including the accession of ten additional Member States in 2004, and entry into force of a multinational economic and monetary union (Merger Reg. 139/2004 (2004)). The Merger Regulation applies only to mergers 'with a Community dimension', defined as concentrations that exceed specified worldwide and Community monetary thresholds unless each of the merging firms does more than two-thirds of its turnover in the same Member State. Mergers below the threshold are reviewed only if the parties do a specified amount of business in at least three Member States (Merger Reg. 1(3) (2004)). The Regulation strikes a balance between the legitimate interests of the Community and its individual sovereign States by enshrining the integrative goals of the Treaty as paramount:

> For the achievement of the aims of the Treaty, Article 3(1)(g) gives the Community the objective of instituting a system of ensuring that competition in the internal market is not distorted. Article 4(1) of the Treaty provides that the activities of the member States and the Community are to be conducted in accordance with the principle of an open market economy with free competition. These principles are essential for the further development of the internal market. (Merger Reg. (1) (2004))

To facilitate efficient review, the Merger Reg. establishes a 'one stop shop' system, with the Commission having exclusive authority to review mergers with the defined Community dimension and delegating other mergers to the antitrust agencies of the affected Member States (Merger Reg. (8) (2004)) who have jurisdiction to apply their own antitrust laws to such mergers (Merger Reg. Art. 4. (2004); Navarro *et al.* (2002); Neven *et al.* (1993)). The Commission also *may* refer a particular merger, even one that has Community-wide effects, to the regulators of a particular Member State if the competitive effects would significantly affect commerce within that country, and must refer it, in whole or in part, to the national regulators if the only competitive effects are limited to one country and the national officials have requested the referral (Case No. IV/M.278 British Airways/Dan Air (1993)). A Member State may refer a merger to the Commission, even if it does not have a Community-wide dimension, if that State believes the merger will affect its own trade with another State (Merger Reg. (15) (2004)). By asserting exclusive jurisdiction over mergers with a Community dimension, but permitting referrals in particular cases, the Commission is engaged in balancing the national and Community interests in applying a uniform substantive legal standard, streamlining the process, and advancing the fundamental goals of the Community, i.e. lowering trade barriers between the Member States, while recognizing interests of the States in transactions of particular significance to their economy. There is real tension in this balancing act, as the Regulation recognizes in Clause 19, which provides:

> Furthermore, the exclusive application of this Regulation to concentrations [mergers] with a Community dimension is without prejudice to Article 296 of the Treaty [security], and does not prevent the Member States from taking appropriate measures to protect legitimate interests other than those pursued by this Regulation, provided that such measures are compatible with the general principles and other provision of Community law. (Merger Reg. (19) (2004))

REGULATION AND PROTECTION OF NATIONAL MARKETS – STATE ACTION

Article 86 (formerly Art. 90) limits the authority of Member States to regulate markets:

> '[i]n the case of public undertakings and undertakings to which Member States grant special or exclusive rights, Member States shall neither enact nor maintain in force any measure contrary to the rules contained in this Treaty, in particular those rules provided for in Article 12 [anti-discrimination on national grounds] and Articles 81 to 89 [competition].'

However, those regulated firms 'entrusted with the operation of services of general economic interest or having the character of a revenue-producing monopoly' are subject to the EU antitrust laws only 'in so far as the application of such rules does not obstruct the performance, in law or in fact, of the particular tasks assigned to them' (Art. 86(2)). The specific sectors subject to State regulation include energy, transportation, telecommunications, agriculture and postal services. Finally, the Commission has the authority to 'ensure the application of the provisions' of Article 86 to the Member States and to issue binding directives to the states (Art. 86(3)). The European experience mirrors, in some respects, regulated industries in the United States and the state action doctrine that exempts firms from antitrust liability if the state government has the authority to regulate, makes an affirmative decision to supplant competition with regulation, and actively supervises the entities (*Parker v. Brown*, 317 U.S. 341 (1943); *California Retail Liquor Dealers Ass'n v. Midcal Alum., Inc.*, 445 U.S. 97 (1980); *FTC v. Ticor Title Ins. Co.*, 504 U.S. 621 (1992)).

Whenever the Commission finds that a Member State has violated its obligations under the Treaty, it has the power to demand an explanation from the State and then may commence infringement proceedings in the European Court of Justice (Art. 226). Court orders are enforceable by the Commission and include penalties and fines (Art. 228). Infringement proceedings have been necessary to compel States to comply with Commission directives in energy and financial markets and its approvals of energy and bank mergers. The number of infringement investigations and proceedings in these two markets indicates that not all the states embrace the liberalization process, especially when particularly important national firms are involved.

Article 87 prohibits State Aid 'which distorts or threatens to distort competition by favouring certain undertakings or the production of certain goods' unless other sections of the Treaty authorize the assistance. Even with the limitations of the Treaty, excessive State Aid can discriminate in favor of national firms, frustrate cross-border competition, and interfere with the Community's goals summarized in Articles 2 and 3, so the Commission has adopted a five-year 'State Aid Action Plan' to reduce governmental aid to firms, promote 'smart' aid limited to responding to market failures without distorting competition, simplify and clarify the rules on aid, and obtain cooperation from the Member States to create a 'level playing field' for all firms in the common market (Commission of the European Communities State Aid Action Plan (2005); Quigley and Collins 2003, pp. 206–209, 228–29, 235–37).

Member States' power to create state-owned monopolies is limited by Articles 31 (formerly 37), 28 (formerly 30) and 29 (formerly 31). Article 31 provides that 'Member States shall adjust any State monopolies of a commercial character so as to ensure that no discrimination regarding the conditions under which goods are procured and marketed exists between nationals of Member States'. This section applies both to monopolies run by the state and any subordinate governmental entity, and also to those private firms that are the beneficiaries of government grants of monopolies. The production and sales of agricultural products receive special treatment throughout the Treaty, and Article 31(3) carves out a rule for government monopolies whose object is marketing or price supports. Finally, Articles 28 and 29, respectively, prohibit 'quantitative restrictions . . . and all measures having equivalent effect' on imports and exports between members of the EU.

Sector Liberalization and State Aid

One of the fundamental objectives of the Union was to equalize and stabilize the economies of the Member States and break down barriers among them (Art. 2). Competition was to be a key method to achieve those goals (Art. 2(g)). However, all countries, including new members, have a patchwork of national preferences and regulations over important sectors of their economies. Deregulation was from the outset part of the mission of the Directorate General for Competition. Article 86 prohibits the Member States from adopting or maintaining any legal preferences contrary to Articles 12 (non-discrimination on the basis of nationality) or 81 through 89 (competition). Therefore, in comparison with United States antitrust law, the European Union explicitly prefers market competition to state regulation, and empowers the competition agency to enforce this position (Art. 86(3)). But this preference for competition is not unlimited. Article 86(2) exempts firms 'entrusted with the operation of services of general economic interest or having the character of a revenue-producing monopoly', making them liable for antitrust violations only to the extent that 'the application of such rules does not obstruct the performance . . . of the particular tasks assigned to them. . .'.

Using its broad authority under Article 86(3), the Commission is in the process of a project of 'liberalization', to promote deregulation and bring competition to the regulated sectors of the Member States' economies. Some industries, and some Member States, have incorporated competition principles more quickly than others. The Commission has issued 18 'decisions' involving regulated industries; five on postal services, four on telecommunications, seven on sea and air transportation, and one each on insurance and broadcasting (Commission of the European Communities, Decisions Pursuant to Art. 86 of the EC Treaty). No formal decisions under Article 83(3) have yet been issued on State efforts to deregulate in the transportation, energy or financial markets, but there are ongoing investigations on the state of competition in these industries. Mergers in the energy and financial services markets have raised particularly provocative issues in the intersection of European competition policy, state aid and liberalization. In response, the Commission has opened Sector Inquiries, or investigations, into the financial services, energy and telecommunications markets.

In 1995, the Commission reported that a key goal for the near term was to bring the benefits of competition to industries that had previously been occupied by state-regulated monopolies sectors. The 1995 Competition Report stated:

> The liberalization of traditionally monopolized markets, such as utilities, is an essential step in the establishment of an internal market. It is strongly believed that, without a stronger and more competitive base in the fields of energy, public transport and telecommunications, the European economy, including consumers and medium-sized enterprises, will be at a disadvantage (European Commission (1995) *XXV Report on Competition Policy*, COM(96) 126).

The Commission warned that after deregulation, strong antitrust enforcement would be necessary to make sure that mergers did not replicate the anticompetitive effects of regulation. Referring particularly to telecommunications, the Commission warned that neither high technology nor global competition were justifications to excuse anticompetitive mergers. The Commission warned that:

> 'newly emerging markets is not a password for approval. While alliances should be allowed, or even encouraged when pro-competitive, they cannot be accepted where they thwart or threaten the demonopolization process. Where big players join forces, the Commission should aim to prevent market foreclosure' (European Commission (1995) *XXV Report on Competition Policy*, COM(96) 126).

The Commission forecast national protection as the most serious threat to competition in airline transportation markets after deregulation scheduled for 1997 (European Commission (1995) *XXV Report on Competition Policy*, COM(96) 126). But, the Commission was more sanguine about the prospects for deregulation and competition in state-controlled industries, finding that:

> [T]he total amount of national aid in the period 1990–1992 has decreased, but at around ECU 94 billion on average per year for the Community as a whole is still too high for the Commission's objectives to be attained, notably with respect to the richer Member States. Vast amounts of state aid are not the way to achieve competitiveness. They delay necessary restructuring, distort competition between the companies and regions, and are a burden on public budgets' (European Commission (1995) *XXV Report on Competition Policy*, COM(96) 126).

By 2004, deregulation and competition advocacy was still at the top of the Commission's agenda:

> Through competition advocacy, good competitive practice in the marketplace can be promoted. Bringing competition to regulated industries is an important aspect of this advocacy task and the relationship between competition authorities and sector regulators plays a key role in it. When regulation is needed, we need to ensure that such regulation is well-targeted and is free of side effects that hold back competition. Both the regulatory framework and its enforcement should favour cross-border competition. Sectoral investigations contribute to our understanding of how particular markets function and help us to identify remaining barriers to free competition – be they the result of business practices, regulation or State subsidy. Sectors which have a direct impact on overall competitiveness, such as financial services and energy will be of prime concern (European Commission (2004) *Report on Competition Policy*, SEC(2005) 805).

MERGERS IN DEREGULATED INDUSTRIES: ENERGY, FINANCIAL SERVICES AND AIRLINE TRANSPORTATION

Although these three market sectors are subject to the same laws and regulatory oversight, the experience of promoting competition and analyzing mergers has diverged in important ways. Airline transportation appears largely competitive. There has been significant consolidation in this sector, and the Commission's decisions reflect an increasingly sophisticated analysis that is approaching harmonization with modern United States merger analysis.

The energy and financial services sectors have been officially liberalized but real competition has been slow to take root. The Commission opened Sector Inquiries, solicited comments and recommendations, and has issued Reports on both of these important sectors, generally finding the state of competition deficient. The Commission has reviewed and approved a number of mergers; however, its work has been frustrated by preferences for national firms and interference by various Member States. Hence, the Commission is in the process of bringing infringement proceedings before the European Court of Justice.

Energy Sector

The Council has been active in deregulating the energy sector, beginning by issuing directives in 1996 on electricity and 1998 on gas, requiring liberalization and single markets for these commodities throughout the EU (Directive 96/92EC [electricity] (2003); Directive 98/30EC [gas] (2003)). Both directives were revised in 2003. Directive 2003/54EC (2003) (electricity); Directive 2003/55 (2003) (gas).

In electricity and gas markets, prices remained high and deregulation was not proceeding swiftly enough; accordingly the Commission opened a Sector Inquiry to investigate the markets, identify competitive issues and make recommendations to national regulators (Commission Press Release IP 05/716 (2005)). The preliminary sector report described high concentration in both gas and electricity markets, uncompetitive wholesale markets caused by vertical integration and long-term contracts that foreclosed entry, vertical integration, barriers to transmission across national borders, and imperfect information that could facilitate collusion. Additional barriers to competition were found in the failure of some Member States to implement the liberalization directives. Of particular concern was the fact that the Commission had been forced to bring, or threaten, proceedings before the European Court of Justice to mandate compliance. Problem areas included gas and electric markets in Spain and Luxembourg, electricity markets in Greece and Portugal, and gas markets in Estonia and Ireland (Communication from the Commission COM(2007) 33 (2007)). The Report concluded that both markets were highly concentrated and characterized by vertically integrated firms that were able to impede new entry. In addition, firms could not easily transmit products across national borders. In the gas sector there was lack of access to transmission networks, pipeline capacity, and storage facilities. Cross-border transmission of electricity lacked transmission capacity and incentives to build additional capacity, discriminatory allocation of transmission capacity, and poor management of congestion. The persistent high concentration led the Commission to offer the possibility of structural, as well as conduct and regulatory, remedies to reform the market (European Commission Energy Sector Inquiry, Preliminary Report, Frequently Asked Questions (2006)).

The Energy Sector Final Report, issued on 10 January 2007, did not find that competition had improved. The Report noted that, despite the 'two waves' of Directives mandating liberalization in gas and electricity markets, many markets were still limited by national or regional borders. These markets tended to be highly concentrated and vertically integrated, resulting in high prices. Further, pricing structures for gas and electric services are so complex that consumers cannot reliably compare and shop for better prices, even if they have a choice among suppliers in their markets. Even though energy markets have become more open to competition, the Report concluded that there is still no competitive European energy market and that most leading national firms in gas and electricity markets do not attempt to compete across their national borders. These national partitions appear to be weakening only between Austria and Germany, where power prices in Germany appear to affect Austrian prices. Kroes (2006) Vienna, Speech/06/137; Kroes (2006) Brussels, Speech/06/92.

In response to the Sector Inquiry, the Commission undertook to review the energy liberalization Directives, aggressively enforce their provisions, and consider new Directives to achieve transparency and free movement across borders. Next, linking high concentration in energy markets to anticompetitive effects, the Commission concluded that effective competition law enforcement at the Commission and national levels is necessary. The Report singled out energy mergers as a special concern and recommended structural remedies including divestiture and review of long-term contracts as remedies to ensure that competition 'does not further deteriorate' (Communication from the Commission Inquiry Pursuant to Art. 17 of Regulation (EC) 1/2003 (2007) pp. 9–10). The Report also suggested structural remedies for violation of the non-merger competition laws (ibid., p. 10). Significantly, the Final

Report recommended that national regulatory bodies have and use more authority to liberalize energy markets. Some of these regulatory actions cited with approval included ceilings on ownership achieved by mandatory divestiture, asset swaps and contract swaps to reduce concentration (ibid., p. 13). In recommending 'substantial strengthening of the powers of regulators' the Commission appears to have chosen re-regulation, rather than deregulation, in energy markets (ibid., p. 12). Commissioner Kroes has also suggested that the Commission 'may even have to review the EU's merger rules, in order to make sure that merger cases get the same strict investigation everywhere, be it at the national or European level' (Kroes Speech to Austrian Chamber of Commerce [2006]).

Since the commencement of liberalization in the energy sector, there have been a number of mergers, only one of which was challenged by the Commission. At this stage of deregulation, however, most of the new competition is still limited to markets entirely or primarily within a single Member State. Therefore most of the merger reviews have been undertaken by the national competition authorities under their national competition laws (Merger Reg. Arts. 4(4), (5), (9)).

Commission Merger Cases

The European structure for merger review creates the likelihood of a major conflict between national and European regulators. Such a case arose in 2005, in a contested acquisition for Endesa, a Spanish gas and electric utility. Initially, Gas Natural, another Spanish energy firm, made a 22.5 billion euro hostile bid to acquire Endesa and notified the Spanish antitrust agency, seeking approval of the acquisition. Endesa petitioned the European Union Competition Directorate, arguing that the merger had a community dimension and therefore the Commission had exclusive jurisdiction to review it. Endesa does business in Portugal, France, Italy, Germany and Poland. The Commission requested the parties to provide information on the scope of their geographic markets to determine its jurisdiction. Gas Natural objected to Endesa's calculations and challenged the Commission's authority. The Spanish competition agency also appeared before the Commission arguing that it was the proper authority to review the merger. This dispute was entirely jurisdictional, based on the amount of Endesa's business within and outside of Spanish borders. The Commission concluded that the transaction lacked Community dimension and deferred to the Spanish competition authority (Case No. COMP/ 37.542 Gas Natural/Endesa (2002)). The Spanish competition agency then approved Gas Natural's bid. Endesa appealed and Spanish national courts reversed the competition agency's decision.

This particular conflict would not have occurred in American merger review. Acquisitions of a minimum size are required to file a pre-merger notification with both US federal antitrust agencies, the U.S. Department of Justice and the Federal Trade Commission. However, any American State affected by the transaction may also review and challenge the acquisition even if the national antitrust authority has declined to challenge the merger (*California v. American Stores Co.*, 495 U.S. 271 (1990)). Therefore, there is a larger risk of conflicting decisions by the antitrust agencies at different levels of government in American merger review than the European counterpart. However, the European Commission's additional authority over liberalization heightens the risk of other conflicts.

Indeed, while Endesa's acquisition by Gas Natural was pending, the German gas and electric utility E.ON AG made a 26.9 billion euro bid to acquire Endesa. This transaction clearly had a Community dimension, so the Commission exercised its merger jurisdiction and approved the transaction. The Commission found that geographic markets in the energy sector were still primarily national in scope. The Commission also found that E.ON was not likely to enter the Spanish market for gas or electricity, so potential competition would not be impaired. Further, the merger was unlikely to entrench Endesa's power in the Spanish markets generation and wholesale transmission of electric power. The merger also did not threaten to foreclose the market for gas procurement because the parties obtained supplies from different sources before the merger so would not gain additional market power after the merger. Finally, the Commission considered whether the merger would be anticompetitive because of the sheer size and geographic scope of E.ON/Endesa, making it a 'pan-European energy operator' distinct from other firms that are limited to national markets. E.ON argued that its share of any such market would be less than 15 per cent and not a competitive concern. The Commission recognized that such an international firm could harm local competitors by blocking their efforts to expand beyond national borders, but found that, first, the concerns were not supported by real evidence and, second, were premature because the pan-European energy markets are theoretical and do not yet exist (Case No. COMP/M. 4110 E.ON/Endesa (2006)).

But the Spanish energy regulatory authority, Comision Nacional de Energia (CNE) imposed conditions on the E.ON/Endesa transaction, requiring E.ON to divest approximately 30 per cent of Endesa's assets. The Commission has exclusive jurisdiction over mergers of Community-wide dimension and individual Member States are generally prohibited from imposing inconsistent conditions although they are permitted to 'take appropriate measures to protect legitimate interests other than those taken into consideration by this Regulation and compatible with the general principles and other provisions of Community law'. These 'legitimate interests' include only security, maintenance of multiple media outlets, and 'prudential rules'. The State must also notify the Commission of its actions and the Commission has 25 days to accede to the conditions (Merger Reg. Art. 21(4)). If a State violates its Treaty obligations, the Commission procedure requires it to review the matter, give the Member State an opportunity to justify its actions and then issue a 'reasoned opinion' giving the State a deadline to comply with the Commission's interpretation of the State's duties under the Treaty. If the State fails to comply, the next step is an infringement action before the Court of Justice (Art. 226).

Faced with incompatible national conditions on a merger approved by the Commission, it opened an official infringement proceeding and issued a 'letter of formal notice', a written demand for justification and withdrawal of the conditions to Spain. The Commission found that CNE's actions violated the Merger Reg. Art. 21 both on the merits and on procedural grounds, and ordered Spain to explain and withdraw the conditions (Commission Press Release IP/06/1265 (2006)). Although Spain did not adequately respond, after an appeal of the Spanish regulatory actions, the Spanish Minister of Industry, Tourism and Trade imposed new conditions. These conditions required Endesa to continue to use its brand name for five years, and to continue using domestic coal, among other things. The Commission preliminarily decided that the new conditions also infringed the Treaty guarantees of free movement of capital and establishment and again requested Spain to justify its actions (Commission Press Release IP/06/1649 (2006)). The response from the Spanish Minister proved unsatisfactory and Commissioner Kroes asserted the primacy of the supranational competition enforcers, stating that:

> I regret that the Commission has once again been obliged to intervene to avoid that a Member State places unjustified conditions on a major European takeover. No one should doubt the Commission's commitment to ensuring Europe's businesses can operate on a level playing field to the benefit of Europe's consumers, businesses and the economy as a whole (Commission Press Release IP/06/1853 (2006)).

This dispute partially arose from a Spanish statute, Royal Decree-Law 4/2005, enacted on 24 February 2006, which expanded the power of the Spanish energy regulatory agency, CNE, over mergers (Commission Press Release, IP/06/569 (2006)). The statute required the approval of CNA of any acquisition of more than 10 per cent of the shares of Spanish energy firms and allowed CNE to consider factors such as the public security and interest in granting or denying approval. The Commission requested information from the Spanish government (ibid.) then rejected Spain's justifications for the statute, and requested the government to modify the statute (Commission Press Release IP/06/1264 (2006)). Spain failed to heed the Commission recommendations. Finally, the Commission took action, formally referring Spain to the European Court of Justice for infringing the Treaty and effectively interfering with competitive acquisitions of electricity and gas utilities (Commission Press Release IP/07/82 (2007)).

This conflict between national and European enforcers over the E.ON/Endesa energy merger is of particular interest because it is unusual. In 2006, the Commission approved six other acquisitions without the friction seen in E.ON/Endesa, requiring divestitures and other affirmative remedies in several cases: Flaga/Progas/JV (Case No. COMP/M.4028 (2006)); DONG/Elsam/Energi E2 (Case No. COMP/M.3868 (2006)) (approved with divestiture of storage facilities and agreement to auction gas to competitors)); Petroplus/European Petroleum Holdings (Case No. COMP/M.4208 (2006)); EBN/Cogas Energy (Case No. COMP/M.4370 (2006)); Edison/Eneco Energia (Case No. COMP/M.4368 (2006)) and Gaz de France/Suez (Case No. COMP/M.4180 (2006)) (requiring divestitures of assets in geographic areas where they overlapped and would gain an excessive market share and to increase investment in an independently-operated gas distribution hub so that other competitors could enter the market). These acquisitions involved firms of the same nationality, operating within the same Member State, although some were subsidiaries of larger foreign firms. These transactions did not raise the E.ON/Endesa problem of an alien firm taking over a domestic champion, which can trigger national regulators to spring into action to protect national interests. The singularity of E.ON/Endesa is unsurprising: a key conclusion of the Energy Sector Inquiry Final Report was that gas and electricity firms at all levels of the chain of distribution still operated at national, or, at best, regional levels. Since liberalization, there have been few cross-border mergers, so the opportunity for conflicts remains limited and competition remains stunted. Only if the Commission is successful at promoting liberalization in the energy sector will European consumers may get the benefit of more choice and competition-driven competitive prices.

The Commission prohibited the merger of Portuguese energy firms, one operating in the wholesale and retail markets for electricity and the other in gas markets (Case No. COMP/M.3440 ENI/EDP/GDP (2004)). EDP was engaged in electricity generation, distribution and supply in Portugal and Spain while ENI was a vertically integrated gas import, transport, wholesale and distribution firm in Portugal. The Commission found that the pre-merger commitments were insufficient to alleviate its competitive concerns, took its objections to a hearing and ultimately blocked the merger. The electricity markets were open to competition before the proposed merger and natural gas markets were in the process of liberalization. In a lengthy analysis, the Commission considered the probable effect of market competition but nevertheless found that the acquisition would have strengthened EDP's dominant position in electricity markets in Portugal and GDP's dominant position in gas markets.

Mergers that do not have a Community-wide dimension are within the jurisdiction of the competition regulators of the various European Member States. Since the EU energy sector liberalization directives, a number of mergers have been reviewed by the respective national agencies, in particular involving firms operating in Belgium, Germany and the Netherlands (a complete discussion of these national mergers is beyond the scope of this chapter, but the transactions are described in more detail in Subiotto and Snelders 2004).

FINANCIAL SERVICES SECTOR

Commission Sector Investigation

In 2005, the Commission opened an inquiry into competition in the retail banking, payment cards, and business insurance markets of the financial services sector. After an extensive investigation, the Commission completed the inquiry and issued a Final Report on the Retail Banking sector in 2007. The Report's conclusions offer some guidance for merger analysis in financial services markets. As an initial matter, the Commission found that cross-border competition was still limited despite the adoption of the common European currency, the Euro. A goal of the 1999 Financial Services Action Plan was European integration of financial markets and harmonization of national regulatory systems. Five years later, the Commission found that integration was still not far advanced and there remained impediments to competition. The market failures in the retail banking industry included high and increasing concentration in some countries due in part to intrastate mergers, barriers to entry, and lack of cross-border mergers. Vertical integration, bank networks, and trade associations were additional structural impediments to competition. A major part of the investigation focused on the payment card industry because the Commission feared that network effects and technology could constitute a barrier to new entry, resulting in higher costs for consumers. Of additional concern, the Commission found anticompetitive conduct in the form of exclusionary behavior by banks against nonbank potential competitors (Commission Press Release IP 06/496 (2006)). Protectionism by national regulators also contributed to the lack of effective competition.

In theory, banks should be able to compete throughout the EU by opening new branches, opening a subsidiary, or by selling services directly to customers without maintaining a physical presence in the country. The last option would be attractive because it would not subject the bank to additional regulation. Banks can also joint venture with a well-known bank in a foreign state, taking advantage of the partner's brand identity, or merge with a foreign bank. The Interim Report on Banking found that these strategies allow quick entry into a new market at sufficient scale to compete successfully and result in more competitive prices for consumers, but that regulatory barriers limited cross-border bank mergers. For more than 20 years, cross-border bank mergers represented no more than 10–15 per cent of all bank merger activity, with exceptions during three periods: the late 1980s, in 1989 after the Financial Services Action Plan, and in 1999–2000 before the introduction of the Euro (Commission of the European Communities (2006), Interim Report II, pp. 32–33). A 2005 survey found five major barriers to cross-border mergers by banks: national regulatory systems that disadvantage new entrants, attitudes including political intervention and consumer distrust of foreigners, taxes, economies of scale, and, to a smaller degree, legal barriers (ibid., pp. 32–33).

The Commission concluded that barriers to interstate mergers should be reduced, even though these transactions may still lag behind intrastate mergers that can consolidate administration and retail services. The national bank regulators were a more serious impediment to multistate mergers than the national antitrust agencies, and reforming the regulatory systems was a high priority. The Commission advised national bank regulators to rely on their counterparts in other countries to apply similar standards to banks, producing sound financial institutions and providing adequate protection to their citizens. The Commission asserted that it was developing 'measures to improve the prudential assessment of cross-border acquisitions in the banking, insurance and securities sectors' (Commission of the European Communities (2006), Interim Report II, pp. 34–35). The Commission also suggested that economies of scale should be made more easily available and tax rules could be amended to facilitate the expansion of financial institutions beyond the borders of a single Member State to create a true European bank (ibid. at p. 35). The Commission concluded that the market for financial services tended to be national in scope and that concentration remained high, especially in the Netherlands, Belgium, Sweden, and Finland. National financial markets in Italy, Spain and Germany appeared to be less concentrated, with the exception of some German regions (ibid. at p. 151).

The Final Report emphasized the importance of retail banking, defined to include financial services for consumers and small- and medium-sized businesses, and found that national borders still represented barriers to European-wide competition for retail banking, payment systems, and credit registers (Communication from the Commission COM(2007) 33 (2007), p. 3).

Commission Merger Cases

Although some mergers involving the financial sector have taken place without controversy, others have involved potentially serious national controversies. In the non-controversial category, the Netherlands firm Fortis Insurance International and the Portugese Banco Comercial Portugues (BCP) agreed jointly to acquire another Portugese financial institution, Millenniumbep Fortis Grupo Segurador, SGPS, S.A. (NHC). Among the acquirers, Fortis participated in the markets for retail and commercial banking and BCP participated in retail, private, and corporate banking, as well as banking products and services. BCP incorporated NHC to hold four insurance companies that BCP previously controlled. In the transaction, BCP sought to transfer control of the insurance companies to NHC; Fortis would then acquire 51 per cent of NHC and BCP would control the remaining 49 per cent minority share. The Commission found, first, that the transaction had a Community-wide dimension and was properly before the European competition agency for review (Case No. COMP/M.3556 Fortis/BCP (2005)). The Commission found the merger did not threaten competition in any case. Even based on the narrowest market definitions, the parties controlled small shares of various insurance products; 15 per cent for retirement products in Portugal, 19 per cent for risk and annuities, 23 per cent for life insurance, 22 per cent in health insurance, and 27 per cent in pension fund management. The Commission's competitive analysis was straightforward and did not highlight either the financial services industry or process of deregulation as significant factors. Instead, the relatively small market shares, the presence of other competitors, and the lack of overlap for all products except pension fund management was determinative. Accordingly, the Commission approved the transaction (Case No. COMP/M.3556 Fortis/BCP (2005)).

The proposed merger of two multinational banks, German HVB and the Italian firm UniCredit, sparked a conflict between the Commission and national regulators resembling the E.ON/Endesa merger in the energy sector and raised the issue of cross-border mergers and national protectionism in the financial services industry. The complex serial mergers began with Italian bank UniCredito's acquisition of a Polish national bank, Polska Kasa Opieke S.A. (Pekao) from the Polish government in 1999. As a part of that acquisition, UniCredito effectively agreed not to acquire any other Polish banks for a 10-year term (Commission Press Release IP/06/277 (2006)). The conflict arose when UniCredito agreed to acquire the German bank HypoVereinsbank (HVB Group), which owned BPH Bank, a Polish bank, in a 20-billion euro deal.

Both UniCredito and HVB banks were full-service financial institutions offering corporate and retail banking services. They operated principally in their home countries but the competition analysis focused on Poland, the Czech Republic and the Slovak Republic. The Commission provisionally defined seven relevant product markets: retail banking (the full line of banking services including checking and savings accounts, ATM services, consumer credit, mortgages, pension funds and securities brokerage), corporate banking, factoring, financial market services for clients, asset management, investment banking and payment clearance. In the Czech Republic and the Slovak Republic neither bank was a dominant firm, each having less than 15 per cent of any of the product markets, and they faced competition from larger firms with international and local reputations.

In Poland, however, the merging firms were the second and third largest banks. The merged firm would have about 20 per cent of the market for retail banking depending on the particular product; and market shares of 15–45 per cent in corporate banking services. In addition to the large market shares, the merged bank would have been magnitudes larger than their competitors in the corporate banking market. Disparity in size is an important factor in assessing the market power of a potentially dominant firm (Case No. 85/76, Hoffmann-LaRoche v. Commission (1979)). Despite the competitive concerns, the Commission concluded that there was sufficient rivalry in Poland for all of the banking products. Moreover, the nature of the industry favors firms with well-developed networks of branches so that retail, corporate, and institutional customers can get service throughout the country. A UniCredito/HVB network would be the largest in Poland, but the Commission found that three other bank competitors maintained viable networks of branches and the next largest would only be slightly smaller than UniCredito/HVB. Therefore, the Commission approved the acquisition and did not order any divestitures or other remedies (Case No. COMP/M.3894 UniCredito/HVB (2005)).

Citing its prior agreement with UniCredito in the 1999 Pekao deal, the Polish government objected to the HVB acquisition and insisted that its national banking regulators prohibit the acquisition. The Commission objected to the Polish government's action and maintained that Poland's agreement with UniCredito became void when Poland joined the European Union in 2004. The Commission commenced an infringement proceeding and argued that it had exclusive jurisdiction over the proposed merger because of its Community-wide dimension (Commission Press Release

IP/06/276 (2006)). The stand-off could have been serious: Commissioner Kroes declared 'I am determined to ensure that Member States do not stand in the way of mergers falling within the Commission's exclusive competence. Otherwise the EU's Single market will descend into chaos' (Commission Press Release IP/06/277 (2006)).

Poland filed a complaint in the European Court of Justice challenging the Commission's approval of the merger. The complaint challenged the antitrust analysis, specifically its market definition and competitive effects assessment (www.eubusiness.com). Ultimately, the crisis was resolved without further judicial proceedings. Poland withdrew its complaint after UniCredito agreed to divest 200 of the 483 BPH branches acquired in the HVB deal to a third party, thus maintaining BPH as an independent bank (*International Herald Tribune*, 11 May 2006; Norris, *NY Times*, 12 May 2006; Case No. COMP/M.3894 UniCredito/HVB (2005)).

European bank merger review looks streamlined compared to the fragmented American system of federal and state regulatory and antitrust enforcement agencies with jurisdiction over mergers of financial institutions. This system has the advantage of clarity, but unsurprisingly it has not eliminated the risk that a Member State will assert its authority over a domestic bank and cause a conflict that can be resolved only by threatening action for infringement. The unitary European system also cannot force banks to diversify across national borders. The Sector Inquiry found that financial institutions still operate primarily within national borders because international branching involves trust as well as legal authorization, so a competitive internal market for financial services has not yet been realized.

TRANSPORTATION SECTOR

Legal Background – Legislation and Regulations

In 1968, the Council began to liberalize the transportation industry, beginning with rail and water transport services (Council Regulation (EEC) 1017/68 (1968) O.J. (L 175) 1–12), and extending liberalization to the airline sector in 2004. Accordingly, the same substantive and procedural antitrust rules, including procedural modernization, apply to competition for air transportation as other industries (Joint Statement of the Council and the Commission on the Functioning of the Network of Competition Authorities (2002) O.J. (L 1) 1–25). The process of liberalization in the airline market has followed a multi-step development: the adoption and enforcement by European authorities of regulations to open access to air carriers of all countries, limitation on State Aid to national carriers and harmonization of national laws and procedures concerning airline transportation (*see* Commission White Paper: European transport policy for 2010: time to decide (2001)).

Any airline licensed by any of the EU Member States is a 'Community air carrier' and may carry passenger, mail and cargo throughout the EU. Importantly however, the license does not entitle the owner the right to serve any particular route. A 'Community air carrier' must be majority owned by either the licensing Member State or its nationals (with exceptions for cargo carriers grandfathered under prior regulations), have its principle place of business in the licensing State, and meet other insurance and safety requirements (Council Regulation (EEC) 2407/92 (1992) O.J. (L 240) 1–7). Beginning in 1993, any licensed Community air carrier was permitted to operate passenger, mail and cargo flights on all routes within the European Union (with temporary exceptions for exclusive contracts in some markets) (Council Regulation (EEC) 2408/92 (1992) O.J. (L 240) 8–14). Accordingly, before the United Kingdom could grant exclusive rights and a government subsidy to secure air service between three pairs of cities in Scotland, it had to make a determination that there was a public need for air service, publicly solicit bids and notify the Commission. Only if no competitor was willing to serve the markets without government compensation, could the UK circumvent the competitive market, grant exclusive rights over the service, and provide a subsidy to protect the public interest and ensure service (UK-Edinburgh: Operation of Scheduled Air Services (EEC) 2408/92 (2006) O.J. (C 186) 17–18).

Since 1993, Community air carriers have been free to set their own fares at any level the carrier deemed appropriate without government oversight by simply filing notice of the rates. This Regulation brought price competition to the airline market but contained the seeds of its own destruction if Member States chose to challenge fares subjectively deemed improper (Council Regulation (EEC) 2409/92 (1992) O.J. (L 240) 15–17). The potential for State interference with the market has not come to pass. The Directorate General for Energy and Transport has reported that no State has ever objected to low fares, as evidenced by the proliferation of discount airlines and the widespread availability of discount fares. The Commission has expressed concern about unfairly high fares on some routes, but, again, neither Member States nor the Commission has sought to block a fare as excessive (Directorate General for Energy and Transport, Air Transport Portal).

Most airline reservations are made through computer reservation systems (CRS), which are jointly owned and operated by airlines. There is a distinct possibility for bias in a CRS, privileging the flights of the owner airlines and discriminating against competitors. A 1989 Council Regulation permitted airline competitors to cooperate to create and operate a CRS, but prohibited bias or discrimination in their operation. Non-owner airlines were guaranteed equal access to list their flights on any CRS. The listing, ranking and display of flights must be neutral, with no preferences for the flights of the CRS operators (Council Regulation (EEC) 2299/89 (1989) O.J. (L 220) 1–7).

An important step towards inter-European competition in air transportation was the introduction of the 'single European sky' concept in 2001. The Commission directed the Member States to adopt structural reforms to implement the concept. Regulations created the framework for a uniform, Europe-wide system of airspace management, coordinated air traffic control, and other multinational cooperation (Regulation (EC) 551/2004 (2004) O.J. (L 96) 20–24; Regulation (EC) 549/2004 (2004) O.J. (L 96) 1–8; Regulation (EC) 550/2004 (2004) O.J. (L 96) 10–19).

Mandating equal access to congested European airports was another critical step towards promoting European competition in airline services. Regulation 793/2004 begins by dividing airports into highly congested (coordinated airports) and more open airports ('schedules facilitated airports') and directed the Member States to categorize each airport in the State in one or other class. Member States were to appoint staff facilitators to manage the schedules. Airlines must obtain a 'slot' in order to take off and land at a congested airport. Competing airlines and the staff facilitators cooperatively agreed upon take-off and landing schedules at the non-congested airports. Such agreements would raise competitive concerns absent the regulatory authorization. The slot allocations and schedules are to be established without discrimination or preferences among the airlines using the airports. Airlines are generally permitted to freely transfer their slots to other airlines or to use their slot for different routes or types of air services, but airlines do not 'own' their slots unless they use them. New entrant airlines must maintain their slots and schedules for two six-month seasons (Regulation (EC) 793/2004 (2004) O.J. (L 138) 50–60). New, unallocated and underused, generally defined as less than 80 per cent of capacity, slots go into a pool and new entrants into the market are entitled to the first 50 per cent of these slots. Finally, airports are prohibited from discriminating in the allocation of slots on the basis of nationality, and must treat the airlines of foreign countries no worse than their domestic air carriers (ibid., at 50–60).

Despite these efforts to create a competitive marketplace for airline transportation described above, the Commission recently concluded that there may be some important limits on the application of antitrust law to airlines. Hard core horizontal restraints of competition, such as price fixing and market allocation, are illegal under Article 81(1), generally in accord with the American antitrust standard. Unlike American practice, the Commission may exempt horizontal agreements from the Article 81 prohibition if it concludes that the pro-competitive benefits outweigh the threatened harm (Art. 81(3)). In the market for airline transportation, the Commission issued a Draft Regulation finding that some horizontal agreements would be both necessary and efficient. Specifically, the Commission found that competitors had to discuss their fares so that passengers could easily travel between their points of origin and destination on more than one airline, termed interlining. These discussions should not be condemned as price fixing or anti-competitive exchanges of information under Article 81. The Commission also found that air carriers should be permitted to discuss schedules and slot allocations at airports without violating the antitrust prohibition against market allocation. Therefore, temporary block exemptions permitted competitors to share price information on interline travel within Europe until 31 December 2006, and with third countries until the end of 2008.

The Commission also has adopted State Aid guidelines that require Member States to give prior notice of any proposed aid to domestic airlines. If the responsible Commission Directorate General concludes, after investigation, that the aid is unlawful, the State has an opportunity to comment, after which the Commission has the power to declare the aid to be illegal and require the State to recover it from the recipient (Council Regulation (EC) 659/1999 (1999) O.J. (L 83) 1–9). The Directorate General for Energy and Transport (DG Tren) is responsible for making decisions on State Aid in transportation sectors, while DG Comp is responsible for most other sectors of the European economy. This is a potentially powerful Regulation that could decrease national protection of domestic firms and facilitate new competitive entry into airline markets throughout Europe. To date, seven national air carriers: Aer Lingus, Air France, Alitalia, Iberia, Olympic Airways, Sabena, and TAP airlines, were permitted to receive State Aid from their respective national governments after the Commission found that the aid was necessary to finance needed corporate reorganizations. Future State Aid decisions will indicate whether this power will be used to promote market competition in the airline transportation sector.

Commission Merger Cases

The Commission has reviewed and approved more than a dozen mergers of air carriers in the past 15 years and has prohibited only one proposed transaction, Ryanair's proposed acquisition of Aer Lingus in 2007 (Case COMP/M.4439 (2007)). However, a number of the approvals were contingent upon important competitive concessions to blunt the anticompetitive aspects of the proposed mergers and others were withdrawn by the parties for unspecified reasons. These transactions include mergers between international airlines that competed in the European Community, such as Delta Airlines and Pan Am (approved in 1991), United Airlines and USAirways (approved in 2001), and Singapore Airlines and Virgin Atlantic (approved 2000), as well as European national carriers, many of which also competed in other international markets, including British Airways and TAT (approved 1996), British Airways and Air Liberté (approved 1997), SAS and Spanair (approved 2002), Air France and KLM (approved 2004), Lufthansa and Swiss (approved 2005).

Product market definition
The Court of First Instance (Case No. T-2/93, Air France v. Commission (TAT) (1994)) and European Court of Justice (Case No. 66/86, Ahmed Saeed Flugreisen and Other v. Zentrale zur Bekämpfung unlauteren Wettbewerbs (1989)) defined product markets for airline mergers as city pairs plus a 'bundle of routes' that are substitutes for particular city pair routes. The Commission employs this market definition, but has applied it with increasing economic sophistication beginning with the 1991 merger between Pan Am and Delta Air Lines. There, the Commission limited the product market to 'scheduled air transportation services' between particular transAtlantic city pairs without significant analysis or consideration of other alternatives such as charter flights or tours. No other methods of transportation were relevant to the product market issue because the only flights that the merging firms offered in competition with each other were transatlantic, eliminating ground transportation and, as a practical matter, water transportation as reasonable substitutes. The Commission also recognized that alternative airports to the ones served by the merging firms might provide competition to particular city pairs because most international transportation was funneled through a relatively small number of gateway cities – 25 in the United States and more than 40 in Europe. Therefore, for example, the Paris/New York city pair might be a reasonable substitute for a London/New York route for some consumers. However, the Commission lacked hard evidence about whether or not consumers actually viewed the 'bundle of routes' as a substitute and was concerned that government regulations on airline routes might make actual substitution infeasible, so it concluded that the decision did not require adoption of a particular product market in order to approve the acquisition (Case No. IV/M.130 Delta Air Lines/Pan Am (1991)).

The Commission added more content to the product market definition in dicta in the KLM/Air UK case. Key overlaps in service existed on routes of the two airlines to and from the five London airports: Gatwick,

Heathrow, London City, Luton, and Stansted. Unlike some United States merger decisions and the DOJ/FTC Merger Guidelines, the Commission obtained and used competitors' opinions on this issue without apparent concern. Some American courts and regulators discount competitors' views on the ground that competitors may be biased against a strong merged firm that would provide fierce competitive pressure or, alternatively, wish to take advantage of the umbrella effect of a dominant merged firm. The results of the consumer survey showed that the product market should be divided between business and leisure travelers because business passengers require flexibility to change their schedules, so would buy full fare tickets, while leisure travelers prefer restricted tickets to obtain discount prices. However, the Commission found that all varieties of tickets and fares were generally available on the overlapping routes and concluded that dividing the market into smaller subsets would not affect its determination that the merger would not significantly harm competition (Case No. IV/M.967 KLM/Air UK (1997)).

The distinction was considered again in SAIR Group/AOM, which involved scheduled airline service and sales to charters and tour operators throughout Europe and the South of France and other 'holiday destinations'. The Commission again found that neither the broader nor narrower market definition would change its final conclusion, so declined to adopt a definitive product market. However, the Commission found that there were important differences in the prices and conditions of travel between tickets sold to individuals and to tour operators, but any individual seat on a scheduled flight to a 'holiday destination' could be bought either by a tourist or a tour operator. The Commission ultimately concluded that no hypothetical narrower product markets would have changed the outcome in any event. Similarly, distinguishing business from leisure travelers, or, to adopt the more accurate language of this decision, 'time-sensitive' and 'price-sensitive' travelers would not have produced a different result (Case No. IV/M.1494 SAirGroup/AOM (1999); Case No. COMP/M.2041 United Airlines/US Airways (2001)). The hypothetical narrow markets which distinguished sales to individuals from block sales to tour operators were again recognized in dicta in SAS/Spanair (Case No. IV/M.1494 SAirGroup/AOM (1999)). In Ryanair, the Commission noted the firm's reputation as a discount airline, but did not define a separate market of 'low cost airlines', finding that it based its prices on competition in the relevant geographic market and because Aer Lingus did not share that reputation (Commission Memo (27 June 2007) Mergers: Commission's prohibition of Ryanair's proposed acquisition of Aer Lingus – frequently asked questions Memo 07/258).

The Commission adopted a different narrower market definition in United/US Air, a case involving transatlantic, not intercontinental, airline service. The Commission had, in prior cases, defined the product market as flights between particular city pairs plus any reasonable substitute cities. The parties in United/US Airways, however, argued that indirect flights, which included a stop, should be part of the city pair market. The Commission recognized important differences between nonstop and other flights: nonstop flights tend to be more expensive but shorter in duration than those that involve a stop. This hypothetical product market therefore tends to converge with other hypothetical narrow markets identified in other airline merger cases, distinguishing time and price-sensitive customers. However, the evidence also showed that even time-sensitive business travelers might be required to accept a somewhat longer trip by their price-sensitive employers, making the transatlantic flight market different from other city pair markets. The Commission also adopted a more precise geographic measure for 'the bundle of substitute cities'. The radius surrounding an airport from which customers are drawn is its catchment area. If the catchment areas of two airports overlap, then customers within the overlap may consider both airports to be substitutes for each other, all else being equal. In this case, the parties sought to broaden the market to include additional cities as substitutes for city pair markets on which they overlapped by proposing large catchment areas. The Commission applied its more precise geographic market definition to the facts presented and defined the markets supported by evidence of consumer substitution. This sharper standard for substitutes more clearly articulates the salient issue for courts, commentators and regulators (Case No. COMP/M.2041 United Airlines/US Airways (2001)). The Commission continued to use catchment area analysis to define the 'bundle of routes' that were adequate substitutes for city pair markets in later airline merger cases, including other factors deemed important to consumers such as the interchangeability of nonstop and indirect flights (Case No. IV/M.1494 SAirGroup/AOM (1999); Case No. IV/M.967 KLM/Air UK (1997)).

Transportation within Europe is unlike its American counterpart; the distances tend to be shorter and rail transportation is more frequent and convenient for many trips. Therefore, the Commission has long considered whether or not railway travel is an adequate substitute for airline service in reviewing proposed airline mergers. Clearly, this would not be relevant for transatlantic or intercontinental routes. In Swissair/Sabena, both airlines served routes between their home countries, Switzerland and Belgium, specifically between Brussels and several Swiss cities. The Commission decided that non-airline travel, including rail service, could be a substitute on these routes but concluded that the price and time differentials made the substitute too imperfect to check any attempted exercise of dominant power (Case No. IV/M.616 Swissair/Sabena II (1995)). Rail transportation within

France was still not sufficient competition for airline service in 1997, when British Airways sought to acquire a controlling share of the insolvent French airline, Air Liberté. Case No. IV/M.857 British Airways/Air Liberté (1997). If high-speed rail transportation via the TGV and Eurostar make significant inroads in the European market, the Commission may change its view and accept this alternative as a reasonable substitute, especially if commuting time to and from airports and airport security delays are considered as part of the total duration of the trip. Time comparability is necessary, but not sufficient, for rail to constitute a legitimate substitute; rail prices must also be comparable to airline prices. It is difficult to predict whether or when this condition may occur – on one hand, gasoline prices have increased significantly, but, on the other hand, discount airlines have proliferated in Europe.

Geographic market definition
AOM/Air Liberté/Air Littoral considers whether different categories of consumers for the 'city pair and bundle of substitutes' product market are in different geographic markets. These merging parties offered transportation between a variety of city pairs in continental Europe, some on scheduled flights and some on charters or group sales by tour operators. The Commission concluded that sales to tour operators and airline charters were different from individual airline tickets purchased by private consumers. This case expands the geographic market definition for the product defined as 'ticket sales to tour and charter operators'. An individual consumer presumably wants to buy a ticket from one point to another, and, other than reasonable substitutes for the origin or destination, no other point will do. By contrast, the tour or charter operator demands a particular point of origin, generally its own location, but considers a variety of substitutes to offer consumers for their vacation destinations. Charter flights to many similar resort destinations may be reasonable substitutes for one other so a tour operator may view an assortment of resorts that share similar characteristics, i.e., warm and on a beach, or snowy and near skiing resorts, in planning a tour. Therefore, the Commission provisionally expanded the geographic market for a defined category of customers, tour and charter operators, to include potentially *all* services that the merging firms offered from a particular point to any other point, or from all of France, for national tour operators (Case No. COMP/M.2008 AOM/Air Liberté/Air Littoral (2000)).

Competitive effects
The Commission recognized 'network effects' as a concern from the earliest reported decision, the Pan Am/Delta merger. In that 1991 case, there were a very limited number of American airports that offered transatlantic

service, so consumers nationwide had to travel to one of those gateway cities. Delta had the advantage of a large American network or routes that would facilitate travel to a gateway. This advantage was unavailable to foreign airlines, which were barred from providing intra-United States service, so the merger, by combining Pan Am and Delta's international gateway cities with Delta's access to domestic United States routes could potentially be exclusionary. However, the Commission concluded that every United States airline possessed this advantage so the merger would not give the merged Pan Am/Delta significant additional power amounting to an illegal dominant position. Moreover, the Commission predicted that liberalization could eliminate some of the regulatory barriers facing European airlines and open up new routes on which they could compete (Case No. IV/M.130 Delta Air Lines/Pan Am (1991)). In fact, in British Airways/TAT, the Commission found that liberalization regulations due to take effect the following year would gradually eliminate the bar to foreign airlines offering point-to-point domestic service out of their home country, and would become fully effective in 1997. This rather distant prospect, plus the presence of strong competitors on the overlapping routes, was sufficient for the Commission to approve the merger, subject to conditions discussed below (Case No. IV/M.259 British Airways/TAT (1992)). Network effects were also no bar to approval of the British Airways/Air Liberté concentration. Although the French airline offered British Airways access to French domestic customers that were otherwise unavailable to BA as a foreign carrier, the total routes in France of the merged firm would be less than 15 per cent of all French air traffic, measured by number of passengers. The Commission used the total market share to measure power over a national network rather than concentration on particular city pairs, found the total power insufficient to raise antitrust concerns, and approved the merger (Case No. IV/M.857 British Airways/Air Liberté (1997)).

In the United/US Air case, the Commission refined its network analysis into an assessment of the 'conglomerate effects' of a merger between a regional US carrier and an international carrier. It was assumed that US Air had provided feeder service to other international airlines, collecting passengers throughout its region and delivering them to the international gateway cities. The competitive risk, then, was that the merger would foreclose competitors of United from access to these US Air customers, weakening the competitors and augmenting United's market position. The Commission summarily rejected this hypothesis, convinced that a significant number of other airlines would continue to provide customers to the competitors of the merged airline (Case No. COMP/M.2041 United Airlines/US Airways (2001)). This analysis is similar to foreclosure analysis under American antitrust law but the Commission, unlike American courts, does not discuss what, if any, market shares or other factors would lead to a finding of foreclosure.

Vertical integration is also a competitive concern to the European competition agency. In the Pan Am/Delta merger, competitors complained that Delta's part ownership of the Worldspan computer reservation network and ability to code-share with other partners would give it exclusionary power and entrench its dominant position. Any vertical anticompetitive effects would not have been caused by to the merger, the Commission found, so the complaints had to be raised in an Article 85 or 86 (now Articles 81 and 82) case rather than as part of the merger review (Case No. IV/M.130 Delta Air Lines/Pan Am (1991)).

In SAIR/AOM, the Commission considered both single firm dominance and collective dominance as potential anticompetitive effects. SAIR was a holding company that included Swissair and AOM was a French airline firm. Single Firm Dominance analysis, or unilateral effects in American antitrust parlance, is a straightforward evaluation of the power of the merged firm compared to other competitors in the market. The Commission assumed that Air France, an existing competitor with 35–40 per cent of the relevant market, would provide sufficiently strong competition to check any unilateral exercise of market power by the merged firm. The fact that Air France's network of flights fed a hub where the merged firm would compete persuaded the Commission that Air France had the incentive to remain in the market and seek to increase its share. The Commission's analysis of potential collective dominance after the merger is more thorough. Under a collective dominance theory, the inquiry was directed to the increased risk of cooperation or parallelism between a combined Swissair/AOM and Air France. First, although prices were publicly available, increasing the risk of conscious parallelism, the Commission noted that not all ticket sales are at the published price because a variety of discounts, incentives, and frequent flier rewards are available. In addition, the airlines compete on non-price considerations including schedules, service, timeliness, and reliability, which are not published and can be used by a competitor to both differentiate itself and increase its share of the market. Finally, demand was increasing, further reducing the motivation or need to cooperate. Since the merger would not change any of these conditions, and since AOM had previously been a Swissair partner, the Commission found no risk of collective dominance and approved the acquisition (Case No. IV/M.1494 SAirGroup/AOM (1999)).

The most recent decision involved point-to-point airline competitors, both based in Ireland and operating throughout the EU. Because neither Ryanair nor Aer Lingus operated a network, the Commission defined the geographic market as the 35 separate routes on which the firms were primary competitors. Finding that the merger would have eliminated a leading competitor on many routes, and the most likely potential entrant on others, the Commission prohibited the acquisition (Case No. COMP/ M.4439 Ryan Air/Aer Lingus (2007)).

Remedies

The Commission has been amenable to 'fix it first' solutions to potentially unlawful mergers from the earliest reported cases. These remedies consistently have involved conduct rather than structural remedies. The first reported case approving such a remedy was the acquisition by British Airways of the French airline TAT. Since BA was not yet authorized to provide intra-France service, the overlaps in service that concerned the Commission involved routes between two French cities and the London airports, Heathrow and Gatwick. Both airports were in the London vicinity and served passengers from London, but Gatwick is located significantly further from the city, thereby requiring more time to commute to the airport. The Commission agreed that the two airports were at least imperfect substitutes for each other. However, that did not alleviate the competitive threat because BA served both London airports, controlled a significant percentage of slots at both congested airports (28.5 per cent and 38 per cent), and customer demand for London to Paris airline service was increasing, making it unlikely that BA would *decrease* its London to Paris flights. To resolve the threatened harm to competition and secure Commission approval, BA agreed that, for five years following approval of the merger, it would make some of its slots available to competitors which could not obtain them through the normal slot allocation process administered by the airports (Case No. IV/M.259 British Airways/TAT (1992)).

Commission merger decisions have analyzed the competitive effects of proposed mergers on the web of airline-related services, including frequent flier programs, airport lounges and ground services, as well as point-to-point transportation between city pairs. United Air Lines was part of the Star Alliance, a group of competitors that code-shared and cooperated in providing other to customers services. In the United/US Airways case, the Commission was especially concerned with additional agreements between United and SAS and Lufthansa airlines beyond cooperation with Star Alliance members. These agreements included code-sharing, and also coordination in pricing, scheduling, marketing, advertising, and new product development. If its proposed merger with US Airways was approved, then that firm would be a party to the cooperative arrangements that United had with Lufthansa and SAS. The Commission found that this set of agreements could give the merged airline excessive power in European airports in Frankfurt and Munich and required commitments from the parties as a condition of approving the merger. The parties were to make slots at the Munich and Frankfurt airports available to *new* entrants only, for a limited time period (Case No. COMP/M.2041 United Airlines/US Airways (2001)).

The Commission has approved mergers to monopoly with sufficient conduct agreements by the parties. The Swissair/Sabena merger is an extreme example; the Commission found that the two airlines were the dominant carriers of their respective countries and some of the airports they served were so congested that slots were relatively difficult for new entrants to obtain. Indeed, the airport congestion was found to be a structural impediment to competition and the Commission characterized 'slot availability' as a factor to be considered in the context of competition on city-pair routes and also independently as an 'essential facility'. To be sufficient, new entry must be possible at sufficient scale to block the exercise of dominance. Sufficient scale requires that new entrants must be able to obtain enough slots at an airport to operate a reasonable schedule of roundtrip flights throughout the day. As a condition of approving the merger in this case, the Commission required remedies from the Swiss and Belgian governments as well as the merging parties. The two governments agreed to amend regulations that limited competition in airports in their respective countries, to eliminate restrictions on passenger capacity, and to allow four new airlines to serve the monopoly routes. The airlines agreed to make a number of their slots available to new competitors on monopoly routes, a familiar remedy that has been seen in other airline mergers, to interline their service, and to open their frequent flier programs to new airline entrants. In addition, Sabena and Swissair agreed not to increase their output, measured in terms of numbers of flights on routes, by more than 25 per cent without prior approval from the Commission. This soundness of remedy can be questioned because it requires regulators to continue to monitor the airline operations after the merger has taken place and artificially limits the merged firm's ability to compete in the marketplace (Case No. IV/M.616 Swissair/Sabena II (1995)).

However, if the proposed commitments offered by the merging parties are found insufficient to protect competition, the Commission may reject the offer and prohibit the merger. Ryanair offered to divest some of its landing and take-off slots at certain airports, but the Commission was not convinced that entry by this mechanism would be sufficient to eliminate the competitive issues on routes served by Ryanair and Aer Lingus. Ryanair proposed an additional 'up front' commitment, to delay its control of Aer Lingus until a new entrant for the slots was found. Although the Commission had accepted similar guarantees in other merger cases, it rejected Ryanair's offer on the ground that new entry would not be sufficient in any case (Memo 07/258).

Two recent cases ratified the traditional Commission standards while adding considerable depth to the analysis and, in the second case, adopting the familiar language of the US DOJ/FTC Merger Guidelines tests. Both mergers were ultimately approved, although both mergers threatened significant anticompetitive effects and were accompanied by agreements from the parties to alleviate the competitive harms.

Air France/KLM

Air France, based in France, and KLM, based in the Netherlands, are international air carriers. Each operated a hub-and-spoke network and each was a member of an international alliance; Air France was part of Sky Team with six other airlines, and KLM had a cooperative relationship with Northwest Airlines. The French government owned a majority share of Air France and the Dutch government owned 14 per cent of the voting rights of KLM (Case No. COMP/M.3280 Air France/KLM (2004)). The Commission's market definition was based on and consistent with prior airline merger decisions, yet more complete and thorough. Markets were defined from the demand side, considering consumers' views on acceptable substitutes, and supply side considerations were also taken into account. The Commission provisionally defined the product market to include of each pair of cities served by the merging firms, the 'point of origin/point of destination (O&D)'. It found that indirect service was unlikely to be a good substitute on short haul flights but could substitute for long, especially transatlantic, flights. Therefore, actual evidence of consumer preferences was required for the Commission to adopt or reject each potential substitute. The airlines defined the market definition and effect on competition from the supply side, arguing that, since each operated a hub-and-spoke network, the networks themselves constituted the correct product markets. The Commission found that most consumers considered alternatives when making their travel arrangements from one point to another, and agreed that such alternatives could be part of the respective airlines' networks, but refused to consider a network to constitute the relevant product market, rejecting the supply side argument. The Commission found that network effects were relevant in the analysis of anticompetitive effects and found that airlines ordinarily choose to enter new markets only if the city connects to one of their hubs and seek to amass market share at their hubs, increasing their market power (Case No. COMP/M.3280 Air France/KLM (2004)).

The merging parties' power was substantially augmented by their partnerships with other airlines, especially Air France's participation in the multi-airline SkyTeam Alliance. The Commission found that the competitive effects would 'not only consist in the elimination of competition between Air France and KLM, but also between their respective partners . . . on the routes falling under the scope of these agreements or directly affected by them as a consequence of the merger'. Therefore, the Commission summed the market shares of the parties and their alliance partners to calculate the relevant market shares. It then reviewed each O&D pair served by the merging parties, expanded to include substitutes, identified the market participants and their market shares, potential competition, and the competitive conditions in the market including regulations that impeded entry or price competition. Based on all of this evidence, the Commission concluded that the merger caused 'competitive concerns' on five of ten short haul O&D pairs and five of 73 long haul routes, but that the network effects of the various inter-airline cooperation agreements did not raise competitive concerns. The potential anticompetitive effects were sufficient for the Commission to conclude that there were 'serious doubts' about the merger and to require the parties to amend the merger agreement to secure approval. In addition, the French and Dutch governments guaranteed that national regulations would not be used to limit competition on certain long haul routes. The parties agreed to give up a number of their slots at up to five European airports without compensation, to interline with new entrants on specific O&D pairs, to cooperate with rail or highway firms on routes between the Netherlands and France and/or Italy (intermodal agreements), and to allow new entrants to join their frequent flier programs. They also agreed not to add additional flights to two city pairs for six IATA seasons (three years). Finally, the parties agreed to reduce fares on the Lyon–Amsterdam city pair, in which the merger resulted in a monopoly, if they reduced fares on the Paris–Amsterdam pair. The Commission pointed out that interlining and inter-modal agreements were standard features of the transportation industry. It justified its limitations on the parties' freedom to reduce prices on two bases. First, because any price reduction in one O&D market had to be matched on the other, predatory pricing would be discouraged. If the parties chose to lower prices on both O&D city pairs, then consumers in both markets would benefit. Second, the Commission believed that the parties would not reduce their prices on these city pairs unless there was new entry in the market, increasing competition to the benefit of consumers (Case No. COMP/M.3280 Air France/KLM (2004)).

Lufthansa/Swiss
The Commission approved the proposed acquisition of Swiss International Air Lines Ltd. by Lufthansa along with a package of commitments by

the firms. Lufthansa, the overwhelmingly larger party and a member of the Star Alliance of 16 airlines, operated worldwide service to 176 points in 74 countries. Swiss provided scheduled and chartered service. This Commission decision adopted an analysis similar to the familiar American step-wise merger analysis: proceeding to define the market, calculate the market shares, and consider ease of entry and the potential competitive effects of the transaction. However, the decision fails to calculate the HHI, either overall or in any O&D city pair market. This case thus demonstrates significant convergence with American-style merger analysis, including some use of economic analysis, while retaining much of the situational narrative discussion of the previous cases discussed above (Case No. COMP/M.3770 Lufthansa/Swiss (2005)).

In defining the relevant markets, the Commission analysis began by defining a provisional market consisting of each D&O (point of destination/point of origin) city pair served in common by the merging firms. These markets were expanded to include those substitutes to which consumers would turn if the price on the D&O pair increased by a small but significant and non-transitory amount (SSNIP). This is the first reported airline merger decision to apply the SSNIP test, which has been adopted by the US DOJ/FTC Merger Guidelines and the Commission Merger Guidelines. In making this determination, the Commission considered the preferences of time-sensitive and price-sensitive consumers and alternatives to nonstop flights. The Commission proceeded to identify the market share of each participant in each market. Both of the merging airlines participated in alliances with other airline partners, Lufthansa in the 16-member Star Alliance and Swiss in the 3-airline Oneworld agreement. The Commission did not define these horizontal networks as relevant product markets as such, but viewed them as potentially increasing the power of Lufthansa or Swiss in a particular city pair market. If, for example, Lufthansa or Swiss did not serve a particular O&D market because of an agreement that one of their partners would do so, then that partner was not a true competitive check on an exercise of power by Lufthansa of Swiss because each had pre-committed not to enter the market of its partner. Accordingly, the Commission added the market shares of the partner airlines to Lufthansa and Swiss, considering them to be functionally equivalent for the purpose of assessing competition in the D&O market.

The Commission recognized five kinds of barriers to entry, some of which would be accepted, some rejected by American courts. These barriers were identified as 'access to airports . . . regulatory barriers . . . economies of scope. . . . branding, promotions, and customer loyalty. . . . [and] network economies and frequency advantages'. The decision found that the ability to obtain a sufficient number of take-off and landing slots at airports in order to provide frequent, regular service was an 'essential condition' for entry and competition. As a matter of fact, the Commission found that some European airports in Switzerland, Germany, Austria, and Scandinavia where the parties operated were congested and slots were unavailable for some or all times of the day. Although the Commission described the intra-EU airline transportation market as 'fully liberalized' for Community licensed airlines, it recognized that international airline service remained heavily regulated. Therefore, the Commission noted that it would consider regulatory barriers to entry as part of its merger review and pointed out its precedent for requiring European governments to agree not to obstruct airlines' ability to set their own prices and serve non-national markets (the so-called 6th and 5th freedoms). Both airlines operated a hub-and-spoke system and also provided other services including aircraft maintenance and ground services. The Commission acknowledged that most 'traditional' airlines use a hub-and-spoke network but recognized that the ability to run one or more large hubs at airports provided cost advantages of economies of scope. Next, the decision defined advertising, promotion and market costs as sunk costs that would not be recoverable in case of market exit, a familiar concept under both the American and European sets of Merger Guidelines. The well-known brand names of these airlines, former national airlines, and their Alliance partners, and their interconnected frequent flier programs also constituted advantages that a new entrant would find difficult to overcome, in the Commission's view. Finally, the Commission found that the hub-and-spoke networks themselves conferred competitive advantages and made entry on single point-to-point routes difficult. It then analyzed each European and intercontinental city pair market, identifying the participants and evaluating their competitive prospects, and concluded that the merger threatened to create or increase illegal dominance in 12 inter-European and seven intercontinental routes. Although these were far from the majority of city pair routes served by the merging firms, the anti-competitive effects on these routes were sufficient to prohibit the merger unless the parties agreed to certain conditions. The parties agreed to the kinds of remedies that have been imposed in other airline cases: making slots available to new entrants at congested airports, interlining and inter-modal cooperation with competitors, access to their frequent flier programs, and termination of agreements with other airlines by Swiss, as Swiss becomes a part of the Star Alliance. The parties again agreed, and the Commission accepted, price controls on two routes where the merger was to create a monopoly for direct flights. Finally, the German and Swiss governments agreed to eliminate regulatory barriers to competition.

CONCLUSION: BALANCING COMPETITION IN DEREGULATED INDUSTRIES AND REGULATION EUROPEAN STYLE

Economic studies agree that deregulating European markets and opening them to competition has a positive economic effect. The OECD quantifies the benefit as yielding a 2–3 per cent annual growth in GDP (Wise 2005). Commissioner for Competition, Neelie Kroes, appointed in 2004, has made liberalization of market sectors and reduction of State Aid important goals of her tenure as head of the Directorate General for Competition. In a 2005 speech, she argued that maintaining the European 'social model' and promoting global competition were not mutually exclusive. Protectionism, in the form of 'economic patriotism' or State Aid 'risk taking Europe into a 1930s-style downward spiral of tit-for-tat' retaliation to the disadvantage of all of the Member States of the EU. She singled out France as a noteworthy offender (Kroes 2005). In the Commissioner's view, the airline market has become more competitive as a direct result of eliminating State Aid and opening European markets to competition, including cross-border mergers in this sector (ibid.). However, consistent with the European Treaty, the Competition Commissioner recognizes the limits of the market and the need for regulation in some segments of the economy:

> '[s]ometimes private markets may not result in greater competitiveness and there may be good reasons to maintain public activities. . . . Some activities may be better placed in the hands of public entities (e.g. education, health care). The same is true for certain R&D activities . . .' (ibid.).

In contrast to current United States antitrust law, Kroes concludes that maintaining the 'European social model' is as important as promoting economic competition for the European market. Thus, at the beginning of the twenty-first century, and after half a century of experience, the European Union antitrust policy continues to promote dual goals of cross-border competition without nationalistic protectionism and a strong model of social welfare administered by government regulation.

REFERENCES

Altunbas, Yerner and Davis Marques Ibanez (2004), *Mergers and Acquisitions and Bank Performance in Europe: the Role of Strategic Similarities*, European Central Bank, ECB Working Paper No. 398.
Budzinski, Oliver (8 December 2005), 'An Economic Perspective on the Jurisdictional Reform of the European Merger Control System,' University of

Marburg, Working Paper Series, forthcoming in *European Competition Journal*, 2(1) 2006.

Drahos, Michael (2001), *Convergence of Competition Laws and Policies in the European Community*, The Hague: Kluwer Law International.

Martin, Reiner, Moreno Roma and Isabel Vansteenkiste (April 2005), *Reforms in Selected EU Network Industries*, European Central Bank, ECB Occasional Paper No. 28.

Navarro Varona, Edurne et al. (2002), *Merger Control in the European Union: Law, Economics and Practice*, Oxford: Oxford University Press.

Neven, Damien, Robin Nuttall and Paul Seabright (1993), *Merger in Daylight: The Economics and Politics of European Merger Control*, London: Center for Economic Policy Research.

Quigley, Conor and Anthony M. Collins (2003), *EC State Aid Law and Policy*, Oxford: Hart.

Subiotto, Romano and Robbert Snelders (2004), *Antitrust Development in Europe 2003* (referred to as *Developments in Europe*), The Hague: Kluwer Law International.

Suedekum, Jens (July 2006), *Cross-Border Mergers and National Champions in an Integrating Economy*, IZA Bonn, Discussion Paper No. 2220.

Van Damme, Eric (2005), *Liberalizing the Dutch Electricity Market: 1998–2004*, TILEC (Tilburg Law and Economics Center), TILEC Discussion Paper No. 2005-009.

Vogelaar, Floris O.W., Jules Stuyck, and Bart L.P. van Reeken (eds.) (2002), *Competition Law in the EU, Its Member States and Switzerland: Law of Business and Finance, Vol. II*, The Hague: Kluwer Law International.

Wise, Michael (2005), 'Competition Law and Policy in the European Union' (referred to as 'OECD Report'), *Report prepared by the Secretariat of the OECD*.

Commission Documents

Joint Statement of the Council and the Commission on the Functioning of the Network of Competition Authorities (16 December 2002), adopted together with Council Regulation ((EC) No. 1/2003) on the implementation of the rules on competition laid down in Articles 81 and 82 of the Treaty (Text with EEA relevance) O.J. (L 1) 1–25; Regulation 1/2003.

European Commission (2004), *Report on Competition Policy, Volume I* (Final Report), SEC(2005) 805.

Communication from the Commission (26 September 1996), Services of General Interest in Europe (96/C 281/03) (O.J. C 281, 26.09.1996, p. 3).

European Commission (1995), *XXV Report On Competition Policy* (Final Report), COM(96)126.

European Commission (1997), *XXVII Report on Competition Policy, Part One, General Report on the Activities of the European Union; Part Two, Report on the Application of the Competition Rules in the European Union* (Final Report), SEC (98) 636.

Commission of the European Communities (7 June 2005), *State Aid Action Plan (Consultation document)*, SEC (2005) 795.

Commission of the European Communities (17 July 2006), *Interim Report II: Current Accounts and Related Services*.

Communication from the Commission (31 January 2007), Sector Inquiry under Art. 17 of Regulation (EC) No. 1/2003 on retail banking (Final Report), COM(2007) 33.

Communication from the Commission (7 January 2007), Inquiry Pursuant to Art. 17 of Regulation (EC) No. 1/2003 into the European gas and electricity sectors (Final Report), SEC (2006) 1724.

Directorate General for Energy and Transport, Air Transport Portal of the European Commission.

Council Regulations

Council Regulation (EC) 1/2003, Council Regulation of 16 December 2002 on the Implementation of the Rules on Competition Laid Down in Articles 81 and 82 of the Treaty, 2003 O.J. (L 1) 1–25.

Council Regulation (EEC) 4064/89, Council Regulation of 21 December 1989 on the Control of Concentrations Between Undertakings, 1989 O.J. (L 395) 1, corrected version in 1990 O.J. (L 257) 13.

Council Regulation (EC) 139/2004, Council Regulation of 20 January 2004 on the Control of Concentrations Between Undertakings (the EC Merger Regulation), 2004 O.J. (L 24) 1–22.

Council Regulation (EEC) 17/62, First Regulation Implementing Articles 85 and 86 of the Treaty, 1959–1962 O.J. Spec. Ed. 87; amended by Council Regulation (EC) 1216/1999, Council Regulation of 10 June Amending Regulation No 17: First Regulation Implementing Articles 81 and 82 of the Treaty, 1999 O.J. (L 148) 5–6.

Council Regulation (EEC) 1017/68, Council Regulation of 19 July 1968 Applying Rules of Competition to Transport by Rail, Road and Inland Waterway, 1968 O.J. (L 175) 1–12; amended by Council Regulation (EC) 1/2003, Council Regulation of 16 December 2002 on the Implementation of the Rules on Competition Laid Down in Articles 81 and 82 of the Treaty, 2003 O.J. (L 1) 1–25.

Rules Applicable to Specific Sectors: Introduction.

Other Sources

European Central Bank (April 2005), *Regulatory Reforms in Selected EU Network Industries*, Occasional Paper Series No. 28.

Kroes, Neelie (3 September 2005), 'Competition Must Drive European Competitiveness in a Global Economy,' Villa d'Este Forum SPEECH/05/477.

Kroes, Neelie (16 February 2006), 'Towards an Efficient and Integrated European Energy Market – First Findings and Next Steps,' European Commission Conference, Energy Sector Inquiry – Public Presentation of the Preliminary Findings, Brussels SPEECH/06/92.

Kroes, Neelie (1 March 2006), 'What's Wrong with Europe's Energy Markets?,' Energy Sector Inquiry Conference, Austrian Chamber of Commerce, Vienna SPEECH/06/137.

Norris, Floyd (3 March 2006), 'It Is European, But It Is Not a Union,' New York, *New York Times* (Late Edition (East Coast)), p. C.1

OECD (26 May 2005), *The Benefits of Liberalising Product Markets and Reducing Barriers to International Trade and Investment: The Case of the US and the EU* ECO/WKP(2005) 19 (referred to in text as OECD Report).

OECD (June 2006), 'Trends and Recent Developments in Foreign Direct Investment,' International Investment Perspectives, 2005 Ed.

Cases

Case No. T-342/99, *Airtours v. Commission*, 2002 E.C.R. II-2585 (annulling Commission Decision of 22 September 1999 (Case IV/M.1524 – Airtours/First Choice)) (*notified under document number C(1999) 3022*), 2000 O.J. (L 93) 1–33.
California v. American Stores Co., 495 U.S. 271 (1990).
California Retail Liquor Dealers Ass'n v. Midcal Alum., Inc., 445 U.S. 97 (1980).
FTC v. Ticor Title Ins. Co., 504 U.S. 621 (1992).
Parker v. Brown, 317 U.S. 341 (1943).
Case No. T-310/01, *Schneider Electric SA v. Commission*, 2002 E.C.R. II-04071 (annulling Commission Decision of 10 October 2001 (Case COMP/M.2283 – Schneider/Legrand)) (*notified under document number C(2001) 3014*), 2004 O.J. (L 101) 1–133; *see also* Commission Press Release, Commission Prohibits Acquisition of Control of Legrand by Schneider Electric, IP/01/1393 (10 October 2001).
Case No. T-5/02, Tetra Laval BV v. Commission, 2002 E.C.R. II-04381 (annulling Commission Decision of 30 October 2001 (Case No COMP/M.2416 – Tetra Laval/Sidel)) (*notified under document number C(2001) 3345*), 2004 O.J. (L 43) 13–87; *see also* Commission Press Release, Commission Prohibits Acquisition of Sidel by Tetra Laval Group, IP/01/1516 (30 October 2001).

Treaty Provisions

Consolidated Version of the Treaty Establishing the European Community (29 December 2006) O.J. (C 321E) [hereinafter cited as EC Treaty; also referred to in text as Treaty of Rome] art. 2(g).
EC Treaty arts. 3(c), (e)-(g), (m), (o), (u); 5; 10; 28 ex 30; 29 ex 31; 31 ex 37; 81 ex 85; 82 ex 86; 83; 86; 87(2)(a)-(c); 87(3)(a)-(d); 93; 226; 228.

Energy Section – Cases

Case No. COMP/M.3440 ENI/EDP/GDP (2004); Commission Press release (9 December 2004), Mergers: Commission prohibits acquisition of GDP by EDP and ENI IP 04/1455.
Case No. COMP/37.542 Gas Natural/Endesa (2002).
● Judgment of the Court of First Instance of 14 July 2006 – Case No. T-417/05 Endesa v. Commission (2006 O.J.) (C 224) 40; *see also* Action Brought on 29 November 2005 – Case No. T-417/05 Endesa v. Commission, (2006) O.J. (C 22) 20–21.
Case No. COMP/M. 4110 E.ON/Endesa (2006); *see also* Commission Press Release, Mergers: Commission Approves Acquisition by E.ON of Endesa, IP/06/528 (25 April 2006).
● Commission Press Release, Free Movement of Capital: Commission Opens Infringement Proceedings Against Spain Regarding Law Amending Functions of Spanish Electricity and Gas Regulator, IP/06/569 (03 May 2006).
● Commission Press Release, Mergers: Commission Rules Against Spanish Energy Regulator's Measures Concerning E.ON's Bid for Endesa, IP/06/1265 (26 September 2006).

- Commission Press Release, Mergers: Commission Informs Spain of Preliminary Assessment That Spanish Minister's Measures in Proposed Takeover E.ON/Endesa Violate EC Law, IP/06/1649 (29 November 2006).
- Commission Press Release, Mergers: Commission Decides That Spanish Measures in Proposed E.ON/Endesa Takeover Violate EC Law, IP/06/1853 (20 December 2006).
- Commission Press Release, Free Movement of Capital: Commission Calls on Spain to Modify the Law Amending the Functions of the Spanish Electricity and Gas Regulator, IP/06/1264 (26 September 2006).
- Commission Press Release, Free Movement of Capital: Commission Refers Spain to European Court of Justice Over Law Extending the Functions of the Spanish Electricity and Gas Regulator, IP/07/82 (24 January 2007).

Case No. COMP/M.3868 DONG/Elsam/Energi E2 (2006); *see also* Commission Press Release, Mergers: Commission Approves Acquisition by DONG of Danish Electricity Generators and Suppliers, Subject to Conditions, IP/06/313 (14 March 2006).

Case No. COMP/M.4370 EBN/Cogas Energy (2006); *see also* Commission Press Release, Mergers: Commission Approves Proposed Acquisition of Cogas Electricity and Gas Retail Supply Business by Electrabel Nederland, IP/06/1279 (29 September 2006).

Case No. COMP/M.4368 Edison/Eneco Energia (2006); *see also* Commission Press Release, Mergers: Commission Approves Planned Acquisition of Eneco Energia by Edison, IP/06/1438 (19 October 2006).

Case No. COMP/M.4028 Flaga/Progas/JV (2006); *see also* Commission Press Release, Mergers: Commission Approves Transaction Between Flaga and Progas in LPG Sector, IP/06/87 (26 January 2006).

Case No. COMP/M.4208 Petroplus/European Petroleum Holdings (2006); *see also* Commission Press Release, Mergers: Commission Clears Acquisition of European Petroleum Holdings by Petroplus, IP/06/691 (29 May 2006).

Case No. COMP/M.4180 Gaz de France/Suez (2006).

- Commission Press Release, Mergers: Commission Opens In-Depth Investigation into Merger Between Gaz de France and Suez Group, IP/06/802 (19 June 2006).
- Commission Press Release, Mergers: Commission Approves Merger of Gaz de France and Suez, Subject to Conditions, IP/06/1558 (14 November 2006).
- Commission Decision of 14 November 2006 declaring a concentration compatible with common market and the functioning of the EEA Agreement (Case COMP/M.4180 – Gaz de France/Suez) (*notified under document number C(2006) 5419*), 2007 O.J. (L 88) 47–50.
- Commission Press Release, Mergers: Summary of the Remedies Offered by GDF and Suez, MEMO/06/424 (14 November 2006).

Other Commission Documents

Communication from the Commission to the Council and the European Parliament (2003), *Report on Progress in Creating the Internal Gas and Electricity Market; Preliminary Report* (Final Report), COM/2005/0568 (see earlier publication at: SEC(2005) 1448).

Directive 2003/54/EC of the European Parliament and of the Council (26 June 2003), concerning common rules for the internal market in electricity and repealing

Directive 96/92/EC – Statements made with regard to decommissioning and waste management activities '2003/54EC,' O.J. (L 176) 37–56.

Directive 2003/55/EC of the European Parliament and of the Council (26 June 2003), concerning common rules for the internal market in natural gas and repealing Directive 98/30/EC '2003/55 EC,' O.J. (L 176) 57–78.

Sector Inquiry Under Art. 17 Regulation 1/2003 on the Gas and Electricity Markets COMP/B-1/39172 (electricity sector inquiry) and COMP/B-1/39173 (gas sector inquiry).

Commission Press Release (13 June 2005) Competition: Commission opens sector inquiry into gas and electricity IP 05/716.

Communication from the Commission to the Council and the European Parliament (31 January 2007), *Sector Inquiry Under Art. 17 of Regulation 1/2003 on Retail Banking* (Final Report), COM(2007) 33.

European Commission (16 February 2006), *Energy Sector Inquiry, Preliminary Report, Frequently Asked Questions.*

European Commission (10 January 2007), *DG Competition Report on Energy Sector Inquiry* (Final Report), SEC(2006) 1724.

Financial Institutions Section – Cases

Case No. 85/76 Hoffmann-LaRoche v. Commission (1979) E.C.R. 461.

Case No. COMP/M.3556 Fortis/BCP (2005); *see also* Commission Press Release, Mergers: Commission Approves Sale by Banco Comercial Portugues of a Stake in its Life Insurance Business to Fortis, IP/05/65 (19 January 2005).

Case No. COMP/M.3894 UniCredito/HVB (2005); *see also* Commission Press Release, Mergers: Commission Approves Acquisition of German Bank HVB by Italy's UniCredito, IP/05/1299 (18 October 2005).

• Commission Press Release, Mergers: Commission Launches Procedure Against Poland for Preventing Unicredito/HVB Merger, IP/06/277 (08 March 2006).

• Commission Press Release, Free Movement of Capital: Commission Opens Infringement Procedure Against Poland in Context of UniCredito/HBV Merger, IP/06/276 (08 March 2006).

Other Commission Documents

Commission Notice on Cooperation within the Network of Competition Authorities (27 April 2004) O.J. (C 101) 43–53.

Commission Press Release (12 April 2006) Competition: Commission Sector Inquiry Highlights Competition Concerns in Payment Cards Industry IP 06/496.

Communication from the Commission (31 January 2007), *Sector Inquiry Under Art. 17 of Regulation 1/2003 on Retail Banking* (Final Report), COM 2007/003.

Airlines Section – Cases

Case No. 66/86, Ahmed Saeed Flugreisen and Other v. Zentrale zur Bekämpfung unlauteren Wettbewerbs, 1989 E.C.R. 803.

Case No. IV/M.130 Delta Air Lines/Pan Am (1991).

Case No. IV/M.259 British Airways/TAT (1992).

Case No. IV/M.278 British Airways/Dan Air (1993).

Case No. T-2/93, Air France v. Commission (TAT), 1994 E.C.R. II-323.

Case No. IV/M.616 Swissair/Sabena II (1995).

Case No. IV/M.857 British Airways/Air Liberté (1997).

Case No. IV/M.967 KLM/Air UK (1997).

Case No. IV/M.1494 SAirGroup/AOM (1999).

Case No. COMP/M.2008 AOM/Air Liberté/Air Littoral (2000); *see also* Commission Press Release, Commission Clears AOM Buy of Air Liberté and TAT European Airlines, IP/00/884 (28 July 2000).

Commission Decision of 11 August 1999 Declaring a Concentration to Be Compatible with the Common Market (Case No IV/M.0019 – KLM/Alitalia), 2000 O.J. (C 96) 5.

Case No. COMP/M.1855 Singapore Airlines/Virgin Atlantic (2000).

Case No. COMP/M.2041 United Airlines/US Airways (2001); *see also* Commission Press Release, Commission Clears Merger Between United Airlines and US Airways Subject to Conditions, IP/01/48 (15 January 2001).

Case No. COMP/M.2672 SAS/Spanair (2002); *see also* Commission Press Release, Commission Clears SAS Majority Stake in Spanair, IP/02/365 (5 March 2002).

Case No. COMP/M.3280 Air France/KLM (2004); *see also* Commission Press Release, Commission Clears Merger Between Air France and KLM Subject to Conditions, IP/04/194 (11 February 2004).

Case No. COMP/M.3770 Lufthansa/Swiss (2005); see also Commission Press Release, Mergers: Commission Clears Planned Acquisition of Swiss by Lufthansa, Subject to Conditions, IP/05/837 (5 July 2005).

Case No. COMP/M.4439 Ryan Air/Aer Lingus (2007) (decision not yet available.

- Commission Memo (27 June 2007) Mergers: Commission's Prohibition of Ryanair's Proposed Acquisition of Aer Lingus – Frequently Asked Questions Memo 07/258.
- Commission Press Release (27 June 2007) Commission Prohibits Ryanair's Proposed Takeover of Aer Lingus IP 07/893.

Regulations

Council Regulation (EEC) 1017/68, Council Regulation of 19 July 1968 Applying Rules of Competition to Transport by Rail, Road and Inland Waterway, 1968 O.J. (L 175) 1–12; amended by Council Regulation (EC) 1/2003, Council Regulation of 16 December 2002 on the Implementation of the Rules on Competition Laid Down in Articles 81 and 82 of the Treaty, 2003 O.J. (L 1) 1–25.

Council Regulation (EEC) 2299/89, Council Regulation of 24 July 1989 on a Code of Conduct for Computerized Reservation Systems, 1989 O.J. (L 220) 1–7.

Council Regulation (EEC) 2407/92, Council Regulation of 23 July 1992 on Licensing of Air Carriers, 1992 O.J. (L 240) 1–7.

Council Regulation (EEC) 2408/92, Council Regulation of 23 July 1992 on Access for Community Air Carriers to Intra-Community Air Routes, 1992 O.J. (L 240) 8–14.

Council Regulation (EEC) 2409/92, Council Regulation of 23 July 1992 on Fares and Rates for Air Services, 1992 O.J. (L 240) 15–17.

UK-Edinburgh: Operation of Scheduled Air Services – Invitation to Tender Issued by the United Kingdom Under Article 4(1)(d) Council Regulation (EEC) No 2408/92 in Respect of the Operation of Scheduled Air Services Between

Glasgow–Campbeltown, Glasgow–Tiree and Glasgow–Barra, 2006 O.J. (C 186) 17–18.

Council Regulation (EC) 659/1999, Council Regulation of 22 March 1999 Laying Down Detailed Rules for the Application of Article 93 of the EC Treaty, 1999 O.J. (L 83) 1–9.

Regulation (EC) 549/2004, Regulation of the European Parliament and of the Council of 10 March 2004 Laying Down the Framework for the Creation of the Single European Sky (the Framework Regulation), 2004 O.J. (L 96) 1–8.

Regulation (EC) 550/2004, Regulation of the European Parliament and of the Council of 10 March 2004 on the Provision of Air Navigation Services in the Single European Sky (the Service Provision Regulation), 2004 O.J. (L 96) 10–19.

Regulation (EC) 551/2004, Regulation of the European Parliament and of the Council of 10 March 2004 on the Organisation and Use of the Airspace in the Single European Sky, 2004 O.J. (L 96) 20–24.

Regulation (EC) 793/2004 of the European Parliament and of the Council of 21 April 2004 Amending Council Regulation (EEC) No 95/93 on Common Rules for the Allocation of Slots at Community Airports, 2004 O.J. (L 138) 50–60.

10. Reflections on mergers and competition in formerly regulated industries

Peter C. Carstensen

The preceding case studies support several important conclusions about the history of revising (or indeed reversing) industry regulation to facilitate greater reliance on market transactions. Certainly, the legal institutions that were responsible for regulating these industries have gone through a Schumpeterian process of creative destruction. The consistent result over the wide variety of industries included here has been the enhancement of efficiency, stimulation of technological innovation and creation of new regulatory challenges.

There is no 'end to history' in a dynamic economy. Every time the legal, technological or social context changes, industries must readjust their activities based on the perceptions of their decision makers, whether government regulators or corporate managers, about both short-term and longer-term strategy. The result is continuing evolution, although there are periods of greater or lesser change. For the last three decades, the United States has gone through a prolonged period of 'deregulation' that is a substantial change in the nature and content of the legal regulations under which these industries operate. In all the case studies except hospitals, there was at least some central planning of this transformation based on assumptions about how the new legal framework would work. One consistent feature of the case studies is the substantial degree of error in those assumptions. Only railroads and gas pipelines seem to have performed largely as predicted. At the same time, the case studies are unanimous in their conclusion that the new legal frameworks did in fact facilitate improvements in the economic performance of these industries. On the other hand, a recurring theme is that the changed regulatory environment has stimulated a rash of mergers that may in the longer run result in the loss of the benefit of a workably competitive market.

While every reader must, ultimately, draw his or her own conclusions from these studies, six results appear to follow from this work:

(1)   The legal conditions under which these industries operate were often poorly designed to facilitate the kinds of market behavior that public policy ostensibly seeks.

(2)   Changes in technology and demand characteristics make accurate predictions of industry behavior very difficult, if not impossible. The resulting unpredictability creates serious problems for public policy makers, especially in evaluating the competitive implications of conduct and merger review.

(3)   In all of these industries, networks and systems encompassing a variety of stakeholders are prominent features of economic activity. Unfortunately this pervasive characteristic has not been very successfully integrated in public policy analysis either in general or in the merger analysis.

(4)   Oversight of mergers and potentially anti-competitive conduct itself has been quite varied and uneven both with respect to the substance of that analysis and its institutional configuration.

(5)   It seems evident that competition policy in general and merger analysis in particular has and probably should involve both some industry-specific standards and recognition of the particular uncertainties and stresses involved in the process of transition to more market-oriented conduct.

(6)   Despite all these concerns, in general, the reduction and redirection of regulation in these industries have produced positive results overall, at least so far. The open question of whether the continued merger activity in these industries will ultimately reverse the effects of increased competition remains.

The remainder of this chapter will elaborate on these six observations.

THE FAILURE TO DEFINE AND IMPLEMENT AN APPROPRIATE LEGAL FRAMEWORK

A striking feature of all of the industries examined in this book is the failure of the reformers to identify and implement an appropriate legal framework to facilitate the operation of the markets being created. The degree of mal-adaption varies from industry to industry. Overall, the case studies demonstrate that the interaction of fundamental industry characteristics and the legal conditions under which market processes go forward are very important to the successful use of market institutions. Workably competitive markets require a legal framework that will constitute such markets in ways that minimize the risk of strategic or opportunistic conduct, facilitate transactions, ensure reasonable access to all would-be participants who have the economic capacity, and establish sufficient transparency that risks and rewards are evident to all stakeholders.

This observation concerning the centrality of law to market facilitation has not been emphasized in most discussions of deregulation. However, it is an obvious feature of the most successful open markets in complex industries. Public capital markets and the markets for commodities (including commodities futures) are powerful illustrations of the importance of market-facilitating regulation. In addition, as both commodities and capital market regulation illustrate, there is need for continued revision and fine tuning of the regulatory process to address new issues as they arise and to revise regulations that have become outdated. All markets are dynamic and the more open and competitive a market is the more likely it is to undergo significant changes over time. In the case of the industries examined in this book, for a variety of social and economic reasons, specialized legal controls will continue to exist that are industry specific. But the dynamic characteristic of all industry makes a continuing process of reevaluating the appropriate oversight and regulation of each industry highly desirable and its absence can and does result in serious costs in both social and economic terms.

Several of the industries considered here have not had the benefit of any significant formal deregulatory legislation. For example, in both gas and electricity, the fundamental federal statutes have not been substantially revised to take account of the radical reorientation of those industries from command and control regulation governing price and interrelationships among firms to the contemporary context of market-driven agreements.[1] In this largely static legislative environment, the relatively more positive outcome in the case of gas pipelines reflects the underlying structure of the industry and the comparatively easy technical steps needed to transform pipelines from merchants of gas to transporters.

The electric industry, as discussed in Chapter 2, faces a much more difficult technological challenge, made even more complex by the ownership organization of the industry and the lack of legal authority of the regulatory agency to command changes. Indeed, one might argue that the apparent success in large regions of the country (i.e., the middle Atlantic states, New England, and parts of the Midwest) in moving the wholesaling of electric power into a workable market context demonstrates that a creative agency (when not obstructed by political forces and despite being armed only with an inapposite and outdated set of legal tools and constrained by anachronistic federalism) can still achieve substantial change. At the same time, the electric industry is the strongest illustration of the problems that result from inadequate and truncated regulatory authority.

The hospital industry reflects a different kind of failure of the legislative process to address the transformation of an industry. No national legal framework exists to promote or organize the provision of hospital services in the course of their transition to a more market-oriented system of pricing services. As noted in Chapter 7, the primary forces shaping hospital billing procedures are the government reimbursement programs. These programs, despite occasional efforts to achieve a more market-oriented approach to health care, lack the will as well as the legal and institutional capacity to provide the oversight for such a massive transition. As a result, health care will continue to exist in a kind of ad hoc state until the crises reach a level that compels action.

The legal framework for airlines reveals a different problem. The failure to embody key legal policy assumptions in the statutory commands resulted in the approval of mergers that produced excessive market power and encouraged exclusionary conduct. The airline experience also suggests the importance of law and regulation in facilitating or frustrating the evolution of desirable market conduct. The lack of regulation of pricing strategies has resulted in highly discriminatory pricing systems that have both excluded competitors and imposed highly differentiated prices on travelers depending on their origins and destinations as well as the duration of their trip.

DYNAMIC TECHNOLOGY AND OTHER SHOCKS TO THE SYSTEM

The changing technology of the industries in question (as well as other shocks to the system) is another force that has played a powerful role in dispelling the rosy predictions about deregulation. Telecommunications is the most conspicuous example of changed technology. This industry has gone through a radical transformation in the period following the breakup of the AT&T monopoly. It is reasonable to infer that the reduction in direct regulation and resulting increased role for competition played a significant part in that process. At the same time, technological change (on top of changes in the legal conditions for the market) creates a very uncertain context within which to evaluate mergers and other competition policy issues.

Banking and health care have also experienced dramatic changes in the technologies and services provided to consumers. In both instances, the changing character of the products and services demanded (as well as the rapid transformation of the technologies used for their production) has resulted in improved service to consumers. However, these innovations have also opened the industries to the potential for a variety of strategic and exclusionary types of conduct. Even if the political will to regulate these activities to protect the public interest once existed, it regularly faced the inherent dynamics in the underlying markets, with the unfortunate result that regulatory initiatives were often outmoded even before they were adopted.

The terrorist attacks of September 2001 transformed demand for airline services for many months. At the same time, the changing capacity of jet planes has opened up the ability of the airlines to restore point-to-point service on more routes, thus further complicating the analysis of competition in that market. The recurring financial crises of the major airlines reflect the economic impact of both of these transformations.

Removing regulatory constraints on markets has had the overall effect of encouraging innovative behavior that increases substantially the dynamics of these markets. Eliminating regulatory constraints alone does not, however, cause innovation. But, increased competition does make it more attractive for firms in the deregulated markets to engage much more actively in innovation. In addition, given at least mildly competitive markets, industry members have much more incentive to bring innovations to consumers in a timely fashion. Thus, eliminating regulation is an important step in inducing both innovation and its dissemination.

THE PERVASIVE ROLE OF SYSTEMS AND NETWORKS IN THESE INDUSTRIES

Although there are distinct differences among the systems and networks that exist in the industries studied in this book, their common characteristic is that each involves a complex and durable set of relationships. In the cases of railroads, telecommunications, airlines, gas and electricity, transporting goods, people or communications between various points is a central component of the service provided. The need for collaboration among enterprises varies from that inherent in moving electricity among the many separate transmission systems in a tightly linked grid to the separate networks that airlines and railroads increasingly have developed. However, conventional market analysis of all these industries typically ignores the networks or integrated systems, overlooks the complexity of the resulting competition and fails to appreciate the implications of specific combinations.

In the case of banking and hospitals, there are systems and networks functioning in the background. For example, smaller banks need to have correspondents to provide some services. Moreover, the credit card and other banking functions often entail complex joint ventures among banks. For this reason, the combination of large banks can create more foreclosure than the apparent market shares.

Similarly, the hospital industry functions as part of a comprehensive health care network in which the hospital has ongoing relations with specific health care provider groups whether HMOs, PPOs or some other financial organizer of health care. If markets are to provide useful services to consumers of health care, there should be negotiation between hospitals and these networks. Hospital organizations function in a way that is very roughly analogous to the railroad or electric grid – each is a core institution that is essential to the operation of the entire system. Once again the role and function of hospitals in the health care system seems to be under-theorized and inadequately understood in merger analysis and competition policy.

The underlying significance of networks for all these industries may explain the impetus that leads to regulation better than any monopoly or conventional market failure model. The concept of networks is an important but relatively new component of public policy analysis of industry. Without a clear model of network interaction and its operational characteristics, policy makers might erroneously seek to regulate the visible issues that arise in such industries while failing to consider the network effects.

Certainly, as the legal system returns to greater reliance on markets and market institutions to regulate the firms in these industries, the relevance of their network characteristics grows. One important attribute of networks is that flows within the networks can be strongly affected by constraints substantially remote from the original locus of concern. Spulber and Yoo (2005) have illustrated this by the use of graph theory (use of mathematical models to identify where in a network the actual constraints may exist). The general implication for public policy formation, and merger analysis in particular, is that the effects of combinations or specific conduct must be appraised in terms of the impact on the entire network and not just in terms of the effects on the most immediate counter parties.

NATURE, SOURCE AND SCOPE OF OVERSIGHT OF MERGERS

Another significant point of difference among these industries occurs in the context of merger review. Here it is necessary to distinguish the formal authority to review the competitive and public interest effects of mergers from the actual practices that have emerged in different industries.

The first important distinction is between exclusive agency review and shared review authority. Currently, merger review power that is exclusively limited to the regulatory agency exists only for the railroad industry. However, the Civil Aeronautics Board (CAB) and later the Department of Transportation had similar exclusive authority over airline mergers for nearly a decade after the end of detailed regulation. The studies of those industries reveal deep reservations about the wisdom of this policy decision On the whole, regulatory agencies with exclusive power to review mergers have approved anticompetitive and undesirable mergers. Indeed, in the case of airlines, the key mergers that the agency approved in that era have had a demonstrably bad effect on prices paid by consumers. The evidence from the railroad sector is inconclusive at this time, because the mergers reducing the competitors from four to two major systems in the western US and from three to two in the eastern US are relatively recent. In addition, as the railroad chapter makes clear, major rail shippers have more bargaining power than do consumers. Therefore, the adverse impact of the railroad mergers on long-run competitiveness may be less dramatic, at least with respect to prices. Nevertheless, if competition is the long-run objective of deregulation, exclusive agency oversight is not good public policy.

At the other extreme, only government antitrust enforcers have authority to review hospital mergers because no federal healthcare regulatory agency has been created. Yet the results are almost as discouraging as those in industries with exclusive agency review. The initial decisions in healthcare markets rested on weak empirical information. At first, courts generally accepted arguments emphasizing the need to retain workably competitive markets despite the asserted merits of concentration in this industry. Over time, the courts have become less skeptical of the claims of hospital managers and consequently have adopted standards that result in approval of all proposed mergers. Whether a hospital regulatory agency would have condemned more of these mergers is, of course, highly speculative. However, it is likely that courts would have treated the opinions of such an expert agency with more deference. Thus an agency could have used its powers to facilitate more competitively desirable mergers and impose conduct-based requirements to ensure that consumers received the benefit of the efficiencies that purportedly arise from such combinations of hospitals.

In the remaining fields, there is overlapping jurisdiction between the regulatory agencies and the federal antitrust authorities. Here there are noticeably different patterns of action depending on the industry sector. In the case of gas, the FTC has been relatively active under a number of presidential administrations. However, despite that apparent vigilance, there has been a marked increase in concentration of ownership of gas pipelines and vertical integration in the generation of electricity. Both types of concentrations create additional competitive risks. Similarly, in the airline industry, there is evidence that the Antitrust Division has continued to monitor airline combinations and has challenged some of them. Significantly, those challenges were effective in keeping overall concentration of ownership from increasing. However, there has been a substantial growth in 'quasi-mergers' in the form of 'code sharing' with little objection from either the Antitrust Division or the Department of Transportation and prices have increased while overall competition has been limited. Finally, the banking industry has seen a very great increase in national concentration, while in regional and local markets concentration has remained static or declined slightly. Again, the issue remains whether the increased dominance of overall banking by a handful of nationwide banks will result in an overall reduction of competition as these banks seek ways to live with each other without vigorous competition or more competition in narrowly defined segments of the banking services market.

In contrast to the gas and airlines sectors, with few exceptions neither the Department of Justice nor the Federal Energy Regulatory Commission (FERC) has been very active in challenging electricity mergers. Indeed, overall, merger enforcement in these areas has not been characterized by significant litigation or any massive settlements. However, as the analysis of electricity markets argued, this is an industry where further consolidation of generators and transmission systems might produce increased efficiency. The vital caveat to that prediction is that the generation of electricity should be separated from the transmission function and perhaps from the local retailing so that all participants have the appropriate incentives to create workably competitive wholesale markets.

The previous observations concerning electricity mergers apply to the relationship between the antitrust enforcement agencies and the Federal Communications Commission (FCC) in the area of telecommunications. In telecommunications, there has been a massive recombination of the firms that were created in the wake of the dissolution of the old AT&T monopoly. At the same time, the rapid technological changes in the industry (such as moving to broadband service and wireless service) have made it particularly difficult to evaluate the probable longer-term impact of the vast increases in concentration in the various segments of the industry and, more recently, in the telecommunications industry overall. As in the case of electricity, the FCC has used its power to approve telecommunications mergers to obtain concessions that opened up segments of the market to more competition. This carrot approach is necessary because neither the FCC nor FERC has sufficient authority to command changes in both structure and conduct that would mandate competitive market conditions.

Overall, there is a recurring concern about the longer-term consequences for competition of both the present and the prospectively higher levels of concentration in these industries. It should be obvious that it is essential to have a reasonably large number of competitors and potential competitors to maintain workably competitive markets. The track record of merger enforcement passivity over the last decade has led to higher levels of concentration in these industries following deregulation. While increased concentration is not necessarily inconsistent with creating and maintaining workably competitive markets, it is problematic. The prior industry structures were the product of a command and control system of overt franchises. Hence, some reorganization and even consolidation were the entirely predictable result of deregulation. However, there is no clear evidence that either the regulatory agencies or the antitrust law enforcers, except perhaps the Surface Transportation Board (STB) and its predecessor the Insterstate Commerce Commission (ICC), ever developed any long-range structural model of the industries that could guide enforcement decisions and direct firms seeking to merge toward combinations that would be likely to facilitate that structural model.

The missed potential for more direction in the transition from strong regulatory controls to a market-oriented system is one of the real gaps in the public policy of deregulation. In the course of a transition from regulation to a market-based system, an agency seeking to optimize competition should have affirmatively undertaken the task of articulating and implementing, to the extent feasible under the law, policies encouraging some types of mergers and discouraging others. However, there is no evidence in any of the case studies that the relevant agencies did more than react to initiatives from the regulated companies. While such industry initiatives may well have an efficient motivation, it is also likely that the proposed mergers sought to create or entrench market power in the transforming industry. The case studies in this book confirm that supposition. When the technological change was very substantial (as in telecommunications) or the market was very unconcentrated on a national basis (as in banking), these efforts, while of concern, have not resulted in much immediate adverse impact. However, the railroads, hospitals and airlines sectors seem to have experienced contrary, and anticompetitive, effects from mergers. The ultimate suggestion must be to emphasize the substantial scope for a more active policy focused on planning the transition to market-oriented activity. The failure of the agencies to perform this kind of proactive planning reflects an underlying failure to appreciate the need to manage the transition to competitive markets in order to gain the greatest benefit for the public.

DIFFERENT STANDARDS FOR MERGERS IN THESE INDUSTRIES

The remedial actions taken by the regulatory agencies discussed in these case studies provide a further contrast to remedies sought by the traditional antitrust enforcement agencies. In general, the regulatory agencies have a strong preference for conduct-oriented regulation that sets future standards of conduct for the merged enterprise. The STB, FERC and the FCC employ this strategy. The banking agencies appear to be less inclined to engage in such controls, but they have not objected to any merger for a long time so these agencies' remedy strategies are largely unknown.

In contrast, the traditional enforcement agencies (the FTC or Antitrust Division) are more likely to insist on divestiture of specific assets in order to retain a market structure that they deem to be workably competitive. However, the FTC's settlement with Time-Warner (2000) in connection with its acquisition of AOL employed basically the conduct regulation model. Despite that one example, generally, the antitrust enforcement agencies will seek a structural remedy aimed a restoring and protecting competition while the regulatory agencies are more likely to allow mergers subject to various requirements as to conduct.

There are institutional and strategic reasons for a regulatory agency to favor conduct regulation. The strongest and best case for conduct remedies is undoubtedly in electricity, where FERC's legal authority to impose a workable market on wholesale electric power remains very limited. Hence, it could only condition approval of mergers on requiring conduct that would facilitate the development of the competitive market. The FCC employed a somewhat similar strategy as it sought to open up competition in the provision of telecommunications services.

On the merits, a dual approach to merger review allows the direct regulator, assuming its commitment to transformation of both structure and conduct to a workably competitive model, to employ a carrot-and-stick approach to the problem of industry transformation. The agency can authorize the merger while at the same time impose conditions that facilitate the transformation of the industry. A good example of this approach is found in telecommunications as discussed in Chapter 4. The STB and FERC have used the same strategy, as noted in more detail in those case studies. In part, FERC's reliance on conditions is a consequence of its limited direct authority to command changes in the fundamental structure of electric markets. However, if an expert regulator can identify the key changes in conduct necessary to promote the transition to a workably competitive environment, there is merit in imposing these requirements as part of approving a merger between self-interested firms in the industry.

The use of conditions also allows the regulator to retain some authority over the ongoing behavior of firms in the respective markets. Transformation of an industry from regulated to fully competitive is a process and the agency must appreciate that the current context is only a transitional stage. At the same time the risk of antitrust liability is a helpful additional source of pressure to induce firms to adhere to the market process.

Regrettably, there does not appear to be clear recognition of the utility of this dual process for bringing about the transformation of regulated industries into market-oriented ones. As a result, there has been no consistent pattern of interaction between antitrust authorities and the relevant agencies. The varied experience of the different industries examined in the preceding chapters suggests that there would be a good deal of benefit for the transition process if this interaction were more carefully structured and worked out.

There was and is substantial potential for the agencies with oversight of these industries to engage in more active planning of the consolidation process. Given their industry expertise and assuming a commitment to developing workably competitive markets, the agencies would be far better positioned than conventional antitrust enforcers to identify the classes of combinations that would assist the transition. The desired transformation thus could be facilitated. However, in actuality, the agencies have not engaged in this kind of transition management, but instead, have largely reacted to proposals initiated by the firms in the industries and generally permitted almost all combinations. The unfortunate result is that planning has not occurred, market structures have become more concentrated than necessary for efficiency and long-run competition may be undermined.

The EU has employed a more holistic approach to the process of transforming formerly regulated or state-owned industries. As described in Chapter 9, there has been much more attention to the transition from command and control regulation to competition relying on market forces. The greater centralization of the EU's economic policy making as well as its more self-conscious response to the institutional challenges of such transformation appear to explain this difference. As a conceptual matter, it is evident that in making policy to govern the transformation of industries, the decision maker should systematically consider a wide range of issues. But this model assumes a degree of foresight that the very transformation sought often defeats. Essentially, the dynamic of markets easily outruns the ability of even the most sophisticated administrative agencies to anticipate change. Hence, despite its better model, the EU does not seem to have had much greater success in channeling overall deregulation.

However, where the issues are recurrent and the regulators can learn from past experience, the more holistic approach of the EU may yield better results. One example of this is in the airline industry. The EU has imposed a number of constraints on pricing, variations in the size of businesses, frequency of service as well as requiring release of landing slots as conditions of approving proposed airline mergers. The result appears to be a more consistently and robustly competitive market in air travel than the US has achieved. Such regulatory constraints would be anathema to American antitrust authorities and the legal authority as well as the willingness of the Department of Transportation to impose any such limits is questionable. Thus, the American air travel market remains much more open to anti-competitive strategic behavior with a consequent limit on the potential for competition on the merits.

One other difference between the EU and the US merits emphasis. The EU system, despite its quasi-federal character, has a strong tendency to grant exclusive control to one level of government. With respect to many deregulatory issues, therefore, the EU Commission has much more comprehensive control than is the case in the US. This is highlighted in the inability of the American national agencies, FERC and the DOJ, to confer effective approval on the proposed merger of Exelon Corp. and Public Service Enterprise Group over the objections of New Jersey to the merger. In contrast, as discussed in Chapter 9, the EU vigorously objected to Spain's effort to block the acquisition of Endesa by a German company, E.ON AG. The Commission's position was that it had exclusive authority to determine whether or not the acquisition should occur. Of course, ultimately, the delays and resistance seem to have resulted in a major transformation of that transaction. Still, there is a strong difference in the relative power of the central authority in the EU when contrasted to that in the US. In addition, authority is much more centralized in the Commission in the EU model, unlike the American model of dispersal among relatively independent agencies.

'DEREGULATION' HAS HAD GENERALLY POSITIVE RESULTS

The primary substantive implication of the various 'deregulatory' actions considered in these case studies is that they have moved the industries in question closer to market-oriented conduct. Moreover, and of great significance, there is general agreement that these changes have had, on balance and despite the many adverse considerations discussed above, a positive impact on the efficiency and dynamics of these industries, ultimately benefiting consumers. The reform movement has not developed a consistent framework of public policies designed to facilitate that transition. Nor has it recognized the potential difficulties inherent in moving industries that historically were organized around varying degrees of command and control regulation into a market oriented framework – both in structure and in conduct. Indeed, in some industries there was no change in the legal system that provided organization and context to the industry. Despite these limitations, the unanimous view of the case studies is that these industries have come closer to serving the public interest in efficient production and innovation as a result of the transformation in regulation. Although the degree of improvement in the functioning of these markets varies substantially among the industries surveyed, it is very significant that, despite the many ways in which these industries have not yet achieved genuinely workable competition, these imperfect market systems have yielded definite gains.

On one side, banking services, natural gas pipelines, railroads, airlines and telecommunications have strongly benefited from being released from the constraints of older regulations. Indeed, many mergers have structurally moved these sectors toward a more efficient and competitive situation. However, the results are more modest than they might have been for two reasons. First, the development of legal conditions under which the newly competitive markets were to operate was inadequate. Second, the responsible regulatory agencies failed to guard against the kinds of mergers that undermine the goal of workable competition.

Because the set of structural and competition regulations that accompanied the commitment to a market-oriented system was incomplete from the outset of deregulation, competition is likely to be less robust. As a result, the pressures for dynamic innovation are less powerful in these industries than they might have been. Nevertheless, using the enormous transformation of the telecommunications sector as an example, it is clear that the pressure of competition has impelled innovation and dissemination of the new products and services to consumers. Yet neither the industry regulator, the FCC, nor the antitrust enforcement agencies have exhibited much concern about the rapid rate of reconcentration that has occurred in that industry in the last decade. Similar innovative promise as well as competitive concerns exist in the banking, gas pipelines, airlines and railroads industries.

Among the less successful efforts to date have been the movements to more market-oriented frameworks in electricity and hospitals. In both cases, as these case studies show, the potential for significant positive results exists. However, for somewhat different reasons the transformation of both industries has lagged substantially. The lack of legal requirements that would more effectively move these industries into a genuine market framework is an underlying institutional problem in both industries.

In the case of electricity, the problem is a combination of the legal context in which the transition is being attempted and the inherent difficulties of constructing a market framework where the laws of physics impose significant constraints on the law of contract. The central difficulty is that in the transmission grid, a classic network system, electrons flow in the line of least resistance despite any contract term requiring them to flow in some other direction. The result is that a workable competitive generation market requires a carefully integrated and consolidated transmission system. FERC lacks the legal authority and the political capital to compel reorganization of ownership or assignment of full control over the system to a central authority. The strong federalism of the current system of oversight further complicates the regulatory situation. The states are no longer natural market areas for generation, but state agencies retain substantial authority over the operation of important components of the system. Until there is a better resolution of the legal authority over the entire electric system and a willingness to pursue the regulations that would fully implement market institutions, the promise of markets in electricity will remain under realized.

In the case of hospitals, the failure of markets also arises from the legal context as well as a continued resistance on the part of the general public to acknowledge and accept the fact that health care is an expensive commodity. Ultimately, it is neither rational nor feasible to have an unlimited supply of health care. Indeed, the realistic viewer in the contemporary world would recognize that services are being rationed, but not in a rational or efficient way. On the legal institutional side, the national entities such as Medicare and Medicaid that finance a vast part of the hospital system lack the authority or the vision to develop a more workably competitive market in hospital services. Such a program would require consideration of both the ownership structure of the industry and the assignment of rights of access to hospitals by doctors and patients.

****

In sum, there has been a broad movement toward greater reliance on market mechanisms to allocate resources in the formerly regulated industries discussed in these case studies. This process holds great promise for further efficiency and innovation that will serve the public interest. The transition has produced massive merger movements within each industry. While many of those mergers have had positive effects, the overall result has been a significant increase in concentration despite the goal of relying on market processes to produce desirable results. Public policy, regulators and antitrust enforcement agencies must become more attentive to the need to create and maintain competitive market structures and competitive conduct. These case studies reveal industries in the process of change. As that process goes forward, the risks of unnecessary concentration will increase. As a result, we risk losing the benefits of the market processes that have been introduced into these industries. Indeed, the one constant is that change will continue. The benefits of competition require an equally dynamic public policy and its implementation.

NOTE

1. As noted in Chapter 2, Congress adopted energy legislation in 2005 that did away with the Public Utility Holding Company Act. That legislation also granted FERC some greater authority to control both interstate electricity transmission siting and reliability. It also expanded FERC authority to authorize the development of liquefied natural gas receiving ports (*see generally* Energy Act 2005).

REFERENCES

Articles

Daniel F. Spulber and Christopher S. Yoo, 2005, 'On the Regulation of Networks as Complex Systems: A Graph Theory Approach,' Northwestern University Law Review, 99:1687–1722.

Statutes

Energy Policy Act of 2005, Pub. L. No. 109-058.

Agency Actions

In the Matter of Time-Warner, Inc., 2000, 2000 WL 1843019.

Index